MIDDLESEX: 1832-1932

■	MIDDLESEX AREAS BUILT UP BEFORE 1882
▦	" " " 1882 - 1907
▤	" " " 1907 - 1932
■	LONDON AREAS BUILT UP BEFORE 1832
▩	" " " 1832 - 1882
▨	" " " SINCE 1882
▒	PUBLIC OPEN SPACES & CROWN LANDS
A	AERODROMES

MIDDLESEX
OLD AND NEW

CHARLES LAMB'S COTTAGE, EDMONTON

MIDDLESEX
Old and New

by

MARTIN S. BRIGGS

Illustrated
BY THE AUTHOR

LONDON
GEORGE ALLEN & UNWIN LTD
MUSEUM STREET

FIRST PUBLISHED IN 1934

PRINTED IN GREAT BRITAIN BY
UNWIN BROTHERS LTD., WOKING

Dedicated to

SIR RAYMOND UNWIN

"The Father of English Town Planning"

PREFACE

IN a little book, *Rusticus: or the Future of the Countryside*, published in 1927, I endeavoured to trace the process of change which has taken place in rural England since the Industrial Revolution, and to make suggestions for the preservation of amenities both rural and urban. The present work is an attempt to apply the same method intensively to that small county of England which, more than any other, has changed its character during the past half-century. Fifty years ago Middlesex was predominantly rural and contained less than a quarter of its present population. Now it is largely suburbanized and partly industrial, with a population which is growing at a sensational rate and is rapidly approaching two millions. It therefore serves as an example for other counties where similar changes are taking place more gradually, and where there is consequently a better opportunity for utilizing town-planning powers and other modern measures of beneficence to regulate haphazard growth.

But this is not to say that all is lost in Middlesex. Much may still be saved from the wreck. Taking the new townships in turn, chapter by chapter, I have shown how each has grown from a single old village, or a group of old villages; why it has grown; what it has lost or gained in the process; and especially what it may still do to preserve its surviving amenities without obstructing reasonable development. It is my hope that this study may create a spirit of civic consciousness and civic pride in the inhabitants, most of whom have come to Middlesex from other parts of England, and thus have no roots in its soil.

The drawings with which the book is illustrated represent typical old buildings and rural scenes, some of which have already disappeared, others which are liable to be destroyed if prompt action is not taken, and others again which have been fortunately preserved as relics of the past.

M. S. B.

THE ORCHARD
MILL HILL
February 1934

CONTENTS

CHAPTER   PAGE

PREFACE   11

LIST OF ILLUSTRATIONS   15

I. MIDDLESEX IN GENERAL   19

II. POTTERS BAR AND SOUTH MIMMS: including Bentley Heath and Dancer's Hill   45

III. ENFIELD: including Botany Bay, Brimsdown, Clay Hill, Forty Hill, Freezy Water, and Ponder's End   55

IV. EDMONTON   70

V. SOUTHGATE: including Bowes Park, Cockfosters, Palmer's Green, and Winchmore Hill   79

VI. TOTTENHAM: including part of Harringay   90

VII. WOOD GREEN   102

VIII. HORNSEY: including Crouch End, Finsbury Park, Fortis Green, part of Harringay, Highgate, Muswell Hill, and Stroud Green   107

IX. FRIERN BARNET: including Colney Hatch ("New Southgate") and Oakleigh Park   119

X. FINCHLEY: including part of Whetstone   123

XI. HENDON: including Burnt Oak ("Watling"), Child's Hill, Colindale, Cricklewood, The Hale, The Hyde; parts of Elstree, Edgware, and the Hampstead Garden Suburb; Golder's Green, and Mill Hill   129

XII. HARROW: including Harrow-on-the-Hill, Harrow Weald, Headstone, Hatch End, Pinner, Wealdstone, Stanmore, Whitchurch, and parts of Edgware and Kenton   142

XIII. WEMBLEY: including Alperton, Kingsbury, Preston, Sudbury, Twyford Abbey; and part of Kenton   154

CHAPTER   PAGE

XIV.   WILLESDEN: including Brondesbury, Dollis Hill, Dudden
        Hill, Harlesden, Kensal Green, Kilburn, Neasden, and
        Stonebridge   161

XV.   ACTON: including Mill Hill Park and part of Park Royal   168

XVI.   EALING: including Greenford, Hanwell, Northolt, Perivale,
        and part of Twyford   177

XVII.   RUISLIP AND NORTHWOOD: including Eastcote   189

XVIII. UXBRIDGE: including Colham Green, Cowley, Harefield,
        Hillingdon, and Ickenham   199

XIX.   YIEWSLEY AND WEST DRAYTON: including Har-
        mondsworth, Heathrow, Longford, and Sipson   213

XX.   HAYES AND HARLINGTON: including Botwell, Cran-
        ford, Dawley, and Yeading   220

XXI.   SOUTHALL–NORWOOD   228

XXII.   FELTHAM: including East Bedfont, Hanworth, and Hatton   234

XXIII. BRENTFORD AND CHISWICK: including Bedford
        Park, Gunnersbury, Strand-on-the-Green, and Turnham
        Green   240

XXIV.   HESTON AND ISLEWORTH: including Hounslow,
        Lampton, Osterley, St. Margaret's, Scrattage, and Sutton   254

XXV.   TWICKENHAM: including Fulwell Park, Strawberry Hill,
        and Whitton   264

XXVI.   TEDDINGTON: including Hampton Wick   274

XXVII. HAMPTON AND SUNBURY: including Chertsey Bridge,
        Lower and Upper Halliford, Kempton Park, Littleton,
        and Shepperton   279

XXVIII. STAINES: including Ashford, Laleham, Poyle, Stanwell,
        and West Bedfont   289

        INDEX   301

LIST OF ILLUSTRATIONS

CHARLES LAMB'S COTTAGE, EDMONTON *Frontispiece*

PAGE

THE CITY BOUNDARY STONE, STAINES 23

HIGH STREET, PINNER 27

HALE END FARM, MILL HILL, 1926 29

EDGWARE: THE HIGH STREET ABOUT FIFTY YEARS AGO 33

LAWRENCE STREET FARM, MILL HILL, 1926 37

HOLCOMBE HILL, MILL HILL, 1926 41

SOUTH MIMMS PARISH CHURCH 46

THE DUKE OF YORK INN ON THE GREAT NORTH ROAD 47

WYLLYOTT'S MANOR, POTTERS BAR 49

DYRHAM PARK GATES, SOUTH MIMMS 53

ENFIELD PARISH CHURCH AND GRAMMAR SCHOOL 56

GENTLEMAN'S ROW, ENFIELD 57

THE MILL, PONDER'S END 59

THE FALLOW BUCK INN, CLAY HILL, NEAR ENFIELD 63

THE MAIDEN'S BRIDGE, FORTY HILL, NEAR ENFIELD 65

THE STABLE COURT GATEWAY, FORTY HALL, NEAR ENFIELD 67

EDMONTON PARISH CHURCH 71

THE RIVER LEA AT EDMONTON 73

SALISBURY HOUSE, BURY STREET, EDMONTON 77

THE OLD SMITHY, SOUTHGATE (DEMOLISHED 1933) 80

"THE THATCHED COTTAGE," PALMER'S GREEN (IN *c.* 1860) 83

BROOMFIELD HOUSE, PALMER'S GREEN, IN 1930 85

ESSEX HOUSE, OLD SOUTHGATE 87

TOTTENHAM PARISH CHURCH 91

TOTTENHAM MILLS ABOUT ONE HUNDRED YEARS AGO 93

BRUCE CASTLE, TOTTENHAM 97

GATEWAY OF "THE PRIORY," TOTTENHAM 99

	PAGE
DEVONSHIRE HILL FARM, WOOD GREEN	105
HIGHGATE HILL	108
THE LAST OF OLD CROUCH END	109
HIGHGATE ARCHWAY IN 1813	113
THE NEW RIVER AND FINSBURY PARK FROM GREEN LANES	115
HORNSEY OLD CHURCH IN 1797	117
ALMSHOUSES, FRIERN BARNET	121
FINCHLEY: DOLLIS BROOK	125
THE SPANIARD'S TAVERN IN 1933	127
GOODHEW'S FARM, MILL HILL, IN 1933	130
GOLDER'S GREEN ROAD, ABOUT 1908	131
MILL HILL "BROADWAY," ABOUT 1906	133
CROSSROADS AT "THE GREEN MAN," MILL HILL, IN 1925	135
COPT HALL, MILL HILL: THE STABLE COURT IN 1926	137
GREYHOUND HILL, HENDON	138
THE "KING'S HEAD," MILL HILL	139
HARROW CHURCH FROM THE WEST	143
HARROW FROM SUDBURY COURT ROAD	145
DEAR'S FARM, BRIDGE STREET, PINNER, IN 1932	147
HARROW SCHOOL: THE OLD BUILDING	149
HEADSTONE MANOR, NEAR HARROW	151
KINGSBURY OLD CHURCH	155
JOHN LYON'S FARM AT PRESTON	157
TWYFORD ABBEY	159
THE "WELSH HARP," OR BRENT RESERVOIR	162
DOLLIS HILL FARM IN 1932	163
MAPESBURY WINDMILL IN c. 1860	165
DOLLIS HILL LANE IN 1932	166
THE LAST OF OLD ACTON: EAST ACTON LANE IN 1933	173
THE CANAL BRIDGE AT PERIVALE	179
PERIVALE CHURCH	181

	PAGE
NORTHOLT CHURCH	183
THE PUBLIC LIBRARY, EALING (FORMERLY PITZHANGER MANOR)	185
RUISLIP VILLAGE	191
THE MANOR FARM, RUISLIP	193
"THE BARNS," EASTCOTE	195
WOODMAN'S FARM, RUISLIP	197
UXBRIDGE HIGH STREET	200
HAREFIELD CHURCH	201
ALMSHOUSES AT HAREFIELD	203
ICKENHAM CHURCH	207
SWAKELEYS, NEAR UXBRIDGE	209
THE GATEHOUSE, WEST DRAYTON	215
HARMONDSWORTH	217
BRIDGE OVER THE CRANE, CRANFORD	221
HARLINGTON CHURCH	223
HAYES CHURCH, THE PORCH	225
NORWOOD GREEN	229
SOUTHALL MANOR HOUSE	231
LOWER FELTHAM IN 1933	237
BRENTFORD: THE MOUTH OF THE BRENT	241
CHISWICK FROM THE SURREY SIDE	243
HOGARTH HOUSE, CHISWICK	245
BOSTON HOUSE, BRENTFORD	247
CHISWICK HOUSE ("LORD BURLINGTON'S VILLA")	251
ISLEWORTH FROM THE SURREY SIDE	255
OSTERLEY PARK	257
THE STABLES AT OSTERLEY PARK	259
HESTON CHURCH, THE LYCH-GATE	261
TWICKENHAM	267
FERRY HOUSE, TWICKENHAM	271
TEDDINGTON LOCK	277

B

PAGE

HAMPTON COURT FROM THE NEW BRIDGE   280

HAMPTON FROM THE SURREY SIDE   281

THE ROYAL MEWS, HAMPTON COURT   283

SUNBURY PARISH CHURCH   285

SHEPPERTON   287

CHURCH STREET, STAINES   291

POYLE   292

STANWELL   293

STANWELL: THE OLD SCHOOL   295

CHERTSEY BRIDGE   297

MAP SHOWING THE GROWTH OF MIDDLESEX: 1832–1932   *Map-endpapers*

MIDDLESEX: OLD AND NEW

CHAPTER I

MIDDLESEX IN GENERAL

MIDDLESEX, smallest but one among English counties, derives most of its fame in history from the fact that, up to some fifty years ago, it contained a large part of London within its borders. In Shakespeare's time London had not spread very far beyond the medieval walls, which themselves marked the limit of the Roman town almost unaltered. On the Surrey side the bridge-head settlement of Southwark had barely begun to grow, though it was attaining some celebrity as the theatrical suburb. The cluster of buildings at Westminster was completely detached from London itself. During the eighteenth century London spread into Middlesex as far as Marylebone Road and City Road on the north, Tyburnia and Sloane Street in the west, and Stepney on the east. The rest of Middlesex remained obstinately rural, and London was still its chief town. But during the nineteenth century the growth of the city was so rapid—sprawling into Essex, Kent, and Surrey as well as into Middlesex—that London became altogether unmanageable.

In 1889 there was formed, to replace a strange hotch-potch of "vestries" and other half-medieval organizations, the new Administrative County of London, and it has hardly found its feet yet. This novel creation included not only a number of metropolitan boroughs—each more or less conscious of its own importance —but also the City of Westminster—with all its long associations with the Abbey and the Crown—and, still more imposing, the ancient City of London itself, complete with its Guildhall, its Lord Mayor, its innumerable regulations and customs, its pageantry and its privileges—veritably an *imperium in imperio*.

The new London County Council, without a county hall or

even a coat-of-arms, laboured for years under the handicap of
frock coats and silk hats as against municipal robes and pomp in
the City; and it continues to do so. In a highly conservative land
like ours, it has to bear the social stigma inevitably attached to
anything that is modern. In like manner, London's own university,
now by far the largest in the country, has suffered for want of a
visible home and trappings, so that it has been unkindly described
as "a brass plate in South Kensington." But already there are
strange rumblings in the bowels of Bloomsbury which will produce,
a few years hence, a block of buildings so gigantic that the Londoner
need no longer apologize for his university. Meanwhile, the huge
London County Hall has recently appeared opposite the Houses
of Parliament, while even a blazon of London arms—a coat of
many colours and of considerable beauty—has been devised
at last.

London, in fact, is coming into its own, and naturally its gain
is Middlesex's loss. The heart of the little county has been wrenched
out, and all its old boundaries and traditions disturbed. The capital
of Middlesex is still nominally at Brentford, as it has been since
that ancient town was the chief town of the Middle Saxons; but
actually the administrative business of the county is carried on
mainly at the Middlesex Guildhall under the shadow of Westminster Abbey in the County of London, and therefore not in
Middlesex at all.

These various administrative anomalies partly explain the
ignorance of so many Middlesex residents about the affairs of their
own county. But that ignorance is increased by at least two other
factors: the centrifugal tendency of London to spread into
Middlesex on the one hand, and the centripetal tendency of
Middlesex to attract immigrants from all parts of England as
residents, working either in that county or in London. It is
commonly known that, during the past few years, the population
of London has begun to diminish at last, while the population of
Middlesex has grown with phenomenal rapidity. At the present
rate of increase, there will be more people in Middlesex than in
London itself thirty or forty years hence. Fifty years ago

Middlesex, outside the London frontier of 1889, was still a rural county where suburban development had hardly begun. To-day the larger part of it is suburbanized and an appreciable area is industrialized. Nothing comparable with this growth (except perhaps the recent and lamentable development of southern Essex) has ever occurred in this country; it is to be hoped that nothing parallel will ever occur again.

Confused by all these abnormal and unnatural movements, it is not surprising that the majority of the inhabitants of Middlesex, born in London or in the provinces and largely employed in London, regard their county of residence as a mere dormitory attached to London. They find it difficult to realize that their own borough or urban district is not an integral part of the metropolis when their letters bear a London postmark and their constables form a section of the London police. Above all, the unbroken lines of tramways and streets and shops that stretch from London itself far into the country have swept away so many local landmarks that the only connecting link between John Citizen and his town hall is the peremptory demand for rates that arrives in his letter-box every six months. On the back of that depressing document are usually printed a few facts about municipal activities, such as the comparative costs of refuse destruction and of education. Hendon, up to recent years, used to add a touch of local colour, giving the highest point above sea-level, and the population of the area. For many otherwise worthy residents in Middlesex this seems to be the extent of their local interest, and it is not widely known that nearly every borough and urban district council in the county publishes an official guide to its area, obtainable gratis at the town hall. The primary purpose of these booklets is, naturally, to attract more people to settle in the locality, and thus to increase local business. The literary style adopted therefore tends to be eulogistic, and a reader may well be staggered to discover, from the persuasive pages of these municipal booby-traps, the unexpected amenities and attractions (such as the municipal bandstand or the fire-station) which surround him on every hand. Yet, apart from this tendency to propaganda, the municipal guide-books generally give some attention to local history and interests, and they have been freely used by the present writer.

Nothing affords clearer evidence of the prevailing apathy among Middlesex people about their own district and county than a simple request at the local bookshop for a local history. If it be a multiple shop, it is probable that its minions—like the stock they sell—have no local colour or interest. Sometimes, it must be admitted, they will produce the desired goods; but only too often, in my experience, they will either profess complete ignorance of any such publication or offer a scarcely veiled hint that the innocent inquirer is a lunatic. Only in two or three Middlesex towns have I found old-established booksellers genuinely interested in the affairs and history of their own neighbourhood. Yet Middlesex does possess numbers of people keenly alive to such things: nearly every public library—where there is one (Harrow and Southgate are unaccountable exceptions) —contains a good collection of maps and pictures of vanished or disappearing landmarks, and nearly every township has a historical or antiquarian society actively engaged in collecting records of the past and of the fast-disappearing present. Moreover, almost every locality has at some time formed the subject of a small history book, often written by a schoolmaster employed in the district.

Middlesex, even when deprived of London, is full of history, and still retains much of its characteristic beauty and charm of landscape. This volume represents an endeavour to rescue, from the apparently irresistible and relentless tide of spreading suburbia, some memory of the scenes and old buildings which are annually becoming submerged and forgotten, if not actually destroyed. For it is possible, given intelligent forethought and knowledge, to avoid many of the mistakes which have been associated with indiscriminate development in the past. The science or art of town-planning, coupled with an increasing concern for the preservation of rural amenities, has made vast strides during recent years. The Middlesex County Council has taken a most active and praiseworthy part in carrying out surveys of various parts of the county which are still capable of sympathetic treatment, and in its policy of preserving a "green girdle" of woodland and pasture within its northern frontier has shown real inspiration. If only the general public could be made to realize how much could be done in this direction with the support of strong local action, and how often it is actually profitable in a financial sense to restrict the senseless methods of ignorant land-sharks and jerry-builders, much of Middlesex might still retain its attractions.

On the bank of the Thames above Staines there is an old

THE CITY BOUNDARY STONE, STAINES

boundary-stone erected in the thirteenth century to mark the limit of the City's jurisdiction over the river (see p. 290). It is inscribed "God preserve ye City of London." It appears to me that at the present day a more appropriate legend would be "God preserve ye County of Middlesex."

*   *   *   *   *

The whole story of the little county's development seems to be indicated by its boundaries, some of which go back to very early times, while others are the result of medieval history or of the modern growth of London. According to Sir Montagu Sharpe,* who has devoted much attention to this question of Middlesex boundaries, the line of demarcation between the *territorium* or province of Londinium and that of Verulamium followed the course of the Rivers Lea and Colne to a point near Hatfield, where they are only a mile or two apart; and the first written reference to the Saxon "province of Middlesex," in a charter of A.D. 704, seems to indicate that its boundaries were identical with those of the former London *territorium*. At that period Middlesex—the land of the Middle Saxons—was a small buffer-state between the three important kingdoms of Essex, Wessex, and Mercia, and shortly afterwards it must have been annexed by Mercia, whose kings held councils at Brentford and Chelsea and in London. Some time about the year 1000 there was a general division (shearing) of Mercia into separate "shires," among which Hertford-shire made its first appearance, and the northern boundary of Middlesex was now pushed southwards, approximately to its present line. In many ways this line forms an excellent natural boundary, running as it does for most of its distance along the high watershed between the Colne and the Brent. From Harefield in the north-west of Middlesex to near Potters Bar in the north-east, this ridge is practically continuous, and along its length is a series of ancient British fortifications, of which the most important is Grim's Dyke, near Pinner. It was a good strategic frontier as well as a satisfactory natural boundary. But this excellent scheme was completely spoiled by the inclusion of Chipping Barnet, East Barnet, and Totteridge (all on the south side, or Middlesex side, of the ridge) in Hertford-shire instead of in Middlesex. This inexplicable mistake seems to have been due to the power of the Abbot of St. Albans, to whom the land within this Barnet "pocket" belonged. Whatever may be the explanation, the result is only too obvious. At the present time Barnet and East Barnet and Totteridge would be more con-veniently administered as part of Middlesex than as part of Hertfordshire, and it is unfortunate that Henry VIII did not

* Sir Montagu Sharpe, *Middlesex in British, Roman, and Saxon Times* (2nd edition, 1932).

arrange a rectification of frontier after the Dissolution of the Monasteries. The remainder of the northern boundary of the county, from Potters Bar to the Lea Valley near Waltham Abbey, runs nearly straight and appears sensible enough.

On its east, west, and south sides Middlesex was continuously bounded by rivers, until the County of London was invented in 1889; and those boundaries are, or were, ideal.* It may be noted here that in several places along the Thames the boundary line crosses the river, i.e. at Staines and Walton, where Middlesex has a small "bridge-head" south of the river, and near Chertsey Bridge, where Surrey takes a bite out of Middlesex. Similarly, the western boundary of the county does not coincide with the main stream of the Colne consistently, sometimes following the course of a tributary brook. The fact is that the Thames has changed its course at several points, which explains these existing anomalies; and doubtless the main stream of the Colne has done likewise. The ancient course of the Lea is submerged beneath huge reservoirs in several places.

Lastly, there is the Middlesex–London frontier, which presumably follows ancient parish boundaries, and runs from the Lea near Tottenham to the Thames at a point between Hammersmith and Chiswick. It is curious to think that this now troublesome boundary line, apparently the result of remote history rather than of modern science, did actually run through open fields for most of its length less than fifty years ago. There were points where London had spread over the line into Middlesex, in Kilburn and in Hornsey, but they were exceptions. So apparently nobody is to blame, though it would be possible now, after the event, to devise a more sensible boundary to get rid of the Kilburn salient and various other inconveniences.

However, that is impracticable, although mention of it reminds us that the Middlesex County Council, in common with other local authorities, has recently made a most drastic revision of nearly all its inter-district boundaries, with a view to economical and efficient administration. Most of the old districts followed the

* But see p. 292 for an anecdote illustrating the drawbacks of a river boundary.

lines of very ancient parish boundaries, many going back to Saxon times or even beyond, and it is only reasonable that they should undergo revision to meet modern conditions. Thus great arterial roads and important railways have been constructed all over the county, radiating outwards from London, and intersecting many old parishes. At the same time districts have been combined together, two old parishes forming one borough or urban district (e.g. Heston–Isleworth, Southall–Norwood, Ruislip–Northwood, and Brentford–Chiswick). These titles seem rather clumsy, but are inevitable unless some clumsier portmanteau-word like "Hestworth" or "Brentwick" be substitued, or unless one partner's name be suppressed. That has happened in the sad case of Kingsbury, a Saxon parish swallowed whole by Wembley (just as so many dismounted Yeomanry regiments lost their ancient titles with their horses during the Great War), while Ealing has engulfed the historic parishes of Perivale, Greenford, Hanwell, and Northolt. It is all very regrettable, and certainly helps to kill local traditions and interest.

Perhaps the next stage in this study is to attempt to forget boundaries for a moment and to recall the general appearance of the county as it was even so recently as fifty years ago, before the cataclysmic growth of the suburbs, most of which has indeed taken place since the war. In 1881 the population of the county was only 355,336, little more than a fifth of the present figure. There were no very large towns anywhere, the chief being (in order) Tottenham, Willesden, Edmonton, Hornsey, Enfield, Acton, Chiswick, Ealing, Twickenham, Brentford, Finchley, and Hendon. Uxbridge had only 7,669 inhabitants, Harrow 5,558, and Staines 4,628. Some of these towns, e.g. Uxbridge, were genuine independent survivals, country market-towns not yet become suburban; others, such as Ealing, Acton, and Chiswick, were developing as London dormitories. But they were still isolated centres, industry had barely begun to rear its factories, and Middlesex was definitely an agricultural county, though rapidly developing a suburban tendency. So recently as 1913, three-fifths of its area was under crops and grass, and even to-day the cultivated area is considerable.

Cornfields are now almost non-existent, though plentiful enough just over the frontiers of Hertfordshire and Buckinghamshire. Yet that is no fault of the soil, for once upon a time Middlesex corn was famous. Norden wrote in 1593 that

The soil of Middlesex is excellent, fat, and fertile, and full of profite; it yieldeth corn and graine, not only in abundance, but most excellent good wheat, especially about Heston, which place may be called *Granarium*

HIGH STREET, PINNER

tritici regalis, from the singularitie of the corne. The vaine of this especiall corn seemeth to extend from Heston to Harrow on the Hill, between which, as in the midway, is Perivale. Yet doth not this so fruitful soyle yield comfort to the wayfaring man in the winter time, by reason of the claiesh nature of the soyle, which, after it hath tasted of the autumne showers, waxeth both dyrtie and deep, but unto the countrie swaine it is a sweet and pleasant garden in regard to his hope of future profite, for

> The deep and dirtie loathsome soyle
> Yields golden gaine to payneful toyle;

and the industrious and paineful husbandman will refuse a pallace to droyle in these golden puddles.

The northern part of the county is largely given up to pasture. It is hilly country, pleasantly wooded—mainly with elms and oaks. At one time the greater part of Middlesex was forest, traversed only by the three great Roman roads: Ermine Street, Watling Street, and the Staines Road. Enfield Chase occupied the whole of the north-east corner, and there was another great forest for hunting at Ruislip, while the "Bishop's Wood," still existing in part between Highgate and Finchley, is a survival of the Bishop of London's hunting park. Further descriptions of all these districts are given in subsequent chapters, but the forests are mentioned here because they account for the wealth of fine old trees in the northern half of Middlesex even to this day. Beeches are rare in Middlesex, presumably owing to the absence of chalk, which lies beneath the London clay and only crops up at Harefield in the north-west and near South Mimms in the north. In the middle and south of the county the characteristic tree is the elm, and any thoughtful person must realize how large a part elms play in the scenery of that area. Yet they are being cut down indiscriminately everywhere to allow of road-widening and speculative building.

One need not be a fanatic to regret this. There is something pathetic as well as ludicrous in the illustrated brochures issued by certain railway companies and other agencies interested in the exploitation of Middlesex. Doubtless the "Cosy Palaces," the "Baronial Halls," the "Tudor Homes," the "Houses of Artistry," the "Wonder Homes,"* and all the other slogans (produced by builders who are surely devoid of humour) make a poignant appeal to the young bride. But the photographs used to lure the home-seeker to "Metroland" mostly represent winding lanes shaded by spreading elms, without a hint of a Baronial Hall (£799), a House of Artistry (£699 19s. 6d.), or a Cosy Palace (£499 19s. 11¾d.). That is where the stupidity of the whole land-shark business lies. He tempts these simple-hearted innocents into the country with pictures of leafy lanes, knowing full well (as they ought also to do) that as soon as he has got them firmly entrapped in a foolproof hire-purchase agreement, he will cut down the elm-trees—and

* These are actual slogans freely employed by builders in my own district.

then the leafy lane has gone for ever with all other traces of the country. The country will never be preserved by such methods. But there are ways by which it can be done. If the theory of satellite towns long advocated by town-planning enthusiasts had been put into operation, every resident in Middlesex could walk into *real* country within a few minutes of his own door, real country that would remain real country. But the time has probably

HALE END FARM, MILL HILL, 1926

passed to cure Middlesex's troubles in this way: the part already developed can only serve as a warning to other districts liable to the same attacks. Yet the lay-out of the Watling Estate between Edgware and Mill Hill (a London housing scheme) shows conclusively that trees need not be cut down, and that they enhance and preserve the amenities of any suburban development.

Up to very recent times, the greater part of South Middlesex— that is, south of the London–Uxbridge Road—was given up to orchards and market gardens. It formed one vast kitchen garden, perhaps 8 miles square, intensively cultivated and, one may imagine, extremely profitable. Here, at London's very door, were being grown huge quantities of fruit and vegetables, which came nightly to Covent Garden in long lines of creaking carts. Twenty years ago, a ride on the top of a tram from Hammersmith or Shepherd's Bush to Hampton Court was a pure joy in May when the blossom was out. And now this thriving area is being blotted out; partly, it must be admitted, by great factories at Hayes and along the Great West Road; but mainly by foolish people who are invited by a builder, with his tongue in his cheek, to "come and live in an orchard." Three months after the agreement has been signed, the orchard has gone; and the surroundings consist of other people's underwear on lines and the screech of innumerable cheap gramophones. Such is life in "London's Country," as the Underground humorously calls it.

Along the river banks poplars and willows share the honours with elms. In later chapters the present condition and future prospects of the Thames Valley scenery will be discussed. It needs separate treatment, for "bungaloid growths" along the riverside have been diagnosed by town-planners as a special disease. Fortunately, the County Councils of Middlesex and Surrey are fully alive to the need for preserving the beauties of the Thames, and are taking measures towards that end. The sad fate of some of the smaller streams, such as Pymme's Brook (see p. 74) and the Moselle (see p. 110), has also led to the acquisition of portions of the banks of the Crane. The Brent has been partly canalized during the last decade, and presents a squalid appearance here and there as a result, but it is not too late to preserve much of its remaining course, and in some parts—notably at Perivale—it is still a beautiful little river. It is to be hoped that the Colne, as yet inviolate, will also be retained as a river rather than a sewer; and that the marshes and banks of the Lea, east of the L.N.E.R., will be retained as public open spaces. (Incidentally, they are unsuited for any other purpose.)

Middlesex has two artificial lakes with natural surroundings: the Brent Reservoir or "Welsh Harp" between Hendon and Willesden, and the reservoir at Ruislip. The latter appears to be saved for all time, with woods down to its edge; the west bank of the former has been secured for recreation grounds by Hendon and Kingsbury, but Willesden has only secured a part of the east bank, the remaining share having been quite needlessly given to factories. They make no use of the water, and the "zoning" of this land for a recreation ground at an early stage would have secured it at slight cost for a densely populated neighbourhood, while the beauty of a fine piece of water would have been unimpaired.

The reservoirs of the Metropolitan Water Board at Littleton and Staines and in the Lea Valley are vast areas of water enclosed by lofty sloping banks partly planted with trees. They have no intrinsic beauty, but are impressive by their great size; they form a refuge for many birds, and they are far less offensive to the eye than the smaller reservoirs at Hampton-on-Thames. (Perivale Wood, north of Ealing, has been acquired by the Selborne Society as a bird sanctuary.)

Besides its natural streams, Middlesex boasts at least three canals in the normal sense of the word: the Lea Navigation on its eastern boundary; the Grand Union (formerly Grand Junction) from Brentford to Southall, Hayes, Yiewsley, and Harefield, where it leaves Middlesex and goes through Watford and Tring to Northamptonshire; and the Paddington Canal, which leaves the Grand Union near Hayes, passes between Southall and Yeading (where there is a horrible refuse-dump) to Northolt, Perivale, and Alperton, and on to the London boundary near Harlesden. Except for the disgusting transport of refuse in strings of open barges, life on the canals is interesting and picturesque.

Then there are some curious half-canals, or aqueducts, wandering across the southern part of the county. The so-called "Longford River," constructed by Charles I, is taken off from the Colne at Longford, east of Colnbrook, and runs south-east across country past Hanworth to Hampton Court, where it reinforces Cardinal Wolsey's original water-supply. Much older is the so-called "Duke's River," which brings water from one of the arms of the Colne into the little River Crane, joining it near Hounslow and forming a chain of picturesque pools at the junction. This canal was constructed by the Abbess of Syon Monastery

(p. 262) to drive a mill at Twickenham, and was afterwards extended to the convent's other mill at Isleworth, where a modern successor still stands. The canal derived its present name from one of the ducal owners of Syon after the Dissolution of the Monasteries.

Lastly, there is the "New River," described in Chapters III and VII. This remarkable engineering achievement, still an important contributor to London's water-supply and, much altered since its original construction in 1609–13, forms a pleasant feature in much of its course through Middlesex, and adds an attraction even to the somewhat dull Finsbury Park.

Middlesex is connected with Surrey by several fine old bridges— at Staines, Chertsey, Kingston, and Richmond—and by fine modern ones at Chiswick, St. Margaret's, and Hampton Court— described in later chapters.

The little old bridges over the smaller streams and canals are fast disappearing under the stringent needs of modern motor traffic, for which they are certainly unsuited, being narrow and steep. But there are still a few surviving examples of some age, such as Cranford Bridge over the Crane, the Maiden's Bridge over Cuffley Brook at Forty Hill, north of Enfield, and the bridge at Mimms Wash on the old road from Barnet to the North. A picturesque example between Hendon and Finchley, Mutton Bridge, has recently been rebuilt. One cannot hope that any of these old bridges will survive another decade unless a modern substitute be built alongside them, as has been done at Stratford-on-Avon and elsewhere; but that seems unlikely.

The roads of Middlesex are probably unsurpassed by those of any other county, but most of them are comparatively modern. The ancient pre-Roman trackways have been described by Sir Montagu Sharpe,* who states that three main tracks led from the great ford over the Thames at "Old England" by Brentford (p. 241): one leading east through Strand-on-the-Green, Chiswick and Fulham, and Chelsea to Charing Cross; another between Hanwell and Ealing, over Horsendon and Sudbury Hills to Brockley

* *Op. cit.*, pp. 3–5.

Hill near Elstree, where there was an encampment (p. 148); and the third past Hanwell Church and Hayes to the ford over the Colne at Uxbridge. But there were many others besides these, and the "Ridgeway" at Mill Hill is believed by some authorities to be of great antiquity.

The Romans constructed three main roads through Middlesex:

EDGWARE: THE HIGH STREET ABOUT FIFTY YEARS AGO
Drawn from a photograph

Ermine Street, from Bishopsgate through Tottenham and Waltham Cross to Lincoln; Watling Street, which really commences at Dover, and passes through London at the Marble Arch, thence through Kilburn and Edgware in Middlesex, leaving the county north of Brockley Hill and continuing through Verulamium to Uriconium (Wroxeter) near Shrewsbury; and the road from London through Shepherd's Bush, Chiswick, Brentford, and Hounslow to Staines. All these wonderful roads are referred to in subsequent pages of this book.

During the Middle Ages another road was used as a means of

access to the north of Middlesex and beyond. According to Norden,* who wrote in 1593, it led "from Clerkenwell to the east of St. Pancras Old Church, thence through Longwich Lane, and skirting to the east of Highgate by Tollingdone Lane (subsequently Tollington), led on to Crouch End. From here the route went by Muswell Hill, Colney Hatch, and Friern Barnet to Whetstone, thence according to Pennant through South Mimms, Ridge, and London Colney to St. Albans. About the middle of the fourteenth century a new way was opened from Highgate running over Finchley Common to Whetstone. At Highgate the Bishop of London had a toll-gate for liberty to pass by this road, instead of using the old way, and the reason why travellers left a section of the old route was, says Norden, on account of its deep and dirty passage in winter." (This old road is further described in Chapters II and VIII.)

The present road from Barnet to St. Albans superseded the medieval road from Barnet to South Mimms just described, and was constructed by Telford in 1826, at a time when many new coaching roads were made. Highgate Archway was constructed in 1813, the new Archway Road beneath it forming another link in the famous route between London and the North. The Finchley Road from the West End to Tally Ho Corner was laid out about 1828, connecting the West End with the Great North Road.

The Uxbridge Road and the Bath Road were among others which became famous during the coaching period, and Hounslow Heath vied with Finchley Common as a scene of the exploits of highwaymen (pp. 125, 257). Both these famous commons have shrunk during the past century, Finchley Common having completely disappeared, while Hounslow Heath is now War Office property and resounds to the tramp of armed men, though it still retains some of the characteristics of the vastly greater wilderness which it was in the past (p. 258). The enclosure of village greens, common land, and the grassy margins of wide roads was a disgrace to our country, and sheds a sinister light on the ethical code of a century ago, when most of it occurred. Twenty thousand acres

* Quoted from Sharpe, *op. cit.*, p. 193.

were thus enclosed in Middlesex between 1800 and 1810.* Incidentally, it also ruined the appearance of many of the beauty spots of Middlesex.

Of the "green lanes" which abounded in Middlesex up to a few years ago, the number is rapidly diminishing as suburbia converts them into neatly kerbed roads lined with stately "Tudor Homes" or "Baronial Halls."

The remarkable series of arterial roads constructed in the county since the war requires no description here, though mention of them is made in later chapters. They comprise the Watford Bypass, the Barnet Bypass, the New Cambridge Road, the North Circular Road, and the Colnbrook Bypass. No seeker after rural peace can pretend to love these roaring great arteries, but they have become absolutely necessary—in Middlesex, at any rate—and on the whole, it may be said that reasonable care has been taken to plant them with trees in such a way that their starkness and straightness is mitigated.

There is nothing much to be said about most of the railways which form a radiating network all over the county, except that the two latest—the extension of the Tube railway from Finsbury Park through Wood Green and Southgate to Cockfosters, and the new line from Wembley Park through Preston and Kingsbury to Canons Park—have just opened up two hitherto rural and some-what inaccessible areas which will assuredly be covered with houses within a decade. But one must admit that the new stations are brightly and admirably designed, a delightful change from the often squalid and now shabby stations of fifty years ago, and that electic traction removes much of the smoke nuisance.

On the other hand, the transmission of electric power for domestic and industrial purposes has involved the erection of lines of huge pylons from Brimsdown in the Lea Valley westwards along the north boundary of the county and thence to Watford, while subsidiary pylons stalk round Harrow, and one of them has been planted in a charming rural corner in Eastcote village. However, it is no use to bewail the advent of this giant "grid,"

* W. Jerrold, *Highways and Byways in Middlesex*, p. 9.

which has obviously come to stay until science can provide us with some less aggressive substitute.

Turning now to the older achievements of man's handiwork in Middlesex, it is good news that the Historical Monuments Commission will soon furnish us, in one of their sumptuous volumes, with an authentic list and an illustrated record of everything notable up to the time of Queen Anne. In the meantime, some description of the chief monuments will be found in the various chapters of this book. "Grim's Dyke," the chief surviving earthwork, has already been mentioned (see also p. 148).

Middlesex, by reason of its proximity to London, has always contained a large number of notable country seats, of which by far the most important and the oldest is Hampton Court Palace (see pp. 284–6). It is certainly the only large house surviving from Tudor times. At West Drayton there is a gatehouse which must be almost contemporary with Hampton Court, but nothing remains of Drayton Hall, to which it formed the entrance. A tower at Bruce Castle, Tottenham, is said to be part of the original building erected in 1514. Among half-timbered and timber-framed houses attributed to the late Middle Ages are Wyllyott's Manor, Potters Bar, and Salisbury House near Edmonton. But it is difficult to date most of these buildings with any precision. Southall Manor House is a fine example, somewhat drastically enlarged and restored; it was erected in 1581. Other timber-framed houses, with plaster panels showing between exposed timbers as at Harmondsworth, Poyle, Pinner, etc., or completely plastered over, still survive in many places, but cannot be dated exactly. Then there are the delightful timber-framed cottages covered with weather-boarding, so characteristic of Middlesex, Essex, and Hertfordshire. The use of weather-boarding seems to have become common in the seventeenth century, and it passed over to America with the Pilgrim Fathers, to become the normal covering of the first New England homes, as I have explained at length elsewhere.*

Brickwork continued to be used for comparatively large houses

* M. S. Briggs, *The Homes of the Pilgrim Fathers in England and America, 1620–1685.*

in Middlesex from Jacobean times onwards. Early examples are the turrets of Osterley Park (1577), Forty Hall near Enfield (1629–32), Boston House near Brentford, Swakeleys near Uxbridge (1638), Copt Hall near Mill Hill (1637), the Church House at Hendon (1676) with its fine chimney-stack, Cromwell House at Highgate, the Cedar House at Hillingdon, and Bruce Castle at Tottenham (1688, etc.). The dates of the following brick houses, which appear to be of the late seventeenth or early

Lawrence Street Farm · Mill Hill
19th September 1926

eighteenth century, are unknown to me: Pymme's Park at Edmonton, afterwards completely transformed by the brothers Adam (p. 77), Broomfield House at Palmers Green, Essex House at Old Southgate, and the Old Court House at Hampton Court, where Wren died in 1723. About this time, too, must have been built Goodhew's Farm, Lower Hale Farm, and Lawrence Street Farm, all near Mill Hill; also Dollis Hill Farm, and Lyon Farm at Preston. Some of the most attractive old streets in Middlesex consist mainly of buildings of this period, e.g. Gentleman's Row at Enfield, the High Street at Uxbridge, and Church Street at Staines. Thatched cottages are now very rare in Middlesex, but there are examples of uncertain date at Heath Row near Harmondsworth and elsewhere. The same period produced some beautiful wrought-iron gates, notably in Enfield, and there is also a fine example at the Priory at Tottenham.

The most striking house of the eighteenth century in Middlesex is Lord Burlington's famous villa, now known as Chiswick House (1730), which is as Italian in spirit as any building in this country. Marble Hill (c. 1725) at Twickenham is a charming and less grandiose design. Hillingdon House was built in 1717, Cranford Park about the middle of the century, as were the mansion in Wrotham Park near South Mimms and Hogarth's house at Chiswick. Robert Adam designed Kenwood, just over the London border, though its stables and outbuildings are in Middlesex; also Syon House near Isleworth; and large parts of the mansions in Osterley Park and Pymme's Park. At the same time Horace Walpole was erecting his ridiculous mock-Gothic house at Strawberry Hill (p. 273), and another very early example of revived Gothic is Twyford Abbey (1807–9). Erected almost at the same time, but in the classical tradition, are Pitzhanger Manor at Ealing, rebuilt by Sir John Soane in 1801 as his country house, and now the Ealing Public Library; Grovelands at Southgate, designed by Nash, the architect of old Regent Street; and Dyrham Park near South Mimms. The great mansions in Trent Park, Gunnersbury Park, White Webbs Park, Canons Park, and Littleton Park are all comparatively modern buildings replacing smaller houses.

Of the three chief public schools in the county, Harrow still possesses its old building of 1615 in a modified form, Highgate retains nothing of the original schoolhouse erected in 1576 (p. 116), and the School at Mill Hill was built in 1825. At Stanwell near Staines is a charming little brick schoolhouse dated 1624. There are Jacobean almshouses in brick at Friern Barnet (1612) and at Harefield, both groups being of considerable interest. There is still a moated house, with a fine example of a moat, at Headstone Manor, but the house itself has little architectural merit; and the very large moated Jacobean house known as Wyre Hall (p. 76) near Edmonton was demolished years ago, the moat having been recently filled in.

Of old timber barns there are still, fortunately, many surviving examples. The most notable is the great barn of the former Priory in Harmondsworth (p. 218), and there are other fine specimens at Ickenham, Headstone Manor, Eastcote, and Ruislip. The second and last of these four are now public property, so will be preserved. Water mills are comparatively rare, and the picturesque mills at Tottenham were burned down about 1850. The large mills at Ponder's End and at Isleworth, covered with weatherboarding, are of no great age but are the chief examples. There is now not a single windmill standing in Middlesex, the familiar landmark at Barnet Gate being a few yards over the Hertfordshire frontier. But they were formerly plentiful enough, as old maps and pictures show, and a fine specimen was standing in Brondesbury so recently as 1860. The village smithy has given way to the suburban petrol pump almost everywhere, but only a generation ago it was a common feature in most parts of the county.

The village inn has made a gallant fight against progress, but is being successfully eliminated in many places by conversion into a modern hotel, thereby assuming the prevailing colour of its environment. Nevertheless, there are numerous picturesque old inns which have still escaped the zeal of the reformer, such as the "Fallow Buck" near Enfield, the "George" at Ruislip, the "Spaniard's Tavern" at Hampstead, and the "King's Head" at Mill Hill. The "Green Man" at the Hale, near Edgware, has now blossomed into a bigger and brighter hostelry, as has the old "Plough" on Kingsbury Green and many another.

All these changes in the interests of business, sanitation, and what-not are gradually eliminating all rural charm from most of the remaining village streets in Middlesex. Of those illustrated here, the High Streets of Pinner, Ruislip, and Uxbridge remain practically as drawn, but the High Road at Edgware is becoming urbanized. The village green at Stanwell is delightful, but that at Ickenham is feeling the suburban draught, and some skill is needed there—as in so many places in Middlesex—to find a viewpoint from which everything in sight is pleasing. In this matter the black-and-white artist has some advantage over a photographer, for, without being deliberately untruthful, he can omit the thirty glaring enamelled signs which proclaim that Goodhew's Farm (p. 130) is now a "service station" which also sells cigarettes, and he can ignore all vulgar screaming slogans about "Baronial Halls" and "Tudor Homes."

He can do all these things, but he cannot help feeling some regret that every village street seems destined—under present conditions—to be sacrificed to a craze for strident and generally futile advertisement. The more hoardings and postings and legends and slogans you plaster on to your walls, the less they can be read, and any sensitive person averts his eyes. The Edgware Road, from Cricklewood to Hendon, displays miles of such hoardings. The banks, the post offices, and telephone exchanges erected during the last few years—together with some multiple shops and some public-houses—are evidence of a conviction in some quarters that taste pays in the end more than American methods of shouting, and they do not insult or bully the charm of the village street. It will be sad if the High Street at Ruislip is to resemble the awful squalor of the Harrow Road within ten years; but it assuredly will, unless the burgesses of Ruislip, who are already banded together to save it from complete uglification, display great ingenuity and persistence. Twenty-five years' study of this changing county have convinced me only too clearly of the grim inevitability with which such things happen in the ordinary course of life.

But even Middlesex need not suffer all these indignities, for it contains, in the Hampstead Garden Suburb, a perfect exemplar—to my mind the best in the whole country—of suburban lay-out. Some people nowadays ridicule the "quaintness" of gabled houses and leaded lights, for fashions change rapidly; others jeer at the little enclosed gardens. But the fact remains that the estate is a most valuable property which is not deteriorating as most building estates do; and the reason why it "keeps up its character" is that, thanks to the artistic vision and foresight of its designer, everything attractive in natural features has been preserved and nothing offensive is allowed to be introduced.

Hardly less attractive is the L.C.C. Watling Estate between

Hendon and Edgware, already mentioned as a place where elm-trees are not cut down. Both these estates have been laid out with great care by trained and thoughtful men, and there are many other excellent examples of lay-out by speculative builders. But a large part of the remaining agricultural and wooded areas of Middlesex will have been completely covered with standardized streets, and stripped of all trees and every feature of natural beauty, unless the authorities move rapidly and decisively. Town-planning

Holcombe Hill · Mill Hill · 1926

experts have reported voluminously; it only remains to decide how far their recommendations can be followed.

The lines of the new main roads are being settled, and perhaps the most important precaution to be taken is the securing—by one means or another—of suitable and adequate public open spaces. In the districts bordering on London, little more remains to be done, for much has been done already, and land is impossibly expensive. There are a few obvious things outstanding, such as the demolition of the hideous and costly Alexandra Palace, which would be an actual economy. But, in the main, the real business lies farther afield. Many of the great private parks mentioned above—Gunnersbury, Broomfield, Grovelands, Chiswick, White

Webbs—have become public property and are secured. Others, such as Syon Park, Osterley Park, Trent Park, Forty Hall, remain in private hands and are liable to be sold at any moment unless they are scheduled as open spaces, private or public, for the future.* All these four parks are of great size and beauty, the first two are nearly surrounded by houses, and the others will be within ten years. In later chapters of this book each district is described and suggestions are made for the preservation of such of its natural features, open spaces, picturesque corners, and old houses, as can be reconciled with modern needs of transport, industry, and housing. Full recognition is given to the excellent work already done in this direction by the county and urban authorities, who are faced with a task in town-planning administration unequalled in urgency and complexity anywhere in England.

It may be observed that no mention has been made in this chapter of the numerous old churches, many of historical interest, which are illustrated in the book. They receive due notice in the individual descriptions of localities which follow, but they raise few problems—as it happens—in connection with the present or the future. For a church is seldom touched in the course of normal housing developments, and, although its picturesque surroundings are often impaired thereby, its possession of a God's Acre planted with yew-trees often makes it a peaceful oasis in the midst of busy urbanity. The old churches of Middlesex are for the most part small, none indeed are large, and in most districts they constitute the only surviving relic of the Middle Ages. Many of them have been over-restored, most have been altered in modern times, but as a whole they have been carefully tended, and are likely to be even more sedulously watched over in the future.

It is therefore clear that the problem of preserving the historical relics of Middlesex is limited to secular buildings and to the natural beauties of landscape which it still retains, to an extent often hardly realized, in so many of its districts.

---

* Trent Park has now been scheduled.

BOOKS ON THE HISTORY AND TOPOGRAPHY OF MIDDLESEX IN GENERAL

ADAMS, THOMPSON and FRY	West Middlesex (Regional Town Planning Report)	1924
ditto	North Middlesex (Regional Town Planning Report)	1928
ditto	The Thames from Putney to Staines (Regional Town Planning Report)	1930
ANDREWS, W.	Bygone Middlesex	1899
BELL, W. G.	Where London Sleeps	1926
BELL, MRS. A.	The Skirts of the Great City	1907
BOSWORTH, G. F.	Middlesex (*Cambridge County Geographies*)	1913
BOWACK, J.	Antiquities of Middlesex	1705
BRAYLEY, E. W., and BRITTON, J.	The Beauties of England and Wales (vol. X, London and Middlesex)	1814–16
BROWN, J. A.	Palaeolithic Man in N.W. Middlesex	1887
CANSICK, F. T.	Epitaphs of Middlesex	1874–5
COOKE, G. A.	Middlesex, Topographical Description of	N.D.
FIRTH, J. B.	Middlesex (*Little Guides*), 2nd edition	1930
FOLEY, H. J.	Our Lanes and Meadow-paths: Rambles in Rural Middlesex	[c. 1887]
GOVER, J. E. B.	The Place Names of Middlesex	1922
GREATER LONDON REGIONAL PLANNING COMMITTEE	Reports (vols. I and II)	1929, 1933
HARPER, C. G.	Rural Nooks near London (Middlesex and Surrey)	1907
ditto	Thames Valley Villages (2 vols.)	1910
HOPE-MONCRIEFF, A. R.	Middlesex (*Black's Colour Books*)	1907
ditto	Black's Guide around London: West Side	1902
ditto	Black's Guide around London: North Side	1903
HUGHES, W.	The Geography of Middlesex	1872
JERROLD, W.	Highways and Byways in Middlesex	1909
KEANE, W.	Beauties of Middlesex	1850
LAWSON, W.	Middlesex (*Collins's County Geographies*)	1872
LONDON AND MIDDLESEX	Archaeological Society's Transactions [*passim*]	1860 *et seq.*

LYSONS, D.	The Environs of London (4 vols.) [Vols. II, III and the Supplement (1811) deal with Middlesex.]	1792-6
LYSONS, D.	. . . Parishes in Middlesex . . . not described [above]	1800
MAXWELL, G. S.	Just Beyond London (Edmonton, Headstone, Gunnersbury, Kingsbury, Osterley, Twyford)	1927
ditto	The Fringe of London (including Wembley and Stonebridge)	1931
[Middlesex]	A Description of the County of Middlesex	1775
MIDDLETON, J.	View of the Agriculture of Middlesex	1798
MOUL, D., and HILL, R. E. H.	Picturesque Middlesex	1904
MURBY, T.	Middlesex (*Murby's County Geographies*)	1874
NORDEN, J.	Speculum Britanniae (vol. I, Middlesex)	1593
PINNOCK, W.	History and Topography of Middlesex	1824
PLARR, V. G., and WALTON, F. W.	A School History of Middlesex	1905
POPE, T. M.	Middlesex in Prose and Verse	1930
SHARPE, SIR Montagu	Middlesex in British, Saxon and Roman Times	1932
SMITH, D. H.	Industries of Greater London (chiefly Middlesex)	1933
SPERLING, J. H.	Church Walks in Middlesex	1849
TAVENOR-PERRY, J.	Memorials of Old Middlesex	1909
THORNE, J.	Environs of London (2 vols.)	1876
VAUGHAN, H. S.	The Way about Middlesex	1896
VICTORIA COUNTY HISTORY	Middlesex [vol. II (vol. I not published)]	1911
VULLIAMY, C. E.	Archaeology of London and Middlesex	1930
WALFORD, E.	Greater London (2 vols.)	1893-5
WOOD, C. A.	Rambles in the Home Counties (Chap. I, "A Streamside Ramble in Middlesex")	1914

NOTE.—The above list does not include books on the Thames, nor articles in periodicals. Useful information will also be found in the volumes of the *Home Counties Magazine*, in *Middlesex Notes and Queries*, and in the transactions and reports of the various local archaeological and historical societies.

CHAPTER II

POTTERS BAR AND SOUTH MIMMS

A PILGRIM through Middlesex may begin his journey from London and work outwards, or approach the metropolis from one of the points where a great road or railway enters Middlesex from the outer darkness. One must begin somewhere, and this district serves as well as any other; or even better, for it retains even now, far more than the suburbanized areas, much of the rural charm that the county as a whole once possessed.

The new double-barrelled name that the authorities have seen fit to impose upon it last year (1933) is clumsy, and somehow grates on the ear. "Potters Bar" is all very well in its way, and presumably it is getting its way as the chief centre of population in a mainly rural area. "It seems probable," writes a local historian,* "that the hamlet derives its name from the pottery which stood near the junction of the Great North Road and Southgate Road, and that a bar, from which the lord of Wyllyott's Manor drew tolls for the upkeep of the road, stood near the pottery." But the historian of Middlesex place-names† says that Potter was an underkeeper at one of the lodges of Enfield Chase (called "Potter's Lodge" in 1635), which stood by the gate or "bar" of the Chase. As for South Mimms, a quaint and beautiful name, that is something of an etymological curiosity.‡ It is spelt "Mimmine" in Domesday (centuries before parvenu Potters Bar was ever heard of), and then appears in all sorts of forms—Mymmis, Mymmys, Mimmis, Myms, Mynes, Menns, Mens, Myns, Minns, Mim, and many more—so that the present official spelling of "Mimms" is as

* F. Brittain, *South Mymms*, p. 32.

† J. B. Gover, *The Place-names of Middlesex*, p. 71.

‡ The name is supposed to have designated "the abode of the Mimmas," perhaps some obscure tribe or family; but one authority suggests *munmus* (Latin = "a mound").

justifiable as the more picturesque rendering "Mymms" favoured
by the historian of the village, who complains that "Mimms"
reminds him of Lewis Carroll's "mimsy borogoves"—whatever
they were, certainly objects of derision. Up to last year the
district in question was "South Mimms Rural District"; from

SOUTH MIMMS PARISH CHURCH

now onwards it becomes "Potters Bar and South Mimms Urban
District," and thus a considerable mouthful.

Its area, now some $9\frac{1}{2}$ square miles, has been varied from time
to time. It remained fairly stable up to 1777, when its eastern
boundary—then formed by the Great North Road—was extended
about three-quarters of a mile by the addition of a strip of Enfield
Chase, over 1,000 acres in all. Southwards the old parish extended
right up to Chipping Barnet Church, thus including a large part
of Barnet and Hadley. But Barnet has successfully nibbled off bits
of South Mimms on recent occasions, and still shows some appetite
for further morsels. It has already been suggested in this book

(p. 24) that Barnet, East Barnet, and Totteridge are geographically part of Middlesex, into which they drain and from which they were detached by the greed of the Abbot of St. Albans a thousand years ago. But conversely, South Mimms, or most of it, is geographically a part of Hertfordshire. The natural boundary between the counties is the road which follows the watershed between the Colne and the Brent, from Elstree through Barnet Gate and Arkley to High Barnet; then the Great North Road to

THE DUKE OF YORK INN ON THE GREAT NORTH ROAD

Potters Bar. Everything south and east of that line ought to be in Middlesex, everything north and west in Hertfordshire. The recent growth of Barnet may have made such a rectification of frontier impracticable for administrative reasons, but it is extraordinary that no attempt at change has been made in the recent game of "general post" among the various local authorities.

South Mimms (and this includes Potters Bar hereafter) had a population of 5,720 in 1931, almost exactly double the figure in 1911 when it had hardly begun to grow. It was 1,698 in 1801. A generation ago there was a very picturesque village at South Mimms, a straggling and rather untidy "suburban" settlement at

Potters Bar, clusters of houses at Dancer's Hill and Bentley Heath. Since those days, except for a few municipal houses and a few bungalows at South Mimms, the development has occurred at Potters Bar, which shows every sign of becoming completely suburban at an early date. A recent announcement that a certain firm are about to commence the erection of 1,100 houses on the Oakmere Estate has an ominous sound, for whatever you call the pioneers, the result is the same ultimately. There will be shops for face powder and gramophone records, loud-speakers will shout American vulgarities at you down the "Parade" and the "Broadway"—to say nothing of "Acacia Gardens"—and the whole place will be crawling with small cars acquired by the newly married settlers. That is the accepted procedure in Disappearing Middlesex.

At the moment, however, most of the district is really beautiful. Its lowest point is 252 feet above sea-level, its highest 433 feet. The chalk appears here, and only in one other place in Middlesex, at Harefield on the western border. There are also gravel beds, but the remainder of the subsoil is the London clay which covers most of the county. It is one of the few districts in Middlesex where corn may still be seen, though Middlesex corn was once famous. Market gardens do not appear, the greater part of the land being either pasture or woodland. Most of the lovely Mimms Wood lies in Hertfordshire, but a portion is in Middlesex. Yet even into that fastness "civilization" is penetrating; for, as Sir Arthur Quiller-Couch has recently written*: "The despoilers come over the ridge to uproot its woodland and wayside flowers: and after these skirmishers all too often follow the heavy municipal hoplites to hew down the trees and plant lamp-posts." Mr. Brittain's book takes up the tale: "It would be a crime if this blue carpet were to be destroyed, and the destroyers would deserve the name of barbarians. Yet its beauty, which depends on the massed effect of the blooms [wild hyacinths], has already been very greatly reduced in area through the depredations of visitors from London. Thousands and thousands of blooms are torn from the ground

* In a Foreword to Mr. Brittain's *South Mymms* (1931).

every year. Many of these are littered along the road to London, 'jewelled plumes at random thrown.' Many are used for 'nature study' lessons in London schools, and thousands of bunches are offered for sale in London streets."

South Mimms is one of the few remaining districts of Middlesex where hounds meet regularly during the season. At least two great estates, Dyrham Park and Wrotham Park, remain inviolate, and

WYLLYOTT'S MANOR, POTTERS BAR

each contains a certain amount of water in the form of ornamental lakes. The only stream in the district is known in various portions of its short length as Trotter's Brook, Mimms Wash, and Mymms-hall Brook. Though properly a tributary of the Colne, it only serves as such in flood-time, its waters normally disappearing into swallow holes at North Mimms.

The railway made its appearance here in 1848, but had little influence upon development for some years, the station (at Potters Bar) being some distance from the string of houses and inns along the Great North Road. But the new electric railway recently opened (1933) to Cockfosters may cause great building activity round Potters Bar as bus services are improved.

The outstanding feature of the district is, and has been for a century, the system of trunk-roads which traverse it. It is, in fact, miraculous that these roads have not caused more housing development than has actually occurred. First and foremost there is the Great North Road itself, renowned in story and song. But it is not a really ancient highway. "Ermine Street," from London through Edmonton and Ware to Royston and Lincoln, and Watling Street, through Edgware and St. Albans to Shrewsbury, carried the north-bound traffic from Roman times for centuries. In the Middle Ages there was a road through St. Pancras, Hornsey, Muswell Hill, and Whetstone to Barnet, whence it seems to have followed the line of the present Great North Road through Hadley and Potters Bar. From Hadley a road to St. Albans wound through Dancer's Hill,* crossed the brook at Mimms Wash by a quaint little hump-backed brick bridge still standing, passed along the main street of South Mimms, and crossed the present Barnet–St. Albans Road, the line of which it rejoined at Ridge Hill. The present wide and well-graded road from Barnet High Street to Ridge Hill was constructed by the famous engineer Telford in 1826. As a result, the main street of South Mimms, which it crossed, ceased to be a traffic artery and was left high and dry. It seems almost incredible that this parish, which had less than 1,700 inhabitants in 1801, at one time actually possessed thirty-eight inns! Yet the local historian gives the name and location of each.† In the words of a contemporary writer, there was "an abundance of such inns as profess to furnish the traveller with comforts only, and leave the elegancies of entertainment to houses of public reception more eligibly circumstanced." But while the construction of Telford's road to St. Albans has left us an almost unspoiled village street at South Mimms, the improvement of the

* Dancer's Hill is so called after a family of that name who lived there before Queen Elizabeth's time, but the inveterate legend-makers have invented a story that its name is due to the fact that she watched children dancing there. What with the beds she slept in all over England, Queen Elizabeth has a lot to answer for.   † Brittain, *op. cit.*, pp. 87–9.

Great North Road has not improved Potters Bar, where, however, one must concede that the large new bus station with its brilliant flower-beds is an attractive modern feature. According to Cary's map of 1800, there was a right-angled bend in the road north of Potters Bar, with a turnpike at the county boundary. The latest road in the district is the Barnet Bypass, a magnificently engineered and well-planted thoroughfare which, at the time of writing, passes through almost entirely open country in its course of 2¾ miles across the district. The history of South Mimms in the past has been largely concerned with famous coaches, inns, highwaymen, and tramps; its future seems to rest mainly with motorists and the speculative builder.

Of ancient buildings, the beautiful parish church of South Mimms is undoubtedly the most important in the district. Its restoration during the nineteenth century by the great architect, G. E. Street, was the cause of long-drawn and violent controversy, for a succession of High Church parsons maintained a ritual often repugnant to a small community in which Nonconformity was active. But they had their way in the end, and the result is one of the finest churches in the county. Its features of interest are described in all guide-books,* but special mention may be made of the Frowyke tomb (c. 1500) and the neighbouring carved screen in wood. There is a noble tower and a painted Calvary in the churchyard.

The site of the Frowykes' manor house is marked by the existing moat in the Old Fold Golf Club. South Mimms had a castle of sorts, briefly described many years ago in an archaeological journal; as it has recently been examined by local antiquaries, we may expect to hear more of it in the future. The old house called Knightsland, near Dyrham Park, is said to date from c. 1500, and contains some fine linenfold panelling. Near Potters Bar station is a curious and very interesting medieval half-timbered house, Wyllyott's Manor. It was given to the Brewers' Company in the seventeenth century, and bought from them in 1924 by Mr. Hugh

---

* See article by the Rev. J. C. Cox in J. Tavenor Perry's *Memorials of Old Middlesex*, pp. 66–8; also J. B. Firth's *Middlesex*, p. 204.

Seabrook, who states that "the original structure consisted of a timbered aisled building, 84 feet long and 28 feet wide, divided into six bays." He had it thoroughly restored, removing the external stucco and thus exposing the timber framing. The interior has interesting features. Other old buildings, of uncertain age and much altered, are Mimms Hall and Blanch Farm. The Battle of Barnet (1471) is commemorated by the obelisk on Hadley Green, and is well described in J. Tavenor Perry's *Memorials of Old Middlesex*, pp. 108–13.

Later buildings of note include the fine old coaching inn, "The Duke of York," at Gannic or Ganwick Corner on the Great North Road, and Bridgefoot House or Farm. The two great country mansions, already mentioned, are Wrotham Park and Dyrham Park. The former was erected by the unfortunate Admiral Byng, who was executed for negligence in his duties, from the designs of the architect Ware in 1754. It is an imposing stone building in the classical style of the period. The military and naval trophies in the pediments seem to have an ironical character in view of their owner's fate. The fine gardens, somewhat informal in treatment, are thrown open to the public periodically in connection with the Queen's Institute of District Nursing Scheme. The whole park has an area of 286 acres, and is still in the possession of the Earl of Strafford, a scion of the Byng family.*

Dyrham Park (170 acres) is another fine estate, and its present owner is a member of a family which bought it in 1798 and rebuilt the mansion at the beginning of the nineteenth century. "Durhams," as it used to be called and is still sometimes known, was originally an Elizabethan house, and has a long history. The most interesting feature architecturally is the triumphal gateway, flanked by lodges, which stands near the Barnet–St. Albans main road. Most guide-books tell us that this was set up in London by General Monk in 1660 to commemorate the first public entry of Charles II after his restoration. But the design suggests a later date, and Mr. Brittain, whose excellent history of South Mimms

* For an illustrated description of Wrotham Park, see *Country Life*, XLIV, pp. 404, 458.

has been frequently quoted in this chapter, writes that "there is no evidence to support this tradition."

Of modern buildings, the Middlesex County Council's Sanatorium at Clare Hall, formerly a private house, is the most important. A melancholy interest is attached to the little cemetery in Mutton Lane, Potters Bar, where lie buried the crews of the two Zeppelins which were brought down in the neighbourhood during the Great War.

DYRHAM PARK GATES, SOUTH MIMMS

When one looks ahead, it will be realized that this district, at present so sparsely populated, can provide space for some 300,000 people on a basis of twelve houses to the acre. Some tens of thousands of them are sure to arrive soon, and it is well to consider some places which should be reserved for public use or—at any rate—as "private open spaces." The Middlesex County Council, in its regional-planning scheme, reserves—under the latter head—Dyrham Park and Wrotham Park, while the valley of the Mymmshall Brook, the area round Kitts End, and several smaller patches are recommended as "public open spaces." It is to be hoped that this provision will be secured, and also that the surviving old buildings mentioned in this chapter will be preserved, to recall something of the present beauty of South Mimms.

BOOKS ON LOCAL HISTORY AND TOPOGRAPHY

BRITTAIN, F.	South Mymms	Cambridge	1931
CASS, F. C.	South Mimms (London and Middlesex Archaeological Society)	Westminster	1877

CHAPTER III

ENFIELD

INCLUDING BOTANY BAY, BRIMSDOWN, CLAY HILL, FORTY HILL, FREEZY WATER, AND PONDER'S END

Most people have heard of Enfield in one connection or another—rifles or Charles Lamb or bicycles or even the famous royal Chase—and those who do not know the district at first-hand will react differently to the mention of its name. Those who have only traversed its eastern quarters will think of it as a crowded town of mean streets, those who have seen only its centre will recall a picturesque market-place with an ancient church, while those who are only familiar with its western and northern half will conjure up a mental picture of hilly and richly wooded country with long views and lordly seats. They will all be right, for Enfield in its wide extent comprises a great variety of scene.

As for its name, it figures in Domesday as "Enefelde," from the Anglo-Saxon *Ænan feld*, which is—being interpreted—"the clear open space of Æna," so the experts say. With the usual variations of spelling, its original name has fluctuated but little in the course of the centuries. Some of the other names at the head of this chapter are more puzzling. Why the cluster of houses on the Ridgeway should be christened "Botany Bay" is not at all clear, and here the invaluable Mr. Gover fails us.* The encyclopedia states that a fruitless attempt was made to establish a penal colony at Botany Bay in Australia in 1787, and that, the name having caught the popular fancy, it was applied to subsequent convict colonies in that newly discovered continent. Certainly the name does not appear on old maps of the district, but a chance reference† to the transportation in 1789 of a pickpocket from Enfield races to "Botany Bay" (i.e. Australia) for seven years leads

---

* J. E. B. Gover, *The Place-names of Middlesex* (1922).
† In J. Tuff, *Notices of Enfield* (1858), p. 30.

me to offer this as a plausible explanation. "Brimsdown," whence all we who dwell in North Middlesex now obtain our electric light and power by means of the "Grid," was formerly "Grimsdown." "Clay Hill" explains itself. "Forty Hill" recalls the mansion of Sir Hugh Fortee, which stood there three hundred years ago. "Freezy Water" defies the etymologists, but as it is a marshy and wind-swept area, the name may be explained on common-sense

ENFIELD PARISH CHURCH AND GRAMMAR SCHOOL, FROM THE MARKET PLACE

grounds. "Ponder's End," a name in use at least as early as 1610, probably indicates a man named Ponder.

Enfield was the largest of the old parishes of Middlesex, and, up to the recent redistribution of areas (1933), was the largest administrative area. It is now, with a revised area of 12,397 acres (about 20 square miles), slightly smaller than the new urban district of Harrow, with 12,558 acres, that is, 16 acres less than Enfield itself was before the rearrangement. Its western frontier to South Mimms has already been described. On the south it is bounded by the old parish of Edmonton, separated into the two districts of Edmonton (Chapter IV) and Southgate (Chapter V) in 1894.

This boundary was very irregular and irrational up to the recent reorganization, when two "salients" at Cockfosters and near Chase Cottage were eliminated—the former going to Southgate, the latter to Edmonton. The remaining part of the southern boundary, from Cockfosters to Hadley, marches with the East Barnet district of Hertfordshire. The northern boundary is nearly straight, and has formed the Middlesex–Hertfordshire frontier since the tenth

GENTLEMAN'S ROW, ENFIELD

or eleventh century, certainly before the Norman Conquest. The eastern boundary, formed by the River Lea, is obvious enough, and is of even greater antiquity, dating from the capture of London in A.D. 886, during King Alfred's wars with the Danes.*

The population of Enfield at the 1931 census was 67,869, and must now be 70,000. It was 56,255 in 1911, so the growth was not especially rapid in the twenty years, compared with many other districts of Middlesex, but is likely to increase greatly in the future owing to the arrival of the new electric railway with stations at

* Sir Montagu Sharpe, *Middlesex in British, Roman, and Saxon Times* (1932), pp. 191–4.

Enfield West and at Cockfosters. It is very rash to prophesy what will be the population of the area a generation hence, but if the whole ground were covered (which God forbid) with "Distinctive Homes" at twelve to the acre, there would be at least 600,000 inhabitants. (Tottenham, with a quarter of Enfield's acreage, already has one-quarter that number of citizens.)

The urban district of Enfield in its 7 miles of length contains, as has been remarked already, a great variety of scenery. Its western half is almost entirely devoid of buildings—this area including the old Chase after its dismemberment in 1777, and several large estates detached from the Chase at that time. It retains a good deal of woodland and much pasture, the subsoil being the London clay interspersed with a few patches of gravel. It is very hilly, and is intersected by several valleys. The eastern half of the district, approximately east of the market-place, is almost dead level, and in a walk of $2\frac{1}{2}$ miles or so from the market-place to the Lea one passes successively over beds of London clay, brick-earth, valley gravel, and (as one approaches the river) alluvium. Up to a few years ago the greater part of this flat area, 3 or 4 miles square, was largely given up to market gardens, orchards, and glasshouses, intersected by a long strip of "ribbon development" on either side of the old Hertford Road. Now all these useful appurtenances of London are being rapidly swept away to make room for more and more "Houses of Artistry," and wider and faster motor-roads. The town-planners' ideal of a great city surrounded by a productive agricultural belt has been sedulously ignored in the development of modern Enfield.

As regards watercourses, Pymme's Brook—which receives some attention in the next two chapters—takes its rise in the charming ponds in Beech Hill Park, now a very beautiful golf course. The Cuffley Brook enters the district near Crews Hill Station, passes White Webbs Park and Forty Hall to Maiden's Bridge, where it is crossed by the Enfield–Theobalds Road, and thence passes beneath the New Cambridge Road, a railway, the old Hertford Road (where it is called "Enfield Wash"), another railway, and at length empties itself into the Lea. From Clay Hill to Maiden's

Bridge its whole course is sylvan and beautiful. Through White Webbs Park, now public property, its banks are preserved, and it is to be hoped that the scheme for including it in the Middlesex "green girdle" will be successful. From Maiden's Bridge to the Lea its appearance progressively deteriorates, and at Enfield Wash it is confined between concrete walls.

The Lea itself must have been a considerable river in the days

THE MILL, PONDER'S END

when "Mr. Piscator" and his friends sallied forth on their early morning expeditions, but its main channel has now been diverted or obliterated for most of its length along the Enfield boundary by the construction of the enormous "King George Reservoir," over a mile and a half long. This artificial lake was opened by His Majesty in 1913 with great pomp and circumstance as befitted the occasion. The other channels and feeders of this part of the Lea have lost much of their former charm, though there is a picturesque reach near the old mill at Ponder's End. In the regional town-planning proposals of the County Council it is proposed to reserve South Marsh and Rammey Marsh as public open spaces, leaving the remaining area between the canal and the railway as an "industrial zone," which indeed it has become already. The great power station at Brimsdown, the gasworks, and factories which occupy part of this belt are an inevitable adjunct to our civilization, and it is no use shedding tears about them.

It is strange that a mere aqueduct should furnish some of the pleasantest riverside scenery in Middlesex. The New River, when it was originally constructed by Sir Hugh Myddelton between 1609 and 1613, was a channel 10 feet wide and about 4 feet deep, carrying water from the springs at Amwell and Chadwell, near Ware in Hertfordshire, to Islington near London. The length of the original course is variously stated to have been 39 and 48 miles, and the fall 2 inches to the mile. Since those days there have been many changes. The width of the stream is now 25 feet, some of the 160 bridges have been removed, and the length of the whole river has been reduced to 28 miles by means of modern engineering. Yet the most remarkable fact to us, in this chapter, is that the whole 7 miles of its winding course through Enfield are now superfluous, and it was proposed some forty-five years ago to drain off the channel. But this purely utilitarian aqueduct was rightly regarded by the inhabitants as a scenic asset to the neighbourhood, and popular agitation defeated the proposal, even in face of those philanthropists who urged that the river's many bends and sheltering trees interfered with the construction of rows of villas.* Thus the New River was not only an engineering triumph for its pioneer, and a source of enormous wealth to his successors, but has become a notable feature in the landscape of Enfield.

It is, however, Enfield Chase that has brought most historical renown to the district. This famous hunting park, consisting of about 8,000 acres, passed to the Crown in 1399, when Henry Duke of Lancaster—who had inherited Enfield Chase through his wife, daughter of De Bohun, lord of the Manor of Enfield— became King Henry IV. Its whole extent remained Crown property until 1777, when it was divided between the King and the surrounding parishes of Enfield, Edmonton, Hadley, and South

* See *The Story of Enfield* (Meyers, Brooks & Co., Enfield, 1930), p. 62.

Mimms. Enfield received over 1,700 acres of the spoils, the Crown retaining some 5 square miles out of its original 12. Apparently the procedure was considered profitable, for Francis Russell —surveyor to the Duchy of Lancaster—received an estate of 270 acres for his share in the transaction, and eventually erected the mansion later known as Beech Hill Park upon the site. According to a map in Whitaker's *History of Enfield*, published in 1911, the Crown owned in 1911 practically all the land, except Beech Hill Park, west of East Lodge, and also the properties known as East Lodge and North Lodge. This area includes Trent Park, Hadley Wood Station, and Botany Bay. At present it is very sparsely populated, but the new stations of Cockfosters and Enfield West on the electric railway are at its door, and presumably there will be a rapid development there in the near future. To-day Hadley Wood is the only part of the old Chase which is in public ownership, and that is in Hertfordshire. This makes it all the more important that some portion of the 5 square miles of its area in Middlesex should be preserved as an open space before it is completely covered with "Baronial Halls." The "green girdle" proposed in the North Middlesex regional scheme includes Trent Park (*c.* 1,000 acres) and Beech Hill Park, now a golf club, as "private open spaces," and the long valley that runs parallel with, and south of, the Ridgeway as a public open space. This is not an excessive provision for a large populated area. It is also proposed to reserve the golf links at Crews Hill, which lies just outside the limits of the Chase proper.

According to the excellent conjectural maps in Captain Whitaker's *History of Enfield*, the whole parish was heavily wooded in pre-Roman times, when there was a continuous forest over most of Middlesex extending into Essex on the east. There was, however, a cleared area between the present line of the Hertford Road and the Lea marshes, marked as "March of the Catuvellauni" on the first of Captain Whitaker's maps. The Lea, crossed by three fords, separated the Catuvellauni of Middlesex from the Trinobantes of Essex. The next map, of Enfield in the Romano-British period, shows the clearing extended west to the site of the present market-

place, in the southern part of the area, and a couple of moated
settlements are shown besides the "Oppidum of Cassivelaunus (?)"
in Old Park. Ermine Street (see page 33) also makes its
appearance, and a Roman villa at "Oldbury." The third map
shows Anglo-Saxon and Danish Enfield with the forest rather more
thinned, the parish church, several manors, and a few tracks on
the present lines of Baker Street, Southbury Road, etc.

The western half of the area remained forest, and this became
the Chase, for a long time crossed by no roads. It was bounded
on the west by the present Great North Road. The north boundary
ran near to the present county boundary, from Potters Bar to
White Webbs. The various gates were Winchmore Hill Gate,
South Gate, Bohun's Gate, Hook Gate, Barvin Gate, Cattle Gate,
White Webbs Gate, Clay Hill Gate, and Filcap Gate. Southgate
and Cattlegate remain as modern names. The four lodges—North
Lodge, South Lodge, East Lodge, and West Lodge—remain as
large private houses with their own grounds, but none of them
seems to have much architectural interest. Other links with the
history of the Chase are to be found in the names of the old inns,
e.g. the "Fallow Buck," the "Roebuck," the "White Hart," the
"Stag," the "Falcon," and the "Greyhound." The King and
Tinker Inn at White Webbs is so called on account of an incident
which occurred in the time of King James I and has been recorded in
doggerel verse, too lengthy to quote here *in extenso*. Briefly, the ballad
relates how the King, when out hunting, stopped to rest at the inn
where the tinker was enjoying a tankard of ale. The tinker remarked
that he had heard that the King was hunting, and would like to
see him. "If you will mount behind me," the monarch replied,
"you shall have your wish." The tinker did so, and off they rode
together. "But how shall I know the king?" said the tinker.
"That will be easy enough," rejoined the King, "because all the
courtiers will be bareheaded." When they finally encountered the
royal attendants, the tinker was at a loss, and asked, "But which
is the king?" "Evidently it must be one of us," said James, "because
everyone else is bareheaded." Whereupon the tinker slid off the
horse and begged for mercy. King James loved a joke, and was so

pleased with this one that he forthwith knighted the tinker, and made him an allowance of five hundred pounds a year for life. Any lover of poetry or royalty may confirm this prosaic paraphrase by calling in person at the "King and Tinker," where for the sum of twopence he can purchase the ballad complete with pictures.

A more authentic picture of the Chase in the seventeenth century appears in John Evelyn's diary for June 2, 1676:

THE FALLOW BUCK INN, CLAY HILL, NEAR ENFIELD

I went with my Lord Chamberlaine to see a garden at Enfield towne; thence to Mr. Sec. Coventry's lodge in the Chase. It is a very pretty place, the house commodious, the gardens handsome, and our entertainment very free, there being none but my Lord and myselfe. That which I most wondered at was, that in the compass of 25 miles, yet within 14 of London, there is not an house, barne, church, or building, besides three lodges. To this Lodge are three greate ponds and some few inclosures, the rest a solitarie desert, yet stor'd with not less than 3,000 deere. These are pretty retreats for gentlemen, especially for those who are studious and lovers of privacy.

The famous Enfield Chase Staghounds have been disbanded since the Great War.

Only one of the roads which traverse the district is old, and that is the main Hertford Road, part of which follows the course of the Roman "Ermine Street" from London through Ware and Royston to Lincoln. Its line coincided more or less with the present road from Bishopsgate through Stamford Hill and Tottenham to near Edmonton. Here the Hertford Road turns slightly north-east and goes through Enfield "Highway," Waltham Cross, and Cheshunt "Street," to Ware. The Roman Road ran almost due north and quite straight from Edmonton, and its course may be traced on a map along bits of road which preserve the line, e.g. on the west of Theobalds Park. The road now called at various points Silver Street, Baker Street, Forty Hill, and Bulls Cross—leading from Enfield Market Place to Theobalds—is an old one. Windmill Hill, the Ridgeway, and the roads across the Chase to Hadley and to East Barnet are said to have been made "at the beginning of the nineteenth century," but are all marked in Cary's Atlas of 1800, so must be earlier. The New Cambridge Road, constructed to relieve the tram-ridden Hertford Road, and the London–Silver Street–Forty Hill Road, was opened a few years ago. Even in its passage through Enfield, market gardens and glasshouses are giving way to fine new factories and schools on either side, with a proportion of small modern houses.

There was a fear, not long ago, that the Baker Street–Forty Hill Road was likely to be widened, with a consequent demolition of the old buildings which still line it, but the local guide-book cheerfully states that: "The Town Planning Act just adopted by Enfield local authorities provides for the construction of a parallel road which will render this widening unnecessary."* It is to be hoped that Enfield will never sacrifice this beautiful thoroughfare, into which is packed so much of its stately history. The map in the North Middlesex regional town-planning report shows two new main roads across the Chase, one from Cockfosters station north-east to White Webbs, the other east-south-east from Cockfosters station to Bush Hill Park.

The advent of the new electric railway to Cockfosters has

* *The Story of Enfield* (1930), p. 49.

already been mentioned; it may be added that the Great Eastern
station was opened in 1849, the Great Northern in 1871, and the
line extended north from the latter in 1910. The number of
historical buildings in Enfield is probably greater than in any other
district of Middlesex, except Brentford–Chiswick. The church is
well placed on the north of the market-place, and its oldest parts
appear to indicate a twelfth-century rebuilding of a pre-Conquest

THE MAIDEN'S BRIDGE, FORTY HILL, NEAR ENFIELD

(i.e. Saxon) church. The main fabric is, however, of the fourteenth–
sixteenth centuries, and has been much altered and restored since.
The exterior is of no great merit; the interior contains a fine
carved organ-case (1752) and a number of interesting monuments,
including a marble altar-tomb with brass effigy of Joyce, Lady
Tiptoft (d. 1446), brass portraits of William Smith (d. 1592) and
Jane, his wife, a tablet carved by Nicholas Stone in memory of
Mrs. Palmer (d. 1617), and an imposing monument to Sir Nicholas
Raynton (d. 1646), Lord Mayor of London, who rebuilt Forty
Hall.

Enfield once possessed quite a number of moated houses, of

which traces remain near the Old Park Farm and (possibly) in "Camlet Moat," a place which stands north of Trent Park and figures in Scott's *Fortunes of Nigel*. There was also a royal palace on the south of the market-place. But in 1928 practically all that remained of this charming building, erected by Edward VI for his sister Elizabeth, consisted of a magnificent panelled room then used as a part of the Enfield Conservative Club, and a particularly fine cedar planted in the garden by the famous horticulturist, Dr. Robert Uvedale, about 1660. The building was demolished in 1928 to make way for a great emporium of feminine adornment, the cedar was felled soon afterwards, and the panelling was appropriately transferred to a house in Gentleman's Row, where it may still be seen by the curious.

Of the Enfield Grammar School, founded in 1557 or (more probably) 1558, a portion remains of the original brick building close to the church and the market-place. It has mullioned windows with dormers in the roof. In 1904 it was considerably enlarged by the Middlesex Education Committee, but the additions harmonize with the old block and form a picturesque whole. The King and Tinker Inn, already mentioned, must be one of the older buildings of the district. The adjoining Fallow Buck Inn is of timber-framing covered with weather-boarding and may be of considerable age, the exact date of these buildings—characteristic of Middlesex, Hertfordshire, and Essex—being always difficult to determine. Other boarded houses in Enfield include a baker's shop and house in the market-place—a fragment of a larger block now destroyed—White Lodge in Silver Street, No. 164 Baker Street, and an old house now occupied by a doctor at the corner of Lancaster Road and Brigadier Hill. To this list may be added the old mill on the Lea at Ponder's End, an unexpectedly attractive group in an industrial district. There are boarded cottages and barns elsewhere in Enfield, and up to a few years ago a boarded windmill was standing on the south side of Windmill Hill, hence the name of that road; but a great many of these timber structures have been destroyed in recent times.

Architecturally, the most important historical monument in

Enfield is Forty Hall, erected in 1629–32 by Sir Nicholas Raynton near, or on the site of, an earlier house belonging to Sir Hugh Fortee. Tradition, repeated by all the local historians, ascribes its design to Inigo Jones. But Mr. J. A. Gotch, the distinguished architectural writer who has recently published a life of Inigo Jones, has reduced the innumerable buildings rashly attributed to

THE STABLE COURT GATEWAY, FORTY HALL, NEAR ENFIELD

that remarkable man down to a mere handful, and Forty Hall is not mentioned among them. It displays certain features which might justify the theory; on the other hand, the beautiful panelling, the richly carved fireplaces, and the strapwork ceilings are all more traditionally Jacobean and less Italian than one usually associates with Inigo Jones. The house has been very much altered and restored since Raynton's time, internally and externally, but is an imposing block with beautiful gardens and a noble park, the whole estate covering over 500 acres. Adjoining the house is a remarkable archway and embattled wall in brickwork enclosing the stableyard. It is difficult to associate this quasi-Tudor design with the academic and Italian taste of Inigo Jones, though it certainly does convey a rustic suggestion of Italy.

Enfield Old Park, which now houses the Enfield Golf Club, was partly built in Queen Anne's reign. It was enlarged in 1838, and again since.* Opposite stands an old house, "The Grove," of which a part is attributed to the time of Elizabeth.†

The remaining old houses of Enfield are mainly brick buildings of the late seventeenth and eighteenth centuries. One of them, formerly used as the first railway station of the G.E.R., was a beautiful design, possibly by Wren, and was erected some time before 1672 for Edward Helder, a bricklayer! It was pulled down in 1872 to make room for the present sordid station building, but the central pediment was fortunately preserved and subsequently erected in the Victoria and Albert Museum. There, that fragment of a bricklayer's house—and possibly relic of Wren's genius—is studied and measured annually by students of architecture.

The same museum contains some specimens of beautiful iron gates and railings from Enfield, but even now a number of fine examples remain *in situ*, e.g. in Gentleman's Row; at Eagle House, Ponder's End (1750); at the Rectory, at "Holmwood," and at Gough Park, all in Baker Street. All the houses just mentioned have historical interest, and to this list may be added "The Hermitage" at Forty Hill—a charming house in the Wren style; Elsynge Cottage, Forty Hill, with dainty windows of the time of Adam; the Rose and Crown Inn at Clay Hill; Capel House (late eighteenth century); Bridgen Hall (*c.* 1750); the Council Offices; and the charming little hump-backed bridge known as Maiden's Bridge over the "Maiden Brook" or Pymme's Brook. One could wish that the inscription formerly affixed to the bridge ("Any person wilfully injuring any part of this County Bridge will be guilty of Felony and upon conviction liable to be transported for life") could be applied at need to those motor-mad people who are now clamouring for the destruction of this, almost the last of the old bridges of Middlesex and the most beautiful corner of old

---

* Illustrated in Whitaker's *Enfield*, p. 102.
† See *The Story of Enfield*, p. 51.

Enfield. Enfield has lost its Palace, its Church Street, and many other things; it cannot save everything. It has preserved Chase Side, White Webbs Park, Clay Hill, and several other beauty spots; it proposes to safeguard Trent Park—perhaps the most magnificent estate in Middlesex—Beech Hill Park and Old Park, and Crews Hill Golf Clubs, as well as the banks of some of its streams. So Enfield is doing well, but here we must put in a plea that Forty Hall and its park, Gentleman's Row, Maiden's Bridge, and as much as possible of the old road from Silver Street to Bulls Cross be added to the list.

BOOKS ON LOCAL HISTORY AND TOPOGRAPHY

ANONYMOUS	Churches of the Deanery of Enfield	Enfield	1898
	Recollections of Old Enfield	Enfield	1911
	The Story of Enfield	Enfield	1932
[ENFIELD U.D.C.]	Official Guide to Enfield	London	N.D.
FORD, E., and HODSON, G. H.	History of Enfield	Enfield	1873
FORD, J. W.	The History of Bush Hill Park	——	1904
HARDY, P.	The Charities of Enfield	——	1834
HYATT, A. H.	Guide to Enfield and its Neighbourhood	Enfield	1908
KEMPE, E. W.	Enfield and its Environments	Enfield	[c.1888]
MACBRIDE, M.	History of Christ Church, Enfield	Enfield	1902
PHILLIPS, M.	Jaunts from Enfield	Enfield	1917
ROBINSON, W.	History of Enfield (2 vols.)	London	1823
ROUND, W.	Rambles Round Enfield	Enfield	1905
SMITH, S.	Short History of Enfield Grammar School	Enfield	1932
SYKES, H. D.	The Old Palace, Enfield	——	1907
TUFF, J.	Historical Notices of Enfield	Enfield	1858
WELD, H. C.	The Charities of Enfield	Enfield	1895
WHITAKER, C. W.	History of Enfield	London	1911

CHAPTER IV

EDMONTON

UNDOUBTEDLY the name of Edmonton suggests literary associations to the average intelligent man: he naturally thinks of John Gilpin's ride, of *The Merry Devil of Edmonton*, and of Charles Lamb. It is quite unnecessary to quote or paraphrase the familiar story of John Gilpin here: every child knows it. *The Merry Devil* is less hackneyed. It is a play, in blank verse, first produced in the early years of the seventeenth century, and revived on a recent occasion by the Dramatic Society of University College, London. The edition of 1631, accounted the best by scholars, bears the title: "*The Merry Devill of Edmonton*, as hath been sundry times Acted by His Maiestie's Servants, at the Globe, on the Bancke-side, London. Printed by T.P. for Francis Falkner, and are to be sold at his Shoppe neere unto St. Margarite's hill, in Southwarke, 1631." It has been attributed to Shakespeare, Michael Drayton, and others. About the same time was published a pamphlet by Thomas Brewer, *The Life and Death of the Merry Devil of Edmonton, with the pleasant pranks of Smug the Smith, Sir John, and mine host of the "George," about stealing the Venison.* The merry devil in question was one "Maister Peter Fabell," a scholar of Peterhouse, Cambridge; "very pleasant, kinde and freehearted was hee to or with his familiars and curteous to strangers and very liberal, full of commisseration and pittie to the poor and needy; both abroad from his purse and at home from his table. . . . In Edmonton he was borne, lived and died in the reigne of King Henry VII." The monument to Fabell in Edmonton Old Church which is mentioned in the prologue of the play, or at any rate the inscription identifying it, has long since disappeared.

But there is no lack of records of Charles Lamb, who went to Enfield to live after his retirement from his post at the India Office in 1825, came to Edmonton in 1833, and died there in December 1834. The house which he and his sister occupied in Church Street is still called "Lamb's Cottage" (see Frontispiece), and has been preserved by its present tenant, so far as possible, in its original condition. Lamb's later years were clouded by the tragedy of his sister's insanity. "I am driven from house to house by Mary's illness," he wrote, and that was why he left Enfield, with which also he had many associations. Edmonton has made the most of Charles Lamb. There is a commemorative medallion on the

EDMONTON PARISH CHURCH

cottage, a bronze medallion portrait and a splendid collection of Lamb prints and documents in the public library, and a Charles Lamb Institute in Church Street. Not all towns in Middlesex have shown so much pride in their association with the lives of great men of the past. But here it must be admitted that the public libraries of Enfield, Edmonton, Tottenham, and the galleries at Broomfield Park, Southgate—to take only this corner of Middlesex —all contain admirable collections of local maps, prints, original paintings and photographs, prehistoric and other antiquities, invaluable alike to their own people and to students, and a great credit to the enthusiasm of the librarians and curators concerned.

The name of Edmonton appears in Domesday as "Adelmetone," and as late as the fourteenth century as "Edelmeton," which seems to mean the "tun," or settlement, of Eadhelm, an Anglo-Saxon personal name. But during the Middle Ages the name of the town approached its present form. Edmonton, it may be noted, was the capital of one of the "hundreds" of Middlesex, including Enfield, Southgate, and most of Tottenham. The civil parish covered some 7,500 acres (about 12 square miles) up to 1894, when Southgate became a separate district and the area of Edmonton was approximately halved. The present district is almost exactly square, with its east boundary formed by the River Lea, and its other boundaries formed by nothing in particular.

Edmonton grew up on the ancient road, a scattered colony of houses, and in 1801 was a small country town, barely suburban, with a population of 5,093, surpassed only by Enfield among neighbouring parishes. (At the same time Tottenham, including Wood Green, had only 3,629 people, Hornsey 2,716, and Finchley 1,503.) The growth of population may be seen from the following figures: 1871, 13,860; 1881, 23,463; 1901, 64,820; 1911, 64,797; 1921, 66,807; 1931, 77,652. It will be observed that there was a very rapid increase in the last thirty years of the nineteenth century, then a period of stagnation which included the Great War, and recently a considerable resumption of building which appears to be continuing without any relaxation at the present time. There is now no clearly marked gap of open country between Edmonton and the three neighbouring districts of Middlesex, though the Lea Marshes—now fortunately secured as an open space—protect it on the east. With a present population of 80,000, and plenty of space left to be "developed," it will become a very large town in the near future, as the construction of two arterial roads across its area will inevitably encourage both industry and housing.

But one cannot feel altogether happy about that development. The prosperous City magnates who formed the chief inhabitants of the little town of a century ago or less have all departed, and their large houses have mostly been demolished or left half derelict.

A large number of streets were built in the late Victorian days when speculative building was, to say the least of it, unimaginative; and, though Edmonton has recently been pronounced a "slumless" town, it contains a lop-sided population which has suffered much poverty and distress of late.

To some extent this is accounted for by natural features. The district is nearly dead level, and somehow that fact tends to a

THE RIVER LEA AT EDMONTON

rather sordid type of development. A hundred years ago it must have been undistinguished flat agricultural ground, traversed by one main road and a few streams. Cary's atlas of 1800, if one studies it with a little imagination, enables one to reconstruct the appearance of Edmonton in those far-off days. There was a scattered string of houses, large and small, along the line of the old Hertford coaching-road, known as Fore Street, with other ribbons along Silver Street, Church Street, and Bury Street, and a cluster of farms (still remaining as part of the modern sewage farm) on Marsh Side. The rest of the area was entirely occupied by fields and market gardens, scraps of which still survive. Windmill Road, off Silver Street, marks the site of the old windmill which once stood near "Huxley Farm." An amusing little pocket-guide to Middlesex, published in 1824, says that "the elegant seats that adorn this neighbourhood are too numerous even to be cursorily noticed."

The Salmon Brook, now partly concealed in a sewer, meanders across the north of the parish, and crosses Fore Street at the picturesque little green, now bisected and almost obliterated, even as a paved space, by a branch line of a railway. The famous Edmonton Statute Fair was not held here but farther south along Fore Street, and is thus described by Lysons, writing in 1810:

A holiday fair of great resort, held in the high road in the town of Edmonton, on the 14th September and the two following days. It is called Edmonton Statute Fair, and was formerly held for the purpose of hiring servants, but that purpose has been for some time discontinued.

It is said that, in its heyday, this fair attracted as many as 30,000 visitors, who spread themselves over the whole district, especially along the busy high road.

Pymme's Brook, also called the Angel Brook, is still to be seen for most of its length, though much of its beauty has vanished. It enters the district from Southgate near the North Circular Road, passes under that roaring thoroughfare, runs south of Silver Street and under it, then through Pymme's Park and behind some houses to the "Angel," where it crosses under Fore Street, and is stowed away in a concrete tunnel under the road for the remainder of its journey to the Lea Marshes. The point where it crosses Fore Street is worth some attention. The "Angel" has been recently and admirably rebuilt, and has a pleasant garden. At the opposite corner of Silver Street a huge super-ultra-cinema has been erected. This is, indeed, a traffic centre of the first order, public lavatories in the centre and so forth, where the North Circular Road crosses Fore Street. Nevertheless, next to the "Angel" there still stands a row of charming little Georgian houses (Nos. 183–201 Fore Street) with a few trees in front, and the Angel Brook opposite to them disappearing into its concrete sewer. Across Fore Street is a still more pathetic group of old cottages, pondering regretfully on the lost view from their doorsteps. A few years ago this spot was an attractive reminder of the eighteenth century: local writers tell us that the "Edmonton Wash" of John Gilpin's ride was in fact the crossing of the Salmon Brook at Edmonton Green farther north:

> And then he threw the wash about
> On both sides of the way,
> Just like unto a trundling mop
> Or a wild goose at play.

There has been so much building in the west half of the district since the opening of the North Circular Road and the New Cambridge Road that it is difficult for those who did not know Edmonton a generation ago to picture its rural aspect; but on the east side there is still a patch of agricultural land, on which three or four farms still stand with their haystacks and elm-trees, though most of the ground is used for sewage disposal. One of them— Cuckoo Hall Farm—has a charming name. North of them is a huge and horrible refuse-dump, which suggests the thought that there must be some better way of dealing with our leavings than has yet been discovered or adopted.

Crossing the canal, known here as the Lea Navigation, one reaches the wide strip of marshland between Edmonton and Chingford—that is, between Middlesex and Essex—which has been recommended for preservation as a public open space. This is a most valuable precaution, for its well-drained meadows provide a splendid playground in the summer for thousands of children from the hot and squalid streets beyond. Meanwhile, their fathers stand in hundreds along the banks of the river and the canal, hopefully angling in spite of the Metropolitan Water Board's curt prohibitions. With its willow-trees and its long, open views, this marsh has a real beauty of its own. At Cook's Ferry the North Circular Road crosses the many branches of the Lea on a fine concrete viaduct with striking pylons. This viaduct involved great engineering difficulties and was long in construction. Near it is a quaint group of old boarded cottages, approached by a footbridge in times of flood.

Besides the old houses already mentioned, there are several others in Fore Street—for the most part in a rather dilapidated and forlorn condition—recalling the stately days of the eighteenth century. Among these may be mentioned Nos. 224, 226 ("Addison House"), 236, 238 ("Elm House"), and Nos. 258 and 260 with good but somewhat decayed iron gates. Opposite them is a large old house with a hipped roof, standing back with a sweeping drive and old trees.

In Silver Street, awaiting demolition, is a small Queen Anne or Georgian building, "Russell House," of good design. In Bury Street, now severed by the New Cambridge Road, is a charming old house, "Bury House," now used as a nurses' home. Bury Hall, formerly the home of the Bowater family—well-known paper-makers—stood opposite this, and was recently demolished. It is said to have been an interesting house, partly Tudor and partly Adam. At the north-west corner of Bury Street and the New Cambridge Road is another old dwelling of some size, obviously doomed to destruction. Farther along Bury Street, going west, is the beautiful gabled building known as Salisbury House, attributed to the fifteenth century, and now standing rather forlorn among rows of "Baronial Halls."

Church Street contains, besides Lamb's Cottage already mentioned, the old Rectory and a few other buildings of some age but no architectural pretensions.

The chief house in Edmonton used to be Wyre or Wyer Hall, situated in the angle between Pymme's Brook and the New Cambridge Road, close to the busy crossing of the North Circular Road. It was a noble Elizabethan or Jacobean building three storeys high, with long gabled façades and mullioned windows. An engraving of 1797[*] shows its appearance then but little altered. It was surrounded by a moat. Some time during the nineteenth century Wyre Hall was demolished and a hideous house erected in its place, the moat being partly filled up. This monstrosity was

* Reproduced on p. 91 of H. J. Griffin's *Old Tottenham and Edmonton* (1926).

still standing in 1933, but "Distinctive Homes," shacks, and hoardings have crept up to it, and there will be no cause for regret when it finally vanishes.

Pymme's Park is the only old house in all Edmonton which still retains some dignity of surroundings, and it is now public property. It is alleged to date back "to the time of Queen Elizabeth," but the greater part of the fabric suggests the late seventeenth century,

SALISBURY HOUSE, BURY STREET, EDMONTON

while the front towards Silver Street is attributed to Robert Adam. The delicate design of the porch certainly supports this ascription. It is a pleasant and dignified building, now used as a clinic, a refreshment-place, and a residence for the park superintendent. Adjoining the house is a beautiful "Old English Garden" enclosed by old brick walls, with formal beds and leafy arbours, a pure joy in a place like Edmonton. The remainder of the Park is, perhaps inevitably, laid out with wide asphalt walks, and may therefore be derided by the elect. But anyone who has seen it crowded, as it always is, with poor but happy children in the hot days of August, will forgive such minor drawbacks and remain content to acknowledge the value of such a playground, with Pymme's Brook winding under weeping willows through its midst, to a crowded industrial area.

Lastly, there is the old Parish Church in Church Street, mainly of the late fourteenth century or thereabouts, judiciously enlarged and restored in modern times. It has a fine tower, but the interior contains little of interest, and the monuments are of no importance. Charles Lamb's tomb in the churchyard is, of course, an attraction to visitors.

Edmonton is now too far developed for any useful suggestions to be offered for the future. Salisbury House should certainly be preserved, also Lamb's Cottage and Bury House. It is perhaps too much to hope for anything to be done to save the mangled group at the "Angel" cross-roads. The Lea Marshes are a priceless asset to the town; anything that can be done to preserve their beauty is worth doing, while possibly the sordid strip of refuse and sewage that separates them from Edmonton may some day prove to be capable of improvement.

BOOKS ON LOCAL HISTORY AND TOPOGRAPHY

[EDMONTON U.D.C.]	Edmonton: Official Guide	London	N.D.
FISK, F.	History of Edmonton	Tottenham	1914
GRIFFIN, H. J.	Old Tottenham and Edmonton	Tottenham	1926
ROBINSON, W.	History and Antiquities of Edmonton	London	1819

CHAPTER V

SOUTHGATE

THE recently incorporated municipal borough of Southgate was detached from Enfield as a separate urban district in 1894. It still contains some of the most beautiful scenery in Middlesex, but there is no part of the county which is more rapidly changing its character at the present time, and a close study of its development is therefore desirable. Its old name, as the "south gate" of Enfield Chase, has already been explained, and needs no further comment here. As regards the names of other places in the area, Bowes Park is the medieval manor of Bowes, of which Mr. Gover writes*: "Bowe or Bowes I take to be a man's name, perhaps originally from Bowes (Yorkshire), which was spelt Boues and Boghes in the thirteenth century, or else from Bow. Or possibly the name may be local, like Bow (East London), from an arched bridge over the stream here, which runs into the Lea."

"Cockfosters," a curious and perplexing name, is variously derived from Old French *bicoque* (= "a little hut or hovel") and from "cock-forester," i.e. ["dwelling of] the chief forester." It contains an inn named "The Cock," which might suggest a third possible origin, but only if that inn is older than the early seventeenth century when first we come across the name "Cockfosters." The word "palmer" in "Palmer's Green" obviously indicates a medieval pilgrim to the Holy Land, and so Mr. Gover explains it. Another writer,† however, considers that it may be "due to the possession of land here by an influential family of the name of Palmer." Winchmore Hill is variously explained as "the hill at the boundary of Wynsige" (the earliest form being

* J. E. B. Gover, *The Place-names of Middlesex* (1922).
† J. Walker Round, *The Story of Southgate and Winchmore Hill* (1906).

"Wynsemerhull"), or as "a tract of moorland upon which the whin or furze flourished abundantly."

So much for speculation. The modern borough, as recently reconstituted in 1933, has an area of about 3,760 acres, or nearly 6 square miles. Cockfosters, previously in Enfield, was added to it in the regrouping of districts, and a ridiculous little tongue of land, three-quarters of a mile long and about 100 yards wide, containing a place known as "World's End," was taken from

THE OLD SMITHY, SOUTHGATE (DEMOLISHED 1933)

Southgate and given to Enfield. Nevertheless, at the end of all this juggling Southgate has a very irregular shape, with boundaries which do not always follow roads or natural features. For the most part it is a hilly district, the subsoil being mainly clay with patches of gravel and sand, but there is a strip of level alluvium on the east of the borough, where the New River runs across the valley of the Lea. The general slope is eastwards, from a height of over 300 feet at Cockfosters to less than 100 feet near the New River, but the irregularities of contour are caused by several small streams with an easterly trend. There is Merryhills Brook in the north, then Houndsden Gutter (which becomes the Salmon Brook or

"Salmon's Brook" near Bush Hill), and Pymme's Brook. None of these has been completely canalized or piped underground, but for some of them that seems to be the ultimate destiny. Pymme's Brook, which in its lower reaches becomes the Angel Brook at Edmonton (see last chapter), is the most important. It enters Southgate from the Hertfordshire district of East Barnet, traverses the whole width of the borough, and passes into Edmonton near the North Circular Road at Chequers Green. Its point of entry, under the bridge at "Waterfall Road," used to be a charming spot, but a prodigal use of concrete has obliterated most of its beauty. The next stage of half a mile, through the preserved fragment of Arnos Park, is still attractive, and should remain so. Then Pymme's Brook picks up a tributary, Bounds Green Brook, which has pursued its short course perilously near a concentration of sewage works serving several districts.* Thus reinforced, Pymme's Brook used to meander along the valley between Broomfield Park and Bowes Road, its banks lined with trees. But now it has been coaxed into a straight concrete channel, its sinuous bed has been filled up with tipped clay, and thus the little valley—at present partly used as allotments—has been converted into an eligible building site. An enormous super-cinema has planted its feet among the pollarded willows, hundreds of "Distinctive Homes" will follow, and soon the disappearing trick will be accomplished. Considering what this part of Pymme's Brook has now become, it is perhaps better to bury it decently, out of sight and out of mind.

There was once a time when the banks of the New River formed a pleasant walk, but now they are necessarily closed to the public, so that Southgate citizens who wish to gaze upon water will have to confine their attention to the municipal lakes in the various parks.

For many centuries the only road which traversed Southgate was the ancient highway from London to Enfield, known as Green Lanes. Other comparatively old roads are Bourne Hill, Fox Lane, Alderman's Hill, Cannon Hill, High Street (Southgate),

---

* These various municipal activities are shortly to be superseded by a regional scheme: let us hope less offensive to one of the senses.

Church Hill, Winchmore Hill Road, Cockfosters Road, Green Dragon Lane, Vicars Moor Lane, Wade's Hill, Firs Lane, Hedge Lane, Hoppers Road, Waterfall Road, and perhaps Bowes Road. Until the railway was opened through the district, just over sixty years ago, Southgate and its satellite villages were almost entirely rural, and practically no other roads existed. At Southgate itself, at Winchmore Hill, and at Palmer's Green there were picturesque greens at the junction of roads. The last-named has now disappeared completely, and the others have lost most of their former charm. The construction of the North Circular Road through the borough has caused a rapid intensification of building in the southern quarters, and the New Cambridge Road has developed the eastern fringe of the district. The opening of stations at Arnos Grove, Southgate, Enfield West, and Cockfosters—all within the borough boundaries—within the past year (1933) has already given a tremendous impetus to the speculator in the north and west, where it is announced that one firm alone has just begun the erection of three thousand small houses. Indeed, there are signs of immense building activity in all parts of Southgate where land is available, except in the small area north of the Enfield–East Barnet Road, where rustic peace still reigns.

The population of Southgate was 14,993 in 1901,* 33,612 in 1911, 39,112 in 1921, and 55,570 in 1931. The increase in the last decennium is remarkable, but it will not be surprising if a comparable increase is recorded in 1941, for it is only during the last three or four years that building has begun to develop in the north and west of the district, or east of Green Lanes. At fifty persons to the acre, the borough can accommodate a population of 188,000.

In face of these facts, it is a good thing that some enthusiasts have begun to collect records of the old and beautiful Southgate that is so rapidly disappearing. The borough has no public library, but one of the rooms at Broomfield House contains a really splendid collection of pictures of the district. This salvage work

---

* Prior to 1894, Southgate formed part of Edmonton, so no separate figures are available.

has been largely voluntary, and shows how much can be done with a little intelligent energy. A number of the pictures are sketches, made in his spare time by Dr. Cresswell, who practised in Winchmore Hill for fifty years, from 1842 till his death in 1892. His daughter has published a delightful study* of life in that primitive village as she and her father knew it long ago. Another excellent little book, Mr. Round's *Old Southgate and Winchmore Hill*—

"THE THATCHED COTTAGE," PALMER'S GREEN, IN *c.* 1860
Drawn from an old photograph

published in 1906 and well illustrated by Mr. Dudley Heath—is now quite unobtainable; and it is significant that practically none of the local booksellers have heard of its existence

Literary references to Southgate are infrequent before the nineteenth century, and the indexes to the diaries of Pepys and Evelyn make no mention of it. In a letter of 1812, Henry Crabb Robinson writes of it as "a delightful village," which has ". . . no distant prospect from the Green, but there are fine trees admirably grouped, and neat, happy homes scattered in picturesque corners

* H. Cresswell, *Winchmore Hill: Memories of a Lost Village* (1912).

and lanes." Leigh Hunt, himself a native of Southgate, wrote at about the same time: "It is a pleasure to me to know that I was ever born in so sweet a village as Southgate. . . . It not only found me cradled in the lap of Nature, which I love, but in the midst of the truly English scenery which I love beyond all other. Middlesex . . . in general is a scene of trees and meadows, of 'greenery' and nestling cottages. And Southgate is a prime specimen of Middlesex. It is a place lying out of the way of innovation; therefore, it has the pure sweet air of antiquity about it."

Charles Lamb, another contemporary, wrote a letter describing: ". . . The way from Southgate to Colney Hatch, thro' the unfrequentedest Blackberry paths that ever concealed their coy bunches from a truant Citizen, we have accidentally fallen upon." And lastly, there is Tom Hood, who lived at Rose Cottage on Winchmore Hill from 1829 to 1832:

Our village, that's to say, not Miss Mitford's village, but our village . . .
Is come into by an avenue of trees, three oak pollards, two elders and a withy;
And in the middle there's a green of about not exceeding an acre and a half;
It is common to all. . . .
Besides a pond in the middle, as is held by a similar kind of common law lease,
And contains twenty ducks, six drakes, three ganders. . . .
Of course the green's cropt very close, and does famous for bowling when the little village boys play cricket. . . .
I can't speak of the stocks, as nothing remains of them but the upright post;
But the pound is kept in repair for the sake of Cob's horse, as is always there almost.

Miss Cresswell's delightfully intimate studies of rural life at Winchmore Hill prove that the development of that district and of Palmer's Green did not begin till sixty years ago.

The charm of Southgate Green persisted, hardly impaired, so recently as three or four years ago. But now one side of the Green is lined with modern houses of creditable design, another with still more modern flats, and part of the third with shops where face powder, gramophone records, and other essentials to present-day

happiness may be obtained. However, it is at the junction of the
old High Street with Chase Side that the most startling change
has occurred, all within a year. Here is a really splendid example
of the very latest cosmopolitan design in the new Underground
station and its surrounding crescent of shops and flats. The old
smithy was demolished in July 1933, and now the buses circle
round a traffic circus in an endless procession. All this is inevitable,

BROOMFIELD HOUSE, PALMER'S GREEN, IN 1930

but, as the lady said in the story, "so sudden." Yet, even now,
the hamlet of Cockfosters remains as beautiful and as undisturbed
as ever, save for another admirably designed station, the terminus
of the new railway.

None of the old buildings in all the district of Southgate is really
ancient, not even the parish church, which was designed by Sir
Gilbert Scott to replace an old chapel of the seventeenth century
and was dedicated in 1861. St. John's Church at Palmer's Green,
a fine building, was erected in 1905. Bowes Manor House,
Minchenden House, Beaver Hall in Waterfall Road, Culland's
Grove on Alderman's Hill, and many other old mansions have

been demolished. Most of the old inns have been rebuilt, but the "Woodman" on Bourne Hill and the "Cherry Tree" on Southgate Green retain some traces of antiquity. Arnos Grove, once known as "Arnold's," was rebuilt on the site of an earlier house in 1720, and enlarged in 1777. It was recently acquired by the North Metropolitan Electric Supply Company as their head offices, and has been so much enlarged and altered that it is not easy to know how much of the original structure remains. A few of the magnificent trees surrounding the house have been left standing, but most of its 260 acres of park have been cut up into building sites, now mostly occupied, and only the lower portion by Pymme's Brook remains as a public park, well wooded, with an area of 44 acres.

Broomfield House is perhaps the chief surviving building, and presented a picturesque Georgian façade in stucco up to two or three years ago, when the authorities were so misguided as to nail strips of flimsy timber all over it with the quite erroneous idea that they were thereby producing a "genuine antique" effect. Nothing could be less genuine or less antique, for such half-timbering as this was never seen in the old days. The interior contains a good seventeenth-century staircase, with blackened paintings on its ceilings and walls attributed to Sir James Thornhill, some panelling, and the fine collection of local pictures already mentioned. The stables and adjoining farm are now the most attractive relics of this once-famous house, but the surrounding public park (54 acres), with its ponds and gardens, is really beautiful.

Grovelands Park (91 acres) contains a lake, and adjoining it is a fine house,* now used as a hospital, which was erected in 1797 from the designs of John Nash, the architect of Regent Street. This park contains the last surviving scrap of the famous Winch-more Hill woods, and authentic bracken is still to be seen here and there among the trees. Of the other open spaces, the newly acquired Oakwood Park (27 acres) in the north of the district is the most important. If Trent Park, in the Enfield district, is to be preserved, the allowance of public open spaces for Southgate is perhaps adequate, especially as Hadley Woods are so near to its boundaries,

---

* Illustrated in Richardson's *Vitruvius Britannicus*, published in 1802.

but the public acquisition of the strip of land between the main road and the county boundary at Cockfosters seems desirable.

Returning to the question of old buildings, it may be mentioned that two fine houses stand on Southgate Green, and appear to be of the early eighteenth century. The flanking garages are cleverly designed to harmonize with the houses themselves. One is called "Essex House," which smacks of the eighteenth century; the other

ESSEX HOUSE, OLD SOUTHGATE

"Arnoside," which does not. Farther along the Green, and somewhat forlorn to-day, is Eagle Hall, previously known as "Leigh Lodge," where Leigh Hunt was born in 1784. His father, a clergyman, had opened a school there in the previous year. It is a stucco-fronted house with a slate roof. Rose Cottage, in Vicars Moor Lane, the home of Thomas Hood the poet from 1829 to 1832, is also standing, in a pleasant garden. It is inhabited and apparently well cared for, but the orchard in front of it has just been cut up into building sites. There are many other old houses of the late eighteenth and early nineteenth centuries, when Southgate and Winchmore Hill were country villages. There is one left on

Cannon Hill, several in Vicars Moor Lane, and a few at the top of Winchmore Hill Green, preserving its old-time quiet. The charming Friends' Meeting House in Church Hill, near these last, stands in a wooded churchyard with characteristically modest tombstones. It is still in use.

Southgate House, from its appearance a building of about 1780 or 1800, has no great merit externally, but perhaps has some artistic interest within. It forms the nucleus of the "Minchenden" Secondary School, a new foundation, with excellent modern buildings, and the large grounds required for playing-fields will preserve permanently a green oasis at a point where shops and cinemas will soon form the surroundings. The grounds contain an oak-tree, the "Minchenden Oak," which is said to be the oldest and largest in the county, with a girth of 27 feet, a spread of 136 feet, and an estimated age of over eight centuries.

The "Thatched Cottage" at Palmer's Green has stood for nearly 150 years beside a thoroughfare which appropriately bore the name of "Green Lanes," but now is a roaring highway packed with trams and buses. The cottage, originally built in 1790, is now the only old building in a row of shops and banks and cinemas. It has been much altered, and looks sadly out of place, but presumably the florist who occupies it finds that its "olde worlde" quaintness makes for the prosperity of his trade. There is another cottage with a thatched roof in Tottenhall Road, near the south-eastern corner of the borough.

Southgate still retains a number of weather-boarded cottages and small houses of uncertain date. The smithy has just been demolished, but there are examples in Church Hill, Winchmore Hill Green, Hoppers Road, and perhaps one or two survivors still in the rapidly disappearing market gardens east of the New River. Hoppers Road also contains a charming little brick building of the Adam period, "Belmont." Soon most of these will have gone, and it seems that all one can hope from Southgate is that some of the beautiful trees—cedars especially—which still adorn the gardens of a more spacious past may be retained to break the monotony of endless rows of "Distinctive Homes."

BOOKS ON LOCAL HISTORY AND TOPOGRAPHY

[ANONYMOUS]	"The Minchenden Oak" (article in *Middlesex Schools' Gazette*)	London	1933
CRESSWELL, HENRIETTA	Winchmore Hill: Memories of a Lost Village (2nd edition)	Dumfries	1912
ROUND, J. WALKER	The Story of Southgate and Winchmore Hill	Enfield, etc.	1906
[SOUTHGATE U.D.C.]	Southgate: Official Guide		N.D.
	Southgate's Charter Day [Programme]	Palmer's Green	1933

CHAPTER VI

TOTTENHAM

TOTTENHAM presents, in many ways, a striking contrast to the borough of Southgate described in the last chapter. For whereas Southgate in 1931 had a density of population of less than fifteen persons to an acre, the corresponding figure for Tottenham was over fifty-two persons, making it the most crowded area in Middlesex. This figure will certainly be exceeded in the next census, but at the present time the district is nearly built up. Again, whereas Southgate has no public library and has a very meagre list of local histories, Tottenham possesses a Central Public Library with splendid local collections and another large collection in the municipal museum at Bruce Castle; while, as the bibliography at the end of this chapter proves, a long list of books and pamphlets going back to the beginning of the seventeenth century records every aspect of its history and topography. The official guide to the district is the best published by any of the numerous townships of Middlesex. And if Southgate is famous as a nursery of cricketers, Tottenham is known everywhere for its Hotspur football club. Tottenham became a borough in 1934.

The name of the district appears as Toteham in Domesday, and is usually explained as the "home or enclosure of Tota" or "Totta." It has some affinity with "Tooting" in South London. Tottenham is now a compact urban area of just over 3,000 acres (about $4\frac{3}{4}$ square miles), measuring about $2\frac{1}{4}$ miles each way. The district of Wood Green, with an area of about 1,600 acres ($2\frac{1}{2}$ square miles), was separated from the old parish of Tottenham in 1888, and is described in the next chapter.

The population in 1801, when Wood Green was a part of Tottenham, was only 3,629. At that date nearly all the houses were spread along the sides of the old road to Hertford, called the

High Road in this part of its course. Cary's atlas of 1800 shows large houses in gardens, beginning at Page Green and extending nearly to the present Park Lane. "Seven Sisters" is marked, but Seven Sisters Road was not constructed till long afterwards. There was a small cluster of houses near the Hale, and Bruce Grove is shown as an avenue, otherwise the whole area is open, and "Woods Green" is barely a hamlet. There is a gap of half a mile or more

TOTTENHAM PARISH CHURCH

between the last house in Stamford Hill (now the London frontier) and the first in Tottenham.

The population had grown to 5,812 in 1821; 22,869 in 1871; and 46,456 in 1881 (including 9,867 in Wood Green). After the detachment of Wood Green, the figures were as follows: 1891, 71,343; 1901, 102,541; 1911, 137,418; 1921, 146,711; 1931, 157,748. As has been already remarked, this last figure is likely to be exceeded in 1941, for building is still proceeding on the few available spaces which are not completely filled up; that is, near the New Cambridge Road, and on the east side of the district near the London and North Eastern Railway. After 1941, the falling birth-rate will probably cause a decline in the total population. This phenomenon has already occurred in London, but has not yet made its appearance in Middlesex.

The figures of population given above indicate that much of the development of Tottenham occurred during the nineteenth century, before modern ideas of housing and town-planning had been evolved. Hence a large part of the area is laid out on "speculative" lines, with small terrace-houses in closely spaced streets. The splendid housing scheme of the London County Council and that of the local urban council in the north of the district, near White Hart Lane, present a welcome contrast to the older streets; and, fortunately, the authorities have wisely secured a reasonably large area of the remaining ground for public open spaces at the eleventh hour, though the southern part of the district is inadequately provided, and there seems to be no chance of acquiring more in that quarter.

Tottenham presents yet another contrast to Southgate in being almost dead level, but a small portion of the district rises to nearly 100 feet at one point on the slope of Stamford Hill. There is a very slight slope downwards from Green Lanes in an easterly direction towards the River Lea. Except in the public parks, where a number of old elms are still standing, in a few wooded avenues such as Bruce Grove, and on the scraps of old "greens" still surviving, the whole area is somewhat short of trees. But an acute observer will find many fine cedars and other exotic trees in the old gardens behind some of the houses in the High Road, in Bruce Grove, and elsewhere. They recall the time when Tottenham was the suburban or country retreat of wealthy City merchants a century ago.

Besides the Lea, there were formerly two small brooks which traversed the district from west to east. One of these, the name of which does not appear to be preserved, is shown on Cruchley's map of 1840. It rose near Crouch End, passed through the grounds of Harringay House, and then ran about half-way between West Green Road and St. Ann's Road. It crossed the High Road a few yards south of the junction with Seven Sisters Road, under the

"Stone Bridge" (now commemorated by Stone Bridge Road), and then ran direct across the marsh into the Lea. It is now completely hidden underground, though many years ago it was visible as it passed through the Chestnuts Recreation Ground in St. Ann's Road.

The other is the Moselle Brook, the name and source of which are dealt with in the chapter on Hornsey. Rising on "Muswell"

TOTTENHAM MILLS ABOUT 100 YEARS AGO
Drawn from an old print

Hill, this once famous but now mainly squalid stream enters the Tottenham district near the junction of Westbury Avenue and Lordship Lane, having crossed Wood Green in a sewer. For about three-quarters of a mile it meanders behind the houses in Walpole Road and across the new Lordship Lane recreation ground, in full daylight. It then goes to earth and turns due north, appearing again in Tottenham Cemetery,* where it runs north-east for half a mile or so to a point near White Hart Lane Station. Here it disappears

* As it passes through the former grounds of Tottenham House, now reserved for cemetery extensions, it widens into a beautiful curved lake beneath fine trees. This portion is well worth preservation as a public park, if not really required for burial purposes.

into a culvert permanently until it finally trickles across the marshes to the Lea. This underground portion of its course may, however, be reconstructed to some extent. Moselle House (707 High Road) and Moselle Street (between 759 and 761 High Road) afford some clue to its whereabouts. It ran south along the side of the High Road to Scotland Green, and then turned east,* regaining the open air at the far side of the railway, whence its course is again easily seen nowadays. This sordid recital has a lesson for us who live in less urbanized parts of Middlesex: it shows that all our brooks are liable to be put into sewers unless they can somehow be introduced as a feature into a proper scheme of town-planning, as has been done, for example, on the Watling Estate at Hendon. Provision has been made for "stream-side reservation" on a large scale in the regional town-planning schemes of the Middlesex County Council; without it, the remaining rural stretches of the Brent, the Crane, and even the Colne will share the squalid fate of the historic Moselle.

As for the Lea, that once wide and pleasant river has been practically obliterated throughout its course through Tottenham, thanks to the huge chain of reservoirs which now draw off so much of its water. The old channel, forming the Middlesex–Essex boundary, zigzags through them. In place of the old Lea, we have a series of artificial channels or canals, with two locks on the main channel, the "River Lea Navigation," in the Tottenham district. Opinions differ as to the spelling of the river's name, the Metropolitan Water Board insisting on "Lee," whereas popular usage generally continues to favour "Lea." But there is no difference of opinion as to the desirability of preserving for the crowded and largely poor population of Tottenham such a magnificent playground as is afforded by such remaining portions of the Lea (or "Lee") Marshes as are not occupied by reservoirs. The sections already acquired, including Broad Mead and Clendish Marsh, have an area of about 135 acres, but the town-planning proposals in the North Middlesex regional report recommend the further

---

* This portion is marked "Garbell Ditch" on Bedwell's map of 1631, and was recently known as "Carbuncle Ditch" until it was covered in, a few years ago.

acquisition of the northern and southern ends of the marshes within the Tottenham district. It is also suggested that a new road be constructed across the northern end of the marsh, from Park Lane in Tottenham to Higham Hill in Essex, thereby providing a much-needed traffic link. At present the only thoroughfare between Tottenham and Essex is the old and formerly narrow Ferry Lane at Tottenham Hale. The picturesque Ferry Boat Inn, now a "Trust House," lies just across the boundary, and is therefore in Essex. Here was found a nest of otters not many years ago. The banks of the reservoirs hereabouts form a bird sanctuary and are covered with wild flowers. The fishing, too, is excellent. The old mills by the side of the Lea were burned down about 1850.

The word "Hale" is defined in the *English Dialect Dictionary* as "flat alluvial land by the side of a river," and this would certainly apply to Tottenham Hale. But the name of "The Hale" near Edgware is more likely to be derived from the Old Mercian *halh* or *hale*, meaning "a nook, corner, retreat." The part of Tottenham between Broad Lane, High Cross Road, and the Hale Station (L.N.E.R.) is now rather squalid, but retains some traces of the past, with a few weather-boarded cottages. Not long ago, a very ancient boat was found during excavations on Tottenham marshes. It is thought that this may be a relic of the Danish invasion in 894, when the Viking fleet sailed up the Lea and was defeated by the strategy of King Alfred, who blocked up the channel and so prevented the enemy ships from returning.

The old roads of Tottenham included the main High Road, Green Lanes, West Green Road, Lordship Lane (marked "Slyfield Lane" on Cary's atlas, 1800), White Hart Lane, Philip Lane ("Hanger's Lane" in Cruchley's map of 1840), Broad Lane, High Cross Road, and Ferry Lane. Seven Sisters Road was constructed in 1831–32. Its name was derived from a group of seven ancient elms, with a walnut-tree in the centre, which used to stand on the east of the High Road at the point where Seven Sisters Road now joins it. They were replaced by a new group of seven trees planted in 1852 by seven sisters of one Tottenham family. The New Cambridge Road is the most important addition to the streets of Tottenham in very recent times. It enters the district in the north-east corner, and soon bifurates into two curved roads forming the beautifully laid out "Roundway." One spur leads through Westbury Avenue to Wood Green and London, the other is intended to be connected with Lordship Lane at the corner of Bruce Castle Park. Fear has been expressed that this extension will disturb the quiet of one of the few remaining quiet corners of Tottenham, but it seems reasonable and inevitable.

From old descriptions of the town it appears that Tottenham once had a dialect of its own. It also had mineral springs which attained some reputation in the late eighteenth century: they were situated on the west side of the High Road, near Philip Lane. Earlier still, we read of a comic tournament being held at Tottenham in the fifteenth century:

> It befel in Totenham on a dere day,
> There was mad a shurting be the hy-way;
> Theder com al the men of the contray,
> Of Hyssylton, of Hy-gate, and of Hakenay,
> And all the swete swynkers:
> Ther hopped Hawkyn,
> Ther daunsed Dawkyn,
> Ther trumped Tomkyn,
> And all were trewe drynkers.

Pinnock, writing in 1824, says that "Tottenham, usually called High Cross . . . is a long straggling village, not remarkable for its beauty nor pleasantness; yet it contains many handsome mansions."

Of the surviving historical buildings of Tottenham, the most important and the oldest is the parish church of All Hallows, which stands in a wonderfully secluded and very picturesque churchyard between Bruce Castle Park and the cemetery.

The local historians state quite categorically that the church was founded and endowed by King David I of Scotland, who, before his accession to the Scottish throne in 1124, "became Lord of the Manor of Tottenham by marriage with the daughter of Earl Waltheof, one of the last of the great Anglo-Saxon nobles."*

* W. J. Roe, *The Ancient Church of All Hallows, Tottenham*, p. 2.

(This is the first of many associations which Tottenham had with Scotland, as we shall see in the subsequent description of Bruce Castle, and may perhaps explain the name of "Scotland Green" as well as "Bruce Grove.") Of that earlier period, probably only the lower part of the tower remains, the brick battlements being obviously much later. The chancel and side chapels in brick are modern, and the nave itself, mainly of the fourteenth century, was extensively restored in 1876–7, so that the whole building,

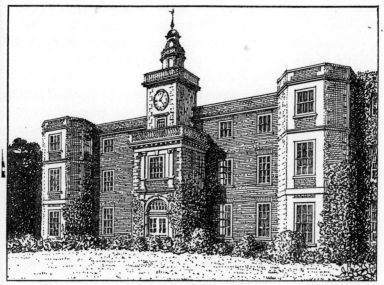

BRUCE CASTLE, TOTTENHAM

though picturesque both internally and externally, is something of an architectural jumble. But the beautiful porch, with a parvise above it and brick diaper patterns, is a fine piece of work and dates from the fifteenth century. The church contains two notable monuments of the seventeenth century and an early brass.

Bruce Castle, which adjoins the church, is said to stand on the site of an earlier house erected by Earl Waltheof, who married a niece of William the Conqueror. From them it descended to the famous "Robert the Bruce" (1274–1329), who became King of Scotland, his rival for the throne, John Baliol, being also the holder of a manor in Tottenham. In 1514 it is said to have been rebuilt by Sir William Compton, and Henry VIII visited it. Of that house only an isolated brick tower in the grounds remains. The building, as we now see it, appears to be mainly of the seventeenth century, but its history is imperfectly known. Its curious interior has been much modified, partly by Sir Rowland Hill and his descendants, who owned and occupied the house from 1827 until 1877. It served as a school under the Hill family and subsequently, until the property with its finely wooded park was bought by the local council in 1891 as a public recreation ground. The house itself contains an excellent museum of local antiquities and natural history, with a large gallery upstairs devoted to the very fine "Union of Post Office Workers (Morten) Postal Collection," appropriately deposited here in the former house of Sir Rowland Hill.

The Priory, which lies west of the church, is obviously an old building, and its exterior suggests an early eighteenth-century date. However, the existence of dated ornament in the internal decorations proves that the house was erected not later than 1620-1, though it has evidently undergone considerable alteration since that time. Of this period are two panelled rooms, some richly decorated ceilings, and a fine oak chimney-piece bearing the owner's name, "Joseph Fenton 1621." Some time between 1720 and 1740 extensive rebuilding took place, and further internal decorations, including a splendid carved pine chimney-piece in the dining-room.* The beautiful iron gateway between the garden and the public road was brought from elsewhere in Tottenham: it is perfectly suited to its position. This house was acquired as a vicarage some thirty years ago, thanks to the enterprise of the vicar who has occupied it ever since, and it is most essential that it be preserved from the hands of the land-shark, here in the one corner of Tottenham that still retains the charm of old days.

The High Cross which stands in the centre of Tottenham on the High Road is not one of the "Eleanor crosses," as is commonly

---

* For description and illustrations of these decorations, see the article by O. Brackett, "Carved Chimney Pieces at Tottenham," in *The Expert*, Vol. I, No. 3 (June 8, 1907).

supposed, nor is it very ancient. There was a cross here in medieval times, but the present structure has a stucco Gothic exterior culminating in a crocketed pinnacle which dates from 1809: the core is formed by a plain octagonal cross* of the beginning of the seventeenth century, which in turn replaced an earlier wooden cross. Near the High Cross is a triangular green, and on it a quaint conically roofed structure sheltering a pump. This green is approached by a wide and tree-lined section of the High Road

GATEWAY OF "THE PRIORY," TOTTENHAM

rising gently from the "Stone Bridge" (now non-existent) to the High Cross: the old "Tottenham Hill," up which Mr. Piscator and his friends used to trudge briskly with their fishing-tackle. It is now lined with the chief public buildings of the town, interspersed with a few dignified old houses, and in spite of endless trams and buses it preserves some of the spaciousness of the coaching days.

Farther along the High Road is Sanchez House, marking the site of a group of eight almshouses which were built in 1596 and demolished recently. Near them used to stand the picturesque

* Illustrated in Oldfield and Dixon's *History and Antiquities of Tottenham* (1790), Plate 7.

Elizabethan mansion occupied and subsequently embellished by Sir Abraham Reynardson, who became Lord Mayor of London in 1648, but was imprisoned in the Tower in the following year for his political views, released shortly afterwards, and died here in 1661. His house* was demolished in 1809, but the Reynardson Almshouses, which were built in 1730 from a bequest in his son's will, still stand in the High Road, with a small chapel as their central feature. They were restored in 1828, and form an attractive block, long and low, with a gable over the chapel and a commemorative tablet recording their history.

Besides the old buildings already enumerated, many others of some interest, if of less antiquity, may be discovered by a systematic tour of the older streets, the High Road itself providing a considerable number. Nearly all of them are the former homes of prosperous middle-class City men, and one must imagine them standing well back from the road, as indeed most of them still do, with little more to disturb them than the occasional rattle of a coach or chaise. Many of the surviving examples are now occupied by doctors or as offices; they have been rendered almost impossible as dwelling-houses by the ceaseless roar of trams, cars, and lorries which continues all through the night. Yet behind them are spacious gardens containing cedars, copper-beeches, and other fine old trees.

The Tottenham Polytechnic, on the Green, occupies a much altered and extended private mansion known originally as Grove House, built early in the eighteenth century, and it contains an alleged cock-pit. From 1828 to 1878 it housed a famous Quaker school with a long list of distinguished "old boys." It is now shared between the Polytechnic and the local Police Court.

Opposite are a few more old buildings, and in Bruce Grove a long row of fine houses, apparently of the eighteenth century, with splendid gardens behind them. Behind Bruce Castle, near the church, is a quaint little wooden cottage. But it is not until one goes farther north that much survives in the High Road. Apart from various quaint cottages, many of them weather-boarded and most of them rather dilapidated, the first old buildings of any

* Illustrated in *Old Tottenham and Edmonton,* p. 37.

distinction as one goes north are Lancaster House (No. 573) and its neighbour, a charming pair of façades with delicate cornices and boldly designed doorways. On the opposite side, No. 630, "Rheola," is typical of the eighteenth century, while No. 632 is probably an early work of the next century. Nos. 672 and 674 are low houses with dormers. Nos. 790 and 792 are a worthy pair, particularly the former. But the finest group of eighteenth-century houses in Tottenham is the series known as Northumberland Row (Nos. 794–802 High Road), opposite White Hart Lane. These five houses appear to be designed as a single composition, and though much of the window-glazing has been replaced by plate-glass, they recall the dignity of their period. The central building, Percy House, is a really noble design with fine gate-piers, scrolls, and ironwork. The connection with the Percy family and the dukedom of Northumberland is not clear.

From this point to the Edmonton boundary the neighbourhood deteriorates, and becomes almost a slum where the site of a little green is now occupied by a builder's warehouse. Nevertheless, Nos. 808 ("Prudhoe House") and No. 810 ("Holly House") have some merits. Across the road, No. 810 has a good door-head, and "Brook House," standing back in a spacious forecourt, is a forlorn reminder of the prosperous and stately days of Tottenham High Road, now gone for ever.

BOOKS ON LOCAL HISTORY AND TOPOGRAPHY

BEDWELL, W.	A brief description . . . of . . . Tottenham	London	1631
COUCHMAN, H.	Reminiscences of Tottenham	Tottenham	1910
FISK, F.	History of Tottenham (2 vols.)	Tottenham	1913 1923
GRIFFIN, H. J.	Old Tottenham and Edmonton	Tottenham	1926
OLDFIELD, H. G., and DYSON, R. R.	History and Antiquities . . . of . . . Tottenham	London	1790
ROBINSON, W.	History and Antiquities of Tottenham	Tottenham	1818
ROE, W. J.	Short History of All Hallows Church, Tottenham	Tottenham	1930
[TOTTENHAM U.D.C.]	Tottenham: Official Guide	London	N.D.

CHAPTER VII

WOOD GREEN

IF mere names had anything to do with it, Wood Green ought to be the most sylvan and beautiful district in all Middlesex, and so it probably was a century ago. The names of its old roads bear out the same conclusion: White Hart Lane, Green Lanes, Wolves Lane, Bounds Green Road, Jolly Butchers' Hill, Lordship Lane. Every one of them recalls the time when the Forest of Middlesex extended over the district. Tottenham Wood, of which it was once often said, "You might as well try to move Tottenham Wood," was the last surviving fragment, and now that has gone too. The patient efforts of speculative builders who for half a century or so have invited the credulous to "build your house in a wood" have been crowned with complete success. Almost every available site has now been occupied, and hardly a scrap of wood has been left standing.

This is not to say that the borough of Wood Green is a poor and crowded area like parts of Edmonton, Tottenham, and Hornsey; far from it. In a sense it is well laid out, and it has no slums. Its innumerable streets are reasonably wide, it has an ample allowance of open spaces, and its public services are doubtless above criticism. It is simply suburban, just that, and the only thing lacking in its lay-out is imagination. It provides a most interesting subject of study to town-planners, because at first sight it appears to be a model town, and yet there is something wrong.

Let us begin with incontrovertible facts. The district of Wood Green was detached from the old parish of Tottenham in 1888, and became an urban district six years later. It has an area of slightly over 1,600 acres (about 2½ square miles), and a density of population—thirty-three persons to the acre—which is not excessive.

The watercourses of the district run mainly underground. The artificial New River bisects the area, entering on the north. It goes to earth under the appropriately named "Myddelton Road," passes through a tunnel two-thirds of a mile long, emerges at Station Road, and then runs between the L.N.E.R. main line and the reservoirs of the Metropolitan Water Board. In Cruchley's map of 1840, however, it is shown winding round the hill to the east, so the tunnel is evidently a modern deviation, saving miles. The Moselle, mentioned in the last chapter, is completely buried. It used to run above ground, entering Wood Green on the south near the present reservoirs. Its whereabouts is indicated by "Brook Road" near Noel Park Station, then by "Moselle Avenue," and at the north end of Westbury Avenue it flows boldly out into the daylight of Tottenham. In old days, travellers along "Green Lanes" crossed the Moselle by a small wooden bridge, while those following Mazes Lane, now "Mayes Road," crossed it by means of stepping-stones.

Let us try to picture Wood Green about the year 1800, when the population consisted of one hundred persons all told, as against fifty in 1619. There was an inn, a forge, several houses, and one or more shops grouped round the green, which lay considerably to the west of the main road known as Green Lanes, and is now represented by the much smaller space alongside Station Road known as "Wood Green Common." This, the original Wood Green, across which the New River meandered, was once some 70 acres in extent, and was approached from Green Lanes by way of Mazes Lane. Duckett's Manor House, which stood a little south of the present "Empire" in Green Lanes, had a moat and a drawbridge but no architectural merit. Going north along Green Lanes from this point, crossing the Moselle and the New River, one arrived at a small common of 11 acres, Else's Green, and ascending Jolly Butchers' Hill, where the new Tube station now stands, one reached the "Roundabout" (as on Robert Morden's map, c. 1690) or "Roundabouts," where was another small common now partly occupied by St. Michael's Church. Here Bounds Green Road, a charming lane up to a few years ago, turned off to "Colney Hatch" as it does now. North of the "Roundabouts" was Wood Green Farm, where now the Fishmongers' and Poulterers' almshouses stand. To the north-west of Wood Green stretched the green slope of Tottenham Wood, reduced to 11 acres. In 1844, when a chapel-of-ease was built, the population had grown to about 400, and when the railway station was opened in 1859 there were more than 3,000 persons living in Wood Green. This number increased to 9,867 in 1881. The 1911 census gives a figure of 49,639; in 1921 the population was 50,707, and in the last census (1931) it was 54,190. Wood Green has not stopped growing, but most of the available ground is now filled, and one speculates with some interest on the future of the only two considerable open spaces which have not yet been definitely reserved.

One of these is the area between Wolves Lane, White Hart Lane, and the north boundary of the district. The ground has a southern slope with extensive views, marred by the Alexandra Palace. This is mainly municipal property, and is now used as allotments and sports grounds. Then comes a strip occupied by tile-makers, next a most untidy and offensive refuse-dump, and in the extreme corner—strange to say—a small and apparently forgotten farm-house, Devonshire Hill Farm, with a fragment of common adjoining where the combined young of Wood Green, Edmonton, and Southgate are permitted to gambol. The farm is hardly worth preserving as a museum-piece, but there will soon be hundreds of Wood Green children who have never seen a farm unless this be done, and at any rate it does possess some trees. The rest of this area certainly needs some thought, especially the dumps. At the other end of Wood Green is the Muswell Hill Golf Club, from which streets of what are called hereabouts "Elegant Houses" are taking such frequent nibbles that one wonders when the golf links will dwindle from eighteen holes to nine, and finally to nil. That may be a matter of no moment, but at present the ground does contain a few of the surviving oak-trees from the long-lost Tottenham Wood, and they at least are worth a little attention.

Wood Green has no historical buildings, every trace of the past having been successfully stamped out. The collection of drawings in the Public Library gives some idea of the district in bygone days. Tottenham Wood House preserved some dignity, but has been eliminated quite recently, and the Town Hall—an early-Victorian survival—is about the oldest thing in the place. Mid-Victorianism is represented by Sir Gilbert Scott's fine tower and spire at St. Michael's Church and by no less than five groups of almshouses which made their way from the noise of the City to the sylvan solitudes of Wood Green at various intervals during the nineteenth century, and unwisely selected sites near the "Roundabouts," where

DEVONSHIRE HILL FARM (THE LAST OF RURAL WOOD GREEN)

now the roar of traffic justifies the name. There are, of course, some well-designed modern churches, houses, and shops in the area and three ultra-modern Tube stations.

Lastly, there is the Alexandra Palace, an offence to the eye for miles around and a heavy charge on the responsible authorities. The first building on the site was opened in 1873, burnt down shortly afterwards, and—most unfortunately—replaced by the present gigantic abortion in 1875. It has a magnificent organ, but the building as a whole has been an unmitigated failure from the outset. Its empty and dilapidated galleries are most depressing to a visitor, and can only be modernized at vast expense. At the time of writing (1934), a scheme is actually being considered to spend a huge amount of ratepayers' money on brightening up this funereal monstrosity. It would be far more profitable (and this opinion is given in all seriousness) to demolish the whole structure, replace it by a small sunken concert-hall, and throw the present floor area into a new terraced garden, thereby enhancing the present charming grounds and affording a fine prospect in all directions. Wood Green is overpowered and vulgarized by the Alexandra Palace.

BOOKS ON LOCAL HISTORY AND TOPOGRAPHY

PEPLOW, W. A.   "Old Wood Green" [three articles in *Middlesex Schools' Gazette*]   1933

[WOOD GREEN U.D.C.] Wood Green: Official Guide   N.D.

CHAPTER VIII

HORNSEY

INCLUDING CROUCH END, FINSBURY PARK, FORTIS GREEN, PART OF
HARRINGAY, HIGHGATE, MUSWELL HILL, AND STROUD GREEN

ALTHOUGH not so famous as Highgate, one of its constituent
areas, Hornsey is a very ancient district, corresponding to the
old parish with some slight modifications. It became a municipal
borough in 1903, two years after Ealing set this fashion for
Middlesex. Since that time, several other urban districts in the
county have obtained corporate powers, and at the time of writing
the habit is spreading like measles.

The name of Hornsey has provoked much research amongst the
learned and is, in fact, a corruption or modification of the much
older name of Harringay, which curiously survives in the title of
one of its wards. Mr. Gover,* who describes the latter as "a
fossilized or preserved form of the original name of the manor,"
adds that the name of Harringay Manor House was so spelt until
the building was demolished about 1870, and that the Great
Northern Railway then adopted it as the name of their new station,
to distinguish it from Hornsey, the next station on the same main
line. He then gives twenty-five variants of the name from its first
appearance as *Haringue* in 1210 to *Hornesey* in 1710, and we see
that *Harensey* appears as early as 1461. The name has nothing to
do with herrings, but is explained as "a patronymic + ey." If this
be so, the suggestion made by Lysons more than a century ago,
that "Hare Ing" means the "meadow of hares," goes by the board,
though hares were certainly hunted hereabouts. Indeed, one
historian of recent times† recalls that when waiting for "the 8.45"
one spring morning in 1866, on the platform of Hornsey station,
he saw an authentic hare chased into the neighbouring meadows
of Harringay. The name "Crouch" in Crouch End and Crouch

* J. E. B. Gover, *Place-names of Middlesex* (1922), s.v. "Hornsey."
† R. O. Sherington, *The Story of Hornsey* (1904), p. 17.

Hill means simply "cross"—the same derivative as "Crutched Friars" in London.

Fortis Green, spelt "Forty Green" on a map two hundred years old, is explained by the same authority as, possibly, "four tree green." He does not, however, seem to realize that Forty Hill at Enfield, which he brackets with this name, derives its name from Sir Hugh Fortee (see page 67). "Finsbury Park" is something of

HIGHGATE HILL

a misnomer, being miles from Finsbury in the City, of which the name means "the stronghold of Fin" or "Finn." The explanation is that when London bought the present large park in 1857, in exchange for the historical playground of "Finsbury Fields" which its citizens had lost, the name of the latter was retained as a memento. Highgate is simply the "high gate," that is, the gate which stood—as explained hereafter—at the top of the high hill on the old road through the Bishop of London's property. "Muswell Hill" marks the former site of the "mossy well" or spring* (spelt

* Gover, *op. cit.*, s.v. "Muswell Hill." There is another "Muswell Hill" near Brill in Buckinghamshire.

mosewella as early as 1152), which was a place of pilgrimage all through the Middle Ages. As for "Stroud Green," that means simply "the green by the marsh," or "the marshy green."*

The borough of Hornsey has an area of some 2,868 acres, about 4 square miles. Although this area has hardly been varied in the recent redistribution of Middlesex districts, the boundaries have undergone some important changes. Finchley has obtained from

THE LAST OF OLD CROUCH END
Demolished for the new Hornsey Town Hall, 1934

Hornsey the ridiculous little salient north of the new North Circular Road, and the whole of Cherry Tree Wood, a small recreation ground; while Hornsey has obtained from Finchley that part of the Highgate Golf Links which formerly lay within the boundaries of the latter district. But many years ago the part of old Hornsey parish which extended south of Seven Sisters Road was given to the County of London. Except for these and sundry minor rectifications, the area of Hornsey has been unaltered for many centuries.

* Gover, *op. cit.,* s.v. "Stroud Green."

Hornsey is a very hilly area, rising to 427 feet at the top of Highgate Hill, where a patch of sand and gravel interrupts the monotony of the London clay. From East Finchley to Muswell Hill runs another spur of high land, averaging nearly 350 feet, from which the ground falls rapidly towards the Lea Valley, reaching a level of less than 70 feet in Harringay. The greater part of the area was formerly wooded, and through the woods ran several brooks which united in the low ground near Hornsey High Street to form the Moselle, a stream mentioned in several previous chapters.

The Moselle proper took its rise somewhere on Muswell Hill, in the "mossy wells" which accounted for its singular name. The site of those wells seems to be completely lost or forgotten, though they were certainly in existence eighty years ago, being then two in number, lined with brick down to the water-level about $5\frac{1}{2}$ feet below ground.* An idea of the direction of the stream is given by the names of "Wellfield Avenue," close to Muswell Hill Station; and "Brook Road," near Hornsey High Street. Somewhere in the valley the Moselle was reinforced by a stream from Queen's Wood, concealed in a pipe about five years ago. The course of this stream may be traced across the Crouch End playing-fields by the surviving line of willows and oak-trees, which nobody has yet had the presence of mind to cut down, until it disappears under the winding course of Park Avenue South. From Hornsey, the Moselle now continues in a sewer over the Wood Green boundary near Noel Park Station.

The situation of the wells on Muswell Hill seems to have accounted for the curious line of what was, in the early Middle Ages, the only road passing through Hornsey. That road left London at Clerkenwell and ran via Gray's Inn Lane, Maiden Lane, Hornsey Lane, and Crouch End to Muswell Hill; thence by Colney Hatch and Whetstone to Barnet. The shrine of "Our Lady of Mosewell," standing on ground given to the Order of St. John of Jerusalem in 1112 by the Bishop of London, Lord of the Manor of Hornsey, was thus conveniently situated for travellers from the North, and—with its wells—became a flourishing place

* See Sherington, *op. cit.*, p. 77.

of pilgrimage. But the road was damp and difficult to maintain, so that the Bishop, about 1386, opened an alternative route over the steep but dry shoulder of Highgate Hill, and placed at the top of it a gatehouse where toll was extracted from all who passed beneath it and through his park on their way between London and the North, or vice versa. It was apparently in Elizabeth's time that this new highway was improved to form the Great North Road, but the local historians are vague on this point. The name of "The Gatehouse" still survives. During the seventeenth and eighteenth centuries the history of Hornsey is largely concerned with highwaymen, fairs, and other incidents of the road at Highgate. At Highgate there was an annual fair held for three days in July, where all sorts of serious and comical sporting events were organized, but the fun was not limited to this occasion alone. In *Poor Robin's Almanack* for 1676 it is written:

> At Islington
> A fair they hold,
> Where cakes and ale
> Are to be sold.
> At Highgate and
> At Holloway
> The like is kept
> There every day.

In those days, and even so late as the beginning of the nineteenth century, there was a curious custom in vogue at Highgate, by which passing travellers were inveigled into one of the nineteen or more inns which stood at the top of the hill in order to spend a shilling for the good of the house. This ceremony was known as "swearing on the horns" (i.e. on the horns fixed over the door of the old Gate House Tavern as a symbol of the right to collect dues from cattle), and one of the mock "oaths" taken was that no man should kiss the maid when the mistress was at hand, but sooner than miss a chance must kiss them both.

Such unhygienic practices, unthinkable in these days of lipstick and the like, ceased when the new Archway Road was opened in 1813 to provide relief to the increasing number of coaches, of

which eighty a day are said to have stopped at the "Red Lion" at
its palmiest period. The archway, a considerable engineering feat,
was replaced by the present great bridge in 1898. The former
structure attained such popularity among suicides that an iron grille
had to be erected over it, and the new bridge is suitably fenced to
avoid accidents. The view of London from the top is really
magnificent on a clear Sunday morning in summer. The Seven
Sisters Road (see p. 95) was driven through the south of Hornsey
in 1832, and nearly a century later the opening of the Barnet
Bypass Road and the North Circular Road has considerably altered
its system of communications.

Hornsey Station on the Great Northern Railway was opened
in the early 'fifties, and a temporary platform or "halt" at Seven
Sisters Road (now "Finsbury Park" Station) in 1861. The branch
to Edgware through Highgate and Finchley followed in 1867, and
the extensions to High Barnet and Muswell Hill in 1872 and
1873 respectively. Stroud Green Station was not opened until 1881,
and Cranley Gardens in 1903. The first Tube railway (the "Great
Northern and City") arrived in 1904 (by which time tramways
had invaded the district), and since that time the Highgate and
Piccadilly Tubes have arrived, with the recent opening of the
remarkable underground station at Manor House on the Cockfosters–Finsbury Park line. There is also talk of making a connection between Highgate Underground and Highgate L.N.E.R.
Stations, a comparatively short distance with, it is said, no insuper-
able engineering difficulties involved. This would certainly be a
boon to suburban travellers, and, by electrifying the L.N.E.R.
branches, would popularize Finchley, Barnet, and Mill Hill. But,
even if that be done, Hornsey has not solved its most urgent traffic
problem: the appalling and dangerous muddle at the tramway-stop
outside Finsbury Park Station. This responsibility it shares with
London.

The growth of Hornsey was most rapid in the last quarter of
the nineteenth century, and was closely connected with railway
developments. The population was 2,716 in 1801, about 5,000 in
1821 (when a fifth of the families were engaged in agriculture),

about 10,000 in 1851, 11,746 in 1871, 22,485 in 1881, 44,523 in 1891, 72,056 in 1901, 84,592 in 1911, 87,659 in 1921, 95,524 in 1931, and is now about 100,000. The density of population was 33·2 persons per acre in 1931. A large part of the available land is now built up, but approximately one-tenth of the total area of the borough has already been acquired for public open spaces.

HIGHGATE ARCHWAY IN 1813
Site of Highgate Underground Station on left

Drawn from an old painting

It seems quite clear that most of Hornsey was covered with forest in the Middle Ages, and certain that the Bishop of London, as Lord of the Manor, used the greater part of it as a hunting park. Coldfall Wood, Bishop's Wood, Highgate Wood, Queen's Wood, Cherry Tree Wood are surviving fragments. North of Fortis Green Road, Finchley Common lay on either side of the Great North Road with an area of 2,000 acres, a paradise for highwaymen. There was also a small common, 3 acres in extent, at Stroud Green. This, and certain other common lands, amounting to more than 100 acres in all, were enclosed after the Hornsey

H

Enclosure Act of 1816. Highgate Wood (69 acres) was acquired by the Corporation of London, and Queen's Wood (52 acres) by the Hornsey Council. The purchase of Finsbury Park (113 acres) has already been mentioned. Compared with the two public woods, thick with oak-trees and still delightfully secluded in spite of their urban surroundings, Finsbury Park is very sophisticated. Bounded by a large and busy railway junction on one side, by crowded and tram-lined thoroughfares on two others, its lay-out is necessarily and rigidly municipal, but its well-kept flower gardens brighten it in the summer, and it is relieved by the New River, which crosses it in one corner. Hornsey possesses some smaller recreation grounds, also a part of the Alexandra Palace Park, and has easy access to the fine grounds of Ken Wood and Waterlow Park, just across the London border. (The stables and a small part of the Ken Wood grounds are, in fact, in Hornsey, as Lord Mansfield diverted Hampstead Lane northwards from the original boundary line after the Gordon Riots at the end of the eighteenth century.) The borough has also recently earmarked the northern part of Coldfall Wood as a public open space for its rapidly developing northern quarters, a wise precaution. Yet in spite of all this commendable provision, it is to be hoped that the huge area of playing-fields between Crouch End and Muswell Hill will be permanently preserved for this purpose, as a "private open space," and that the really beautiful area of the golf links, with such part of Bishop's Wood as lies within the Hornsey boundaries, may be similarly treated. Both these reservations are recommended in the North Middlesex Regional Town-Planning Report. On "Lodge Hill," which lies within the golf course, stands a portion of the moat which once surrounded the Bishop's hunting lodge which once stood here. This house is said to have been demolished before the sixteenth century, the material being used for building Hornsey Church in 1500. Norden, writing in 1593, mentions the ruins, with bricks, tiles, and slates still visible. The moat is marked on the large-scale ordnance map, and is still partially visible, but a recent cursory inspection failed to reveal any traces of the building.

The amenities of Hornsey are considerable, and on the whole

the district is attractively laid out, being mainly a product of the last fifty or sixty years. Further development will be mainly confined to the small open areas remaining on the north, next to the frontier of Finchley and Friern Barnet. Much good building has been done in the district recently, the blocks of flats on Fortis Green Road forming a typical example of the best work.

Hornsey possesses only one old ecclesiastical monument in all

THE NEW RIVER AND FINSBURY PARK FROM GREEN LANES

its area of 4 square miles, the tower of St. Mary's Parish Church, near Hornsey Station. Once upon a time the New River wound round it, and hayfields reached to the walls of the churchyard. In 1832 all the old church was demolished, except the picturesque brick and stone tower, and a new church erected. This in turn was demolished in 1888, and a fine stone building erected from the designs of James Brooks. It still lacks the lofty tower and spire which were intended to complete the building.* Within the new church are some interesting monuments removed from the

* Design illustrated in *The Builder*, May 12, 1888.

old one. There is a fine incised slab (apparently sixteenth century) with life-sized effigies of George Rey of "Higate" and his two wives; a splendidly designed marble effigy and monument of Francis Musters (d. 1680); and two smaller tablets of the seventeenth century. The chapel which once stood on Highgate Hill, adjoining the school, was built in 1576 and demolished in 1834.

All the original school buildings have also disappeared, and most of the present school premises are in Victorian Gothic. The neighbouring almshouses in Southwood Lane, originally erected by Sir John Wollaston in 1658, were rebuilt in 1722. Cromwell House, on Highgate Hill, is the most important old domestic building in the borough. Early historians of Highgate connected the building, quite groundlessly, with Cromwell; but Mr. Philip Norman has proved that the house was built early in the seventeenth century by Robert Sprignell of Hornsey, who died in 1624, or by his son, Sir Richard Sprignell, Bart. (d. 1656), of Highgate. The ceiling of the principal room bears the Sprignell arms, and Sir Richard was a close friend of some of Cromwell's supporters. The beautiful staircase of this house is certainly of early seventeenth-century date, and is decorated with carved figures in pre-Cromwellian costume. The house is now used as a hospital. Most of the other historical houses of Highgate, on Highgate Hill and in South Grove, are on the London side of the county boundary—which runs down Highgate Hill from Hampstead Lane—and are therefore not described here. There are few houses of architectural interest on the Middlesex side of the road.

Southwood Lane contains several old houses (Nos. 2–12) at its south end, a picturesque house at the corner of Jackson's Lane, then Southwood House—a large brick house with flanking wings and a forecourt, apparently of the eighteenth century—and some quaint cottages. On North Hill there are quite a number of houses of the eighteenth and early nineteenth centuries. Byron Cottage and the fine house north of it may be even older. Farther north, and close to the Finchley boundary, stands the "Old Manor House," a dignified design of c. 1690, with fine ironwork over its gate and a little forecourt. Measured drawings of it have been

made by members of the London Society, but it seems unlikely
that it will resist the housebreaker for long. Muswell Hill seems
to contain no relics of antiquity, Crouch End has an old boarded
house in its centre—on the site where the new Hornsey Town

HORNSEY OLD CHURCH IN 1797

Drawn from an old print

Hall is to be erected,—there are some decrepit cottages in Tottenham Lane, and opposite the parish church in Hornsey Lane two
or three houses of some antiquity: one of them, Eagle House, is
now occupied by the Hornsey Constitutional Club.

BOOKS ON LOCAL HISTORY AND TOPOGRAPHY

GIBSON, W. S.	History and Antiquities of High-gate	London	1842
[HORNSEY BOROUGH COUNCIL]	Hornsey: Official Guide	London	N.D.
HOWITT, W.	Northern Heights of London	London	1869

JEALOUS, W. K.	Highgate Village	London	1919
LLOYD, J. H.	History of Highgate	Highgate	1888
MARCHAM, F., and W. McB.	Court Rolls of the Manor of Hornsey, 1603–1701	London	1929
NORMAN, P.	Cromwell House, Highgate	London	1917
	Cromwell House, Highgate (London Survey Committee)	London	1926
PRICKETT, F.	History of Highgate	Highgate	1842
SHERINGTON, R. O.	The Story of Hornsey	London	1904
SIDEY, C. J. M.	Short History of Hornsey Old Church	London	1911

CHAPTER IX

FRIERN BARNET

THE small urban district of Friern Barnet does not appear to have found a historian, and indeed its only distinctive feature is its name. The friary in question, of which all visible trace has long since disappeared, belonged to the Knights of St. John and passed, at the Dissolution of the Monasteries in the fifteenth century, to the Dean and Chapter of St. Paul's Cathedral. "Colney Hatch" is an old name, though not so ancient as many in Middlesex, and occurs as early as the beginning of the sixteenth century. It is nowhere near the River Colne, so the name can have no affinity with Colney Heath and Colney Street, a few miles north in Hertfordshire. The word "Colney" in this case is given two possible derivations by Mr. Gover*: either "island of Cola," or else from the Middle English word "coni" or "conni" (= coney, i.e. rabbit). "Hatch" means "gate": that is, one of the numerous gates of Enfield Chase, of which "Southgate" was another. This quaint old name, the "Rabbits' Gate," would seem to be attractive enough to satisfy any inhabitant, however fastidious. However, when the huge County Lunatic Asylum was established here in 1851, a very different significance was attached to the name, and the mere mention of "Colney Hatch" gave rise to loud laughter. So the villagers rebelled, and their hamlet came to be rechristened "New Southgate," a harmless and respectable name. As for Oakleigh Park, that sounds suburban enough, and does not appear to have any historical tradition.

The urban district of Friern Barnet is a very small one, with an area of rather more than 2 square miles. The population increased from under 15,000 in 1911 to 17,375 in 1921 and, much more rapidly, to 23,081 in 1931. It has since continued to

---

* J. E. B. Gover, *Place-names of Middlesex*, p. 18.

grow. On the basis of fifty persons to the acre, the district could accommodate over 65,000 people; but a considerable area, including the large grounds of the Mental Hospital, is not available for building, so that it is unlikely that the population will ever exceed 50,000. Presumably it is partly for this reason, and partly because of the awkward shape and configuration of the area, that the Ministry of Health has recently recommended that the district of Friern Barnet should be amalgamated with the new borough of Finchley. This suggestion would result in the creation of an enlarged Finchley with an area of about 5,000 acres (say $7\frac{1}{2}$ square miles) and a population which was about 90,000 in 1931, so will be about 100,000 at the present time.

The only stream within the district is the Bounds Green Brook, which runs beside or beneath the new North Circular Road at the south end of the area, where there is low-lying ground. At this point are concentrated several sewage farms from which rise odours that offend the sensitive nostrils of the newly arrived settlers. This was formerly a secluded corner of Middlesex, and it was not considered important that the feelings of the unfortunate inmates of "Colney Hatch" should be regarded. However, all this unpleasantness is to disappear shortly—or so we are told—when the new county drainage scheme is completed; "Distinctive Homes" will blossom everywhere, and, in fact, all's well that ends well.

Apart from sewage farms and the extensive demesne of the Mental Hospital, Friern Barnet possesses 51 acres of public allotments and 67 acres of public open spaces—including Friary Park and Bethune Park—also the large and attractive North Middlesex golf course. If the district is to grow as rapidly as now seems probable, it is to be hoped that this golf course with its fine trees will be preserved to recall—together with Friary Park adjoining—the attractions of a district which was secluded and rural a generation ago. The golf course has been scheduled as a "private open space." Some excellent modern housing development has taken place in the northern part of the district, but the picturesque aspect of the Great North Road at Whetstone is rapidly fading.

Friern Barnet contains few notable relics of its past. The picturesquely placed old church is small, and has been so extensively restored that not much remains of the ancient building except a Norman doorway. There is a row of charming brick almshouses, built in 1612 by Laurence Campe, "citizen and draper" of London. Restored in 1843 and in 1897, they bear the arms of their founder, the City of London, and the Drapers' Company. No trace remains of the Friary buildings, but it is stated that the present club-house

ALMSHOUSES, FRIERN BARNET

in Friary Park occupies their site, and that the building known as "The Priory" (now used as District Council Offices) at the corner of Friern Lane and Friern Barnet Lane is connected with the Friary by "subterranean passages," while from the Friary itself to the old parish church, along the line of the present fine avenue of elms and beneath it, "is supposed to be a secret passage which the monks used on their way to vespers, emerging from an opening in the church at the back of the chancel"! Alleged secret passages are as common as bedrooms in which Queen Elizabeth is alleged to have slept, and these local traditions are seldom founded on fact. It is time that some competent historian should turn his attention to the fast-disappearing traces of Friern Barnet. There was a time in the Middle Ages, as was related in Chapter VIII, when the road from London to Chipping Barnet and the North ran through Crouch End, past the shrine and spring of "Our Lady of Mosewell," through Colney Hatch and Friern Barnet and Whetstone, whence it followed the line of the present Great North Road; and surely there must be material in the history of the district to give its inhabitants some sense of their inheritance.

BOOKS ON LOCAL HISTORY AND TOPOGRAPHY

NIL.

CHAPTER X

FINCHLEY

T HE borough of Finchley obtained its charter on October 5, 1933, and celebrated the event cheerfully, but wisely refrained from roasting an ox as its neighbour, Hendon, did in like circumstances. The name of Finchley does not occur in Domesday, but appears in the thirteenth century as "Fynchesleye," which means "the pasture or clearing of Finch," obviously a personal name. Whetstone, which lies partly in Finchley and partly in Friern Barnet, is found in the fifteenth century, is a name of uncertain derivation. Two alternatives have been suggested:* a large white stone, which is or was to be seen outside the Griffin Inn, on which it is said that soldiers whetted their swords and battle-axes before the battle of Barnet; or the whetstone which was once awarded as a prize for lying, in certain villages.

Before the recent revision of boundaries, Finchley had an area of 3,384 acres. As a result of revision, a portion of Hendon, including the grounds of Nether Court which Finchley had previously acquired as an open space and is at present used as a golf course, was added; but the Ministry of Health declined to approve the transfer from Hendon to Finchley of the portion of the Hampstead Garden Suburb included within the boundaries of the former borough. Feeling ran high on this question, Finchley contending that the whole of the suburb ought to be under one authority, while Hendon argued that its own half of the suburb was satis-factorily administered and that the inhabitants had no reasonable grievance. It may be observed that the suburb, admirably laid out in such a way that its high rateable value is likely to be maintained, is obviously a prize which arouses the cupidity of any municipal body; and this fact is a powerful argument in favour of wise town-

---

* J. R. Biggers, *Finchley and Neighbourhood* (1903).

planning. A further proposal, already mentioned in the previous chapter, suggested the addition of the urban district of Friern Barnet to the borough of Finchley. Excluding Friern Barnet, but including the part of Hendon just added, Finchley now has an area of about 3,600 acres, or 5½ square miles.

The borough has an irregular shape, rather like a ham, with the frilly end at Whetstone and the other end at Hampstead Heath. Its length is 5 miles from north to south, its greatest breadth nearly 2½ miles. The Dollis Brook forms a part of the west boundary, and separates Finchley from Hertfordshire. The Finchley Road forms a further section of the west boundary, from the "Naked Lady" (as the tram conductors persist in describing the War Memorial statue), to the Tube station at Golder's Green. The east boundary of the borough has recently been modified, but remains irregular and follows neither roads nor natural features.

The population of Finchley was 1,503 in 1801, 2,349 in 1821, 3,610 in 1841, 4,937 in 1861, 7,146 in 1871, and 11,191 in 1881. Then the increase became more rapid: 16,344 in 1891, 22,126 in 1901, 39,419 in 1911, 46,716 in 1921, and 58,961 in 1931. Evidently the period 1901–11 was the growing time for Finchley. Building is still proceeding rapidly in several parts of the district, and, though the large amount of public spaces and the strictly limited spacing of houses on the Garden Suburb will prevent a very dense population in the future, it seems probable that the present population of over 61,000 will increase to 80,000 at least, even without the addition of Friern Barnet. Theoretically, Finchley could accommodate 180,000 people, at fifty persons per acre; and a further 65,000 if Friern Barnet be added.

Of the important trunk roads which traverse the borough, only a few are ancient. The North Circular Road is the most recent, with its spurs leading to Hendon and Highgate. The Finchley Road, from Regent's Park and West Hampstead to Tally-Ho Corner, was opened just over a century ago, though part of its length, still known as "Ballard's Lane," is much older. The Great North Road, from Holloway and Highgate to Finchley and Whetstone, is older still, but not so old as the lane which passed through Crouch End, Muswell Hill, and Friern Barnet, mentioned in the previous chapter. Rocque's map of Middlesex (*c.* 1754) shows the Great North Road, Ballard's Lane (continuing as Hendon Lane over Finchley Bridge), East End Road, Long Lane, Summers Lane, Dollis Lane, and Nether Street; while the modern "Squires Lane" appears on the map as "Place Lane." Cary's atlas of 1800 shows almost the same number of roads.

FINCHLEY: DOLLIS BROOK

On both maps the most striking feature is the huge expanse of Finchley Common, which extended from Fortis Green Road in the south to near Totteridge Lane in the north, occupying practically all the land east of the Great North Road and a wide strip west of it. According to a recent official publication, the Common area covered about two-thirds of the acreage of the parish. Dr. Hunter, writing in 1810, stated that Finchley Common was "a place formidable to travellers from the highway robberies of which it has been the scene" and that it was "estimated to contain 2,101 acres, the waste and uncultivated state of which so near the metropolis is disgraceful to the economy of the country." Lysons, writing fifteen years earlier, gives the area as 1,010 acres. This suggests a misprint, but it seems probable that the area of the Common was over 2,000 acres before the eighteenth century, and it is stated elsewhere that the area had been reduced to 1,243 acres in 1743. The final enclosure took place early in the nineteenth century. Finchley Common was 3 miles long and 1½ miles broad when Cary made his survey in 1800, and covered the whole of the space now occupied by East Finchley and North Finchley.

Although "Turpin's Oak" still survives in Oak Lane, modern historians are inclined to discount the exploits of that legendary hero, including his famous ride to York on Black Bess, and to dismiss him as a common rascal. But there is no doubt that Finchley Common vied with Hounslow Heath (which will be described in a later chapter of this book) as a place of real terror for travellers. Dick Turpin and Jack Sheppard were only two of the highwaymen who regularly operated on its desolate and oak-scattered expanse, and nobody knows at whom the bullets were fired that have been extracted from the gnarled trunk of "Turpin's Oak." A gibbet used to stand at the south end of the Common, close to the site of the East Finchley Congregational Church. Three robberies are recorded in 1740, others in 1762 and 1776. In 1776 and 1778 highwaymen attempting to rob the Derby stage coach were shot, on one occasion by the guard, whose office in those days was no sinecure. In Lord Lytton's *Paul Clifford* and in Fielding's *Tom Jones* there are stories of highway robberies on Finchley Common. Now that famous waste is partly occupied by houses, but the greater part is devoted to such beneficent uses as sewage farms, allotments, recreation grounds, and enormous cemeteries. An open-air swimming bath stands in one corner, and it is rumoured that Finchley's future town hall is to be located on the small portion still left vacant.

The borough contains a generous allowance of open spaces, amounting in all to more than 400 acres. The most interesting of these reservations is the "Brookside Walk" along the courses of the Mutton Brook and the Dollis Brook, a distance of 4½ miles in all.

The north part of this strip, the Whetstone end, is sufficiently broad to give a feeling of space, which is lacking when a stream-side walk is bounded on either side by the back fences of villas only a few yards apart, and is apt to become a mere dumping-ground for domestic rubbish. It is to be hoped that the grounds of the Hampstead Golf Club will never be built upon. The wood that stands in the angle between Colney Hatch Lane and Woodham

THE SPANIARD'S TAVERN IN 1933

Road, above the sewage works and the North Circular Road, should most certainly be preserved.

Historical buildings are scarce in the borough of Finchley. There is the attractive old parish church of St. Mary, with a squat stone tower. It has been much restored, and in 1932 was enlarged by the addition of a well-designed south aisle. It contains some interesting memorial-brasses, the best being dated 1610. In the gallery are two noteworthy monuments, to Sir Thomas Allen of Finchley (d. 1681) and his wife; and to "Alexander Kinge, Esq., one of His Majesty's Auditors" (d. 1618). Both these are marble memorials, characteristic of their day. The Manor House in

East End Road, a large brick building about two hundred years old, is now "the Convent of Marie Auxiliatrice"; it contains a fine panelled room, where the owner once administered justice. "The Squire's Lane," which once ran from the Manor House between a great fish-pond on one side and the village pond on the other, is now a very ordinary suburban street. Then there is the Spaniard's Inn, with its turnpike-lodge in Hampstead Lane; Park House (No. 56, Hendon Lane), a charming and well-preserved Georgian brick building; a few other old houses, such as Woodside House at Whetstone; and, here and there, forlorn boarded cottages, as in Granville Road. But the old coaching inns have gone, smothered and blotted out by the vulgar line of hoardings, petrol stations, blatant shops, and muddle of all kinds, that desecrate the stately and historic highway known as the Great North Road.

BOOKS ON LOCAL HISTORY AND TOPOGRAPHY

BANKS, C. O.	The Finchley Manor, I	Finchley	1929
BIGGERS, J. R.	Finchley and Neighbourhood	London	1903
[FINCHLEY BOROUGH]	Official Souvenir of the Charter of Incorporation	Finchley	1933
[FINCHLEY U.D.C.]	Finchley: Official Guide	London	N.D.
LATIMER, DR. A.	The Illustrated Story of Finchley	Birmingham	N.D.
PASSMORE, W. B.	"Bygone Finchley" [in *Home Counties Magazine*]	London	1897– 1903
PEACOCK, T. F.	Finchley (London and Middlesex Archaeological Society)	London	1872
WALKER, H.	Glacial Drifts of Muswell Hill and Finchley	London	1874

CHAPTER XI

HENDON

HENDON, already one of the largest and perhaps destined to be the largest of all the new boroughs of Middlesex, makes many claims to our notice. It provides the most sensational example of rapid growth in recent years, its area is considerable, it still possesses some of the most attractive rural scenery in the country, it contains some of the best examples of modern building, it has a splendid library with a good collection of local relics and drawings, and it celebrated its recent grant of a charter in 1932 by the public roasting of an ox. This last barbarous performance, culminating in the distribution of thousands of beef sandwiches to its carnivorous citizens, was unworthy of so civilized a community, and has not been imitated by any subsequent recipients of municipal status.

The name of Hendon appears long before Domesday, and means simply "high down" or "hill." "Burnt Oak," which also occurs at Pinner, recalls the Roman custom of burning an oak-tree on one side to mark a boundary line. That line was "Watling Street," the famous Roman road from Londinium to Verulamium, which also served as the boundary of the Danelaw at the Treaty of Wedmore in 878, and has recently been utilized as the name of the large L.C.C. housing estate at Burnt Oak. "Child's" Hill may be taken to preserve the memory of a man called Child, and Colindale presumably has a similar origin, also "Golder's" Green. Cricklewood, so described for more than two centuries, may have some affinity with the Dutch *krinkel* (= "twist") or the old English *crickle* (= "tangle"), thus coming to mean a "tangled wood." The word Hale, which as we have seen had another significance at Tottenham (see page 95), is interpreted in this case by Mr. Gover* as "a nook, corner, or retreat"; while "Hyde" may recall an Anglo-Saxon name for a measure of land, usually 100 to 120 acres, and is found in the familiar name of Hyde Park. "Edgware," spelt *Ægces wer* in the tenth century and *Eggeswere* in the twelfth, does not indicate the edge of anything, but means "Ecg's weir" or fishing-pool, Ecg being a man's name. "Elstree"

GOODHEW'S FARM, MILL HILL, IN 1933
Used as a garage and disfigured with placards.

has an even more complicated origin: it is spelt *Tioulfes treow* in the eighth century and *Tidulvestre* in the twelfth, which is, being interpreted, "at the tree of Tidwulf." The name of Mill Hill seems to require no explanation whatever. It almost certainly means exactly what it implies—a mill on the top of a hill—and there was a mill there long ago, marked on an old map and commemorated in the "Old Mill Field" opposite Belmont. On the other hand, it has been suggested that the origin is "mile," the Ridgeway at Mill Hill being a mile long: or that it may recall the

* J. E. B. Gover, *Place-names of Middlesex*, s.v. "Hale," etc.

name of one "Miles," who, centuries ago, owned the orchard where I live, and who presumably had something to do with "Milespit Hill" close by.*

The present borough boundaries, which have been readjusted in minor details lately, include an area of more than 10,000 acres (almost exactly 16 square miles). The maximum length is over seven miles, extending from Hampstead to Elstree, and the maxi-

GOLDER'S GREEN ROAD, ABOUT 1908
(Trees now removed)

mum breadth between three and four miles. Up to 1931 the district boundaries were identical with those of the old parish of Hendon, but in that year the parish of Edgware was added. This greatly increased the acreage (previously 8,000), but it must be remembered that this addition only includes Edgware *east* of Watling Street. All the town west of the road is in the new district of Harrow, and forms part of the parish of Little Stanmore (see page 144). The straight line of Watling Street thus serves as the

* N. G. Brett-James, *The Story of Mill Hill Village*, p. 27. D. G. Denoon, *How Mill Hill got its Name*, passim.

west boundary of Hendon from the London frontier at Hampstead to the Hertfordshire frontier at Elstree, except for a distance of about a mile near the "Welsh Harp," where Hendon crosses the road. The recent redistribution of boundaries (1933) has given to Finchley the grounds of Nether Court, a fine golf course recently purchased by Finchley as an open space; but has refused to deprive Hendon of its share of the Hampstead Garden Suburb, which is a great financial asset to the borough, thanks to its admirable lay-out.

Hendon contains some of the highest ground in the county, along the ridge from Barnet Gate (463 feet) to Brockley Hill (440 feet), at Highwood Hill (452 feet), at Mill Hill (400 feet), and at Hendon Church (287 feet). The subsoil everywhere is the London clay, but there are patches of gravel on most of the hills and some valley gravel near Brent Bridge; while the Bagshot sand occurs in the south of Hendon, on Hampstead Heath. The removal of gravel here and there accounts for the Burroughs Pond at Hendon, and for the Angel Pond and the "Sheepwash" on the Ridgeway at Mill Hill. The watercourses of the district consist of a large number of brooks which join in the "Welsh Harp" reservoir (otherwise known as "Hendon Lake" or the "Brent Reservoir") and form one arm of the Brent River. There is the Dollis Brook which separates Finchley from Hendon and is joined by the Mutton Brook near Mutton Bridge, a well-designed and inevitable modern affair replacing a quaint little brick structure that existed up to very recent times. Higher up the Dollis Brook is a weir, formerly an attractive spot where the water widened to form a little lake crossed by Finchley Bridge, but now overshadowed by an arterial road. Descending the Dollis Brook from Mutton Bridge one passes through the "Decoy," and soon Brent Bridge is reached. The bridge itself has been rebuilt and the large old house adjoining it has been converted into a hotel catering for the lighter pleasures of the borough and equipped with a modern dance hall. To provide a romantic "Olde Worlde" setting for love-stricken sitters-out, the Dollis Brook has here been made to pass over an elaborate picturesque waterfall, suitably equipped with fairy lights and a summer-house that is far too rustic to be rural. From Brent Bridge to the reservoir the errant stream has been shepherded into a straight concrete channel and will doubtless be covered in eventually. The other stream feeding the reservoir is formed by the confluence of several tributaries. One is the Dean's Brook, which rises in Nut Wood, part of the beautiful Moat Mount estate recently acquired by the borough as a public open space, and here there is a charming lake. It then passes under the Barnet Bypass Road,

MILL HILL "BROADWAY", ABOUT 1906
(From the bottom of Station Road)

picks up some other brooks, and forms another very attractive lake haunted by wildfowl, runs beneath the Watford Bypass, and reaches Hale Lane. Here there used to be a charming "water-splash," but that too has been replaced by a culvert so that buses and other traffic may pass over it. It next pursues a devious course east of the two stations at Edgware, and receives the waters of the Edgware Brook. From this point to the reservoir it is known as the Silk Stream. It traverses the Watling Estate, sometimes in its natural state, sometimes restrained in a concrete channel. As for the reservoir itself, that was a beautiful lake some forty years ago, and fortunately the Hendon and Kingsbury authorities have lately acquired most of its west and north banks as public open spaces, thus preventing any further building. But in the naughty nineties or thereabouts a regrettable outburst of very shabby building occurred at West Hendon, between Watling Street and the lake. The little patch of mean houses will stand there until some fierce reformer of the future calls for their removal. At the Watling Street end of the reservoir there is now displayed the following self-explanatory legend:

OLDE WELSH HARP
MOTOR-BOAT WATERDROME
OUR BREEZY BRACING THRILLS
SAVE YOU £s IN DOCTOR'S BILLS.

Meanwhile the old white house shown on page 162 has been converted into a service-garage and is adorned with the usual crop of advertisements. Across the road is a queer little café frequented by lorry drivers, and thus announced: "DRIFT INTO CHARLES' FOR TEA AND EATS." So does the Oxford manner penetrate to the purlieus of West Hendon.

These vulgarities may suggest the need of stream-side control advocated by all town-planning enthusiasts, but in practice the application of that control is very difficult. The mere fencing-in of a narrow strip of ground on either side of one of these charming brooks is quite useless so long as the barbarous inhabitants of "Distinctive Homes" on the banks are so uncivilized as to throw their domestic rubbish over the fence; and that is what happens. I have seen a youth in an indisputable blazer hurling the lumber of his garage into the neighbouring Dean's Brook, yet doubtless he and his kind journey miles to find the authentic country. One cannot patrol the banks of all these streams for offenders of this calibre.

Hendon possesses, in Watling Street, already mentioned, one of the oldest roads in England. Another ancient highway is that which goes from Hampstead Heath to Barnet Gate and is known at various stages of its length as North End Road, Golder's Hill, Golder's Green Road, Brent Street, Parson Street, Holders

Hill, Bittacy Hill, Drivers' Hill, The Ridgeway, Holcombe Hill, Highwood Hill, and Hendon Wood Lane. Among other old roads in the borough may be mentioned Hoop Lane, Bridge Lane, Bell Lane, Church Road, Hall Lane, Page Street, The Burroughs, Colindeep Lane, Finchley Lane, Child's Hill, Bunns Lane, Daws Lane, Wise Lane, Hammers Lane, Hale Lane, Frith Lane, and Burton Hole Lane. The Finchley Road was opened in 1825 or

CROSSROADS AT "THE GREEN MAN," MILL HILL, IN 1925
Nothing illustrated here now survives

1826. Very little construction of main roads took place during the next century, and even minor streets were few up to 1900 or later, but recent times have seen the making of the North Circular Road, Watford Way, the Watford and Barnet Bypasses, and many others. Some extension of main roads from east to west in the north of the borough will soon become inevitable.

The L.M.S. main line railway and the L.N.E.R. branch line through Mill Hill to Edgware were both constructed in the years 1867–9. There was then perfect calm, except for the construction of tramlines along the Finchley Road in 1905–10, until the Tube for Hampstead to Golder's Green arrived in 1907. The new station at Golder's Green was then situated in completely open country, with hardly a house in sight. The spate of building which followed led to the extension of the Tube to Edgware between 1922 and 1924, since when development has been phenomenal, fomented by an increasing system of scarlet buses.

Bearing these dates in mind, it is easy to see from the following figures how much the growth of Hendon has been due to the activity of the Tube railway, and how little the older lines have had to do with it. The population of the district was only 1,955 in 1801, 2,589 in 1811, 3,100 in 1821, 3,110 in 1831, 3,333 in 1851, 6,972 in 1871, 10,484 in 1881, 15,843 in 1891, 22,450 in 1901, 40,039 in 1911, 57,529 in 1921, and 115,682 in 1931. It is now increasing by leaps and bounds, and there is plenty of room. At the moderate and enlightened allowance of fifty persons to the acre, the borough could accommodate half a million people; packed as tightly as the inhabitants of the slums of Leeds, it could hold the entire present population of the County of London.

It is to be hoped that even the former alternative may never occur, but the risk leads us now to consider open spaces. In this matter Hendon has done very well and has looked far ahead. At the time of writing (1934) the public open spaces amount to over 900 acres, to which must be added 167 acres of the Moat Mount golf course (a private open space) and 123 acres of allotments. Besides all these, the Council's town-planning scheme provides for the reservation of a large area of woodland and pasture as part of the "Green Girdle" (see page 22), between Scratch Wood and Elstree: also for other reservations elsewhere. In addition to these public spaces, it must be remembered that the borough contains several large properties which are likely to remain open, such as the extensive grounds of Mill Hill School and the area surrounding Mill Hill Barracks. Then there is the enormous but unlovely area of the Hendon aerodrome, which may perhaps be considered untouchable, though the neighbouring private aerodromes at Cricklewood and Stag Lane have both been sold for building land. In view of this generous provision, it may seem greedy to ask for more, but to

anyone who has grown up in the district from boyhood it is sad to
think that Wilberforce's beautiful home at Hendon Park on Highwood Hill is liable to be cut up into small slices some day, its lovely
trees felled, and the pond where the water-hens paddle about filled
up for ever.

But it is unlikely now that such carelessness will occur again as
allowed the village green at Mill Hill to be enclosed a century ago.
Now it carries on its small area a chapel, a shop, and a dozen houses

Capt Hall: Mill Hill: The Stable Court
23rd May 1926

—an almost incredible achievement. Golder's Green in those days
was a wide strip of grass a mile along, on either side of the present
"Golder's Green Road" from Brent Bridge to the Hippodrome.

Considering its size and age, Hendon does not possess a large
number of old buildings. The Parish Church is very interesting,
but was much altered and enlarged in 1915. It must be admitted
that the work was most skilfully done, indeed several discoveries
made at that time and since have increased our knowledge of the
ancient church, which contains fragments of a Norman building
and is said to have had a Saxon origin. The font is a fine specimen
of Norman work, there are remains of thirteenth-century masonry
and carving in the chancel, and an arcade of the same century in

the nave. The tower, the beautiful roof, and the north aisle are
later Gothic work. The interior of the church as altered is spacious,
light, and admirably decorated. It contains some notable monuments and in the churchyard are some well-designed tombstones.
Edgware Parish Church has a fifteenth-century tower of stone, but
is otherwise of no architectural importance; and as for St. Paul's at
Mill Hill, erected by the saintly William Wilberforce in 1833, the

GREYHOUND HILL, HENDON
The old Church House on the right

less said about it the better. St. Alban's at Golder's Green is a noble
building recently erected from the designs of Sir Giles Scott, R.A.

Of old domestic buildings, several are scattered about the district.
In the south of the borough, Avenue or Cowhouse Farm at
Child's Hill was demolished in 1932, and Clitterhouse Farm—of
some historical importance but no intrinsic merit—is still standing.
Wylde's Farm, a delightful little boarded house near Hampstead
Heath, still remains, though drastically altered. There Sir Raymond
Unwin settled to plan out the Hampstead Garden Suburb in 1907,
and there he still remains. Part of the old White Swan Inn in
Golder's Green Road is surviving, but Hodford Farm near Golder's
Green Station has gone years ago. At the Burroughs there is a line

of old buildings, Nos. 42–52, of which the best, No. 42, is now
used by the Public Health Department of the town. The terribly
defaced old, low buildings adjoining serve as a garage. Opposite are
three quaint old houses (Nos. 11–15). At Church End are the brick
Daniel Almshouses built in 1729, and repaired in 1853 and 1893.
Near the church are some delightful wooden cottages, and, adjoining them on Greyhound Hill, the beautiful Church House Farm,
a seventeenth-century gabled house with a magnificent brick

THE "KING'S HEAD," MILL HILL

chimney-stack.* Not far away is Hendon Hall, an imposing mansion
occupied by David Garrick from 1756 to 1779, with a striking
portico said to have been brought here from Canons Park. It is
now a residential hotel and has been much altered. Opposite,
across Parson Street, is Tenterden Hall School, a dignified white
building of the eighteenth century, occupying the site of the old
Hendon manor house. Most of the surviving old buildings of
Edgware are west of Watling Street, and therefore outside the

* It seems worth recording that, in the fields adjoining Hendon Grove,
between the fire station and the church, Highland cattle are still grazing in this
year 1934, but the land has been sold for building.

Hendon boundary, but there is a group of four almshouses at Stone Grove, east of the road, founded in 1680, by Samuel Atkinson, a bricklayer of Waltham Cross who was born in Edgware. The building has a tiled roof and a picturesque "Dutch" curved gable in the centre of the front. Nearer to Edgware, and on the same side of the road, is a row of eight ugly Gothic almshouses erected in 1828.

At Mill Hill there are the Nicoll Almshouses near the Angel Pond, founded in 1697; the mutilated shell of Copt Hall (1637), built by a member of the Nicoll family; the large house known as "Littleberries" and now forming part of St. Vincent's Convent, on the Ridgeway; Hale End Farm, on the way to Edgware; Lawrence Street Farm; and Goodhew's Farm, near Copt Hall. All these are brick buildings, and the last named is a charming design, utterly ruined now by some seventeen enamelled iron advertisements of various brands of motor spirit and cigarettes. The King's Head Inn, on the Ridgeway, is another old brick building. Hendon Park, on Highwood Hill, is rather later in date, and is covered with stucco. The charming house known as "Jeannette's" on the Ridgeway was demolished lately, also the Green Man Inn. Goldbeaters' Farm, which contained a few relics of its great antiquity but was otherwise unimportant, was demolished in 1928 when the Watling Estate was nearly completed. Mill Hill also still retains a number of old boarded houses and cottages, including "Rosebank" and "The Grove" on the Ridgeway. The Three Hammers Inn, "Cherry's Farm" near Lawrence Street, "Pursley House" in Dole Street, and several specimens on Milespit Hill and on Holcombe Hill. Edgwarebury Farm is vaguely associated with Dick Turpin. The main block of Mill Hill School was erected in 1825 from the designs of Sir William Tite, to replace the far more ancient Ridgeway House. It is a very dignified building, and it could be wished that the miscellaneous collection of subsidiary buildings, that have grown up around it, had preserved some harmony of style with it.

In its most recent development, consisting mainly of dwelling-houses and shops, Hendon has maintained a notably high level of building. The Hampstead Garden Suburb was inspired by Dame

Henrietta Barnett, and first laid out by Sir Raymond Unwin in 1907. Building is still in progress. It presents the outstanding example of financially successful private enterprise on such a scale, and there seems no reason to anticipate that the property will deteriorate in value, as most built-up areas tend to do eventually. Fashions do change; thus, the fact that the first houses had no garages is a drawback to the average modern newly wed, but not to all of the intelligentsia who are said to predominate in "The Suburb," and this beautiful area is still regarded as a most desirable place of residence. The Watling Estate of the London County Council at Burnt Oak, with over 4,000 houses, is an equally admirable example of municipal housing. Together, these two estates provide an excellent model for the Hendon of the future.

BOOKS ON LOCAL HISTORY AND TOPOGRAPHY

BARNETT, DAME H.	Growth of the Hampstead Garden Suburb	——	1928
BRETT-JAMES, N. G.	History of Mill Hill School, 1807–1907	London	N.D.
	History of Mill Hill School, 1807–1923	Reigate	N.D.
	The Story of Mill Hill Village	Reigate	N.D.
	The Story of Hendon	Hendon	1929
	Some Extents and Surveys of Hendon	London	1933
CLARKE, A. G.	Story of Goldbeaters and Watling	Mill Hill	1931
DAVEY, E. J.	Golder's Hill and Wylde's Farm	Hampstead	1907
DENOON, D. G.	How Mill Hill got its Name	Mill Hill	1932
DEXTER, B. W. [Ed.]	Cricklewood	Cricklewood	1908
EELES, F. C.	Parish Church of St. Mary, Hendon	Hendon	1931
EVANS, E. T.	History and Topography of Hendon	London	1890
[HENDON U.D.C.]	Hendon : Official Guide	London	1931
HOWKINS, F.	The Story of Golder's Green	Golder's Green	[1922]
RELF, T. J.	Ye Booke of Olde Edgware	Edgware	[1924]
WHITING, J. E.	Golder's Hill, Hampstead	Hampstead	1909
WILSON, M. E.	Wylde's and its Story	London	1904

CHAPTER XII

HARROW

INCLUDING HARROW-ON-THE-HILL, HARROW WEALD, HEADSTONE, HATCH END, PINNER, WEALDSTONE, STANMORE, WHITCHURCH, AND PARTS OF EDGWARE AND KENTON

To many people Harrow must still be synonymous with the great school established on its hill more than three hundred years ago; and indeed "The Hill"—which has given a title to a novel of Harrow school life—is still very largely monopolized by the school, but it is becoming more and more an island surrounded by an endless sea of "Distinctive Homes." Almost exactly the same thing has occurred at Mill Hill, but there the hill is less of an island. Yet in each case, in order to keep itself unspotted from the world and, by preserving its rural amenities, to maintain a steady flow of fee-payers, the school has had to buy large tracts of land on the skirts of the hill where it stands. These purchases have been of great value to the rapidly growing districts of Harrow and Hendon respectively, for they have secured open spaces which, if not actually public, do greatly enhance the attractions of the neighbourhood. The nightingale still returns every spring to the wooded slopes of Harrow Hill.

It is only during 1934 that the huge area of twentieth-century villadom surrounding Harrow—including the old villages named at the head of this chapter—has been formed into one district with Harrow-on-the-Hill forming its centre and providing its name. Harrow is no longer, as one Pinnock described it in 1824, "a large and populous village celebrated for its important Scholastic establishment . . ." with a parish church which is ". . . a respectable edifice." It is a community of over a hundred thousand persons, inchoate and unwieldy as yet. It has no public library and no public collection of local pictures and relics. Indeed, it was in this district that a local bookseller, so-called, greeted my request for a guide-book

with a scathing reference to "fanatics interested in antiquities."
This, by the way, was in Edgware, of which more will be said in
this chapter. As a matter of fact, Harrow-on-the-Hill is the best
place in Middlesex in which to buy old books. It has an "Architectural Club," and there is also a very active Edgware and Stanmore
Historical Society. So there is some hope that interest in local
affairs and local history will be maintained in this huge new
artificially-created "town" of Harrow.

HARROW CHURCH FROM THE WEST

The name Harrow first occurs as *Hergae* in 767, then as *Herges*
in Domesday, and as *Harrewe* in 1216–1307. Mr. Gover explains
this as "a heathen temple or place of worship," often on the top of
a hill; and adds that "Peperharow" in Surrey has the same derivation. "Weald," in "Wealdstone" and "Harrow Weald," is an
Anglo-Saxon word meaning "a wood" or "wooded country," and
in later times "wild open country." For the origin of "Headstone"
the same writer suggests the Anglo-Saxon *hecg tun* = "farm
enclosed by a hedge." Hatch End is easily explained, for "hatch"
means "gate" or "wicket," and "end" usually indicates a point on a
boundary. "Pinner" might mean "the bank of the river Pin," but

Mr. Gover considers that "the river name must be a back formation, and the prefix represent a personal name Pinna." "Stanmore," which first occurs in Domesday as "Stanmere," obviously means "a stony mere," and Whitchurch "a white church."

The new district, known hereafter as the "Urban District of Harrow," has the very large area of 12,558 acres; that is, about 19½ square miles. It thus surpasses, by a small margin, the acreage of Enfield, previously the most extensive in the country. This new Harrow comprises the former urban districts of Harrow-on-the-Hill (2,129 acres) and Wealdstone (1,061 acres) and the former rural district of Hendon (9,230 acres), but considerable rectification of the boundaries with adjacent areas has also taken place, small portions of Ealing and Wembley being annexed in the process. Practically all the Harrow School playing-fields area, formerly more in Wembley than in Harrow, has thus been brought into the latter district. Roughly speaking, the new district of Harrow comprises the old parishes of Harrow, Pinner, Great Stanmore, and Little Stanmore (otherwise known as "Whitchurch").

The natural features of the area provide a great range of natural scenery. On the north, where there are patches of sand and gravel, the ground reaches the height of 505 feet, hence the somewhat bombastic title of "The Alpine Hut" given to a café at this point, on the top of Stanmore Heath. This is the highest point in Middlesex, and there is a stretch of magnificent wooded common all along the ridge from Stanmore Heath to Grim's Dyke, with a smaller area on Pinner Hill. It is intended that eventually all this area shall become public property and form part of the "Green Girdle," mentioned on previous occasions in this book. The highest point on Harrow Hill is marked on the map as 407·9 feet (and one admires the surveyor who possessed the nerve to record it thus, and not make it a commonplace 408 feet). But the land surrounding it is so flat that Harrow Hill does resemble an island, seen from any aspect, and its elevation appears even greater than it is. Nearly all the area comprised in the new district, except the wooded belt on the north, was given over to pasture up to a few years ago; but now the cattle are everywhere being displaced by estate agents' screaming placards and builders' growling concrete-mixers.

There are several small brooks in the area, but no watercourses of any importance, and no lakes larger than those of Canons Park and Harrow School. The Yeading Brook rises on the western slopes of Harrow Hill, picks up the Pin, and in its lower reaches becomes the River Crane. The Wealdstone Brook runs into the Brent via Wembley, the Edgware Brook becomes the Silk Stream

HARROW FROM SUDBURY COURT ROAD

after crossing Watling Street and also joins the Brent, while a few small streams on the north of the Stanmore–Harrow Weald ridge find their way into the Colne. For reasons given in the previous chapter, it seems hopeless to attempt any "stream-side reservation" where these various brooks pass between the back fences of suburban citizens with hooligan ideas of refuse disposal, and only where a stream passes through a public park is it worth leaving uncovered.

The oldest highway in the district is, of course, the Roman "Watling Street" which forms its eastern boundary for some miles. Robert Morden's map of 1695 indicates the following additional roads: Edgware–Stanmore–Watford; Harrow–Bushey–Watford;

Brockley Hill–Stanmore Common–Harrow Weald Common; Stanmore–Pinner–Ruislip ;   Wembley–Preston–Kenton–Pinner. Cary's atlas of 1800 also shows the Harrow–Greenford, Edgware–Whitchurch, and Harrow–Headstone–Hatch End roads; while Pinnock's little map of 1824 actually marks Honeypot Lane as well as the Harrow–Northolt road. These were the principal thoroughfares a century ago. Many of them were narrow, most of them had sharp corners, and all were lined with thick, tall hedges and trees. Honeypot Lane is practically the only survivor, and within two years at most it will have lost all its character, when it is widened and kerbed and its hedges and trees swept away. Recent new trunk roads in the district include a short length of the Watford Bypass and a number of important widenings, but several new arteries are proposed, including main roads direct from Wood End to Pinner, from Kenton to Edgware, from Harrow via Hatch End to Pinner, and from Blackbird Farm to Honeypot Lane.

The first railway constructed out of London, the "London and Birmingham Rail Road," afterwards known as the L.N.W.R., and now the L.M.S.R., passes near Harrow, but not through the town. The Metropolitan Railway is a comparatively modern upstart, but has had a far greater influence on the development of the town because from the outset it has made full use of such slogans as "Metroland," "Beechy Bucks," and the like, to tempt people to live in the country that its servants have done so much to obliterate. The pages of *Metroland*, one of its publications, are filled with irresistible pictures of country lanes, rustic stiles, and thatched cottages bowered in roses—just the very things that the motorist and the house agent and the builder between them have practically destroyed throughout the nearer parts of "Metroland" itself. It may be highly beneficial to humanity, as it certainly is to the pockets of shareholders, that these vast migrations should take place; but the language of hyperbole so freely employed in the process jars upon a sensitive ear, and even the helpless victims of the campaign must feel some regret in seeing the countryside receding so rapidly from them. The recent extension of the "Met." to Canons Park and Stanmore will certainly expedite the movement.

Such reflections naturally lead us to consider the growth of population in the area, which has been nothing less than phenomenal. The combined population of the four parishes of Harrow, Pinner, Great Stanmore, and Little Stanmore was 4,392 in 1801; 8,252 in 1851; 9,583 in 1861; 13,042 in 1871; 14,970 in 1881; 18,114 in 1891; and 28,419 (a very rapid rise) in 1901. In 1911 the combined population of the four constituent parishes was 42,052; in 1921 it was 49,210; and at the 1931 census it leaped

DEAR'S FARM, BRIDGE STREET, PINNER, IN 1932

up to 96,984, thus showing an increase of about 100 per cent. in ten years. So far as one can judge, this rate of progress is continuing at the present time, and it may be some satisfaction to the builders of "Houses of Charm and Character" (as they are known in this refined neighbourhood) to realize that the area of the district can accommodate 600,000 people on the luxurious basis of twelve houses to the acre.

At least, that would be the position if no allowance were made for open spaces. But fortunately the local fathers have long been aware of needs in that direction and have prepared town-planning schemes by which provision has been made for ample reservations. Coupled with their commendable activity has been the fine scheme of the County Council to secure the famous "Green Girdle," to say nothing of the successful efforts of Harrow School to preserve its beautiful surroundings. The open spaces acquired or reserved by the Hendon R.D.C. alone up to 1931 amounted to about 860 acres, while even in 1928 Harrow-on-the-Hill had reserved about 110 acres and Wealdstone about 50 acres. Add to these public spaces—over 1,000 acres in all—the enormous area of the proposed "Green Girdle" and the 400 acres or so acquired by the governors of Harrow School, and it is clear that a substantial portion of this beautiful district is safe for all time.

Apart from this question of open land, one could wish that such charming village streets as we find still at Pinner could be safeguarded, but if the lamentable change of the Edgware High Street from its former appearance to its present-day activity is to be a criterion, there is not much hope.

As for individual buildings of historical interest, they are falling down like ninepins before the housebreaker's pick. The two most ancient relics of the district are Grim's Dyke and the site of Sulloniacae, the Roman station on Brockley Hill. A scrap of the former has been preserved on newly acquired public ground, but nothing remains of Sulloniacae but a memorial obelisk near the Grove at Stanmore. The few old parish churches—at Harrow, Pinner, Great Stanmore, and Whitchurch—are not likely to suffer any ill-treatment in the future, and the authorities may be trusted to look after them. Harrow Church, with its fine spire, is more than a landmark, and is one of the most important in Middlesex. It has formed the subject of a large volume by Mr. Gardner and needs no description here, but it may be remarked that its architecture and its memorials are full of interest, while Byron's tomb in the churchyard will always serve as a lure to the romantically minded. Pinner Church looks charming from the High Street, but does not contain many features of note. The old parish church of Great Stanmore, consecrated by Archbishop Laud in 1632, is now disused, abandoned, and ruined, and ought never to have been allowed to become so. Churches of the period are very scarce, and this one is a fine specimen of seventeenth-century brickwork. It is also an example of the transition period when the Renaissance had just made its appearance in England and had not yet been adopted whole-heartedly for churches; St. John's Church at Leeds— another very rare specimen—was built in 1634 in pure Gothic. The old church at Stanmore is an interesting hybrid, the battle-mented tower with its turret staircase and massive staircases being Gothic in form, while the rest of the structure and all the doors and windows are decidedly Roman. It was built for Sir John

HARROW SCHOOL: THE OLD BUILDING

Wolstenholme (d. 1639), whose beautiful marble effigy by Nicholas Stone* is regarded as one of that sculptor's best works, and is now placed in the new church, together with a fine marble font by the same hand, and a very striking coloured memorial to John Burnell (d. 1605). The new church, erected in 1849, is a smug Gothic affair. St. Lawrence, Whitchurch—the parish church of Little Stanmore—has a fifteenth-century tower, but the rest of the structure dates from 1715, when the celebrated Duke of Chandos

---

* The label in the church ascribes the effigy to *Thomas* Stone. This is incorrect. Nicholas Stone's own diary says that he was paid £12 for the effigy and also mentions the font. (See the article by W. L. Spiers, "The Notebook and Account Book of Nicholas Stone," in the 7th volume of the Walpole Society, 1919.)

rebuilt it in the style of his period. It contains wall and ceiling paintings of some note, a gallery for the Duke, a grandiose mausoleum where that nobleman and his wives are interred, and an organ-case carved by Grinling Gibbons, together with some good ironwork and the original oak pews. The organ has acquired some fame for the church, for here Handel acted as organist from 1718 to 1721. It is a quaint little instrument, with a keyboard of only three octaves and six stops. Behind the church are some old almshouses.

Apart from churches, the chief historical monument is the Old Building of Harrow School erected in 1608–15. It contained three storeys and an attic. The lowest floor provided only storage for fuel, the next floor the large schoolroom known as the "Fourth Form Room," and on the second floor were three rooms for the master, the usher, and the governors respectively. The large schoolroom (60 by 24 feet) contained the whole of Harrow School for many years, but in 1650 the master flitted to a house of his own, the usher gave up his room shortly afterwards, and thus three classrooms were available; until at last, in 1819, an extension was made by which the old building became the west wing of the present block with its two fine oriels and noble central steps, as shown on my sketch. The Old School was described by a writer of 1818 as "a building little calculated to call forth the admiration of a casual spectator by any Architectural embellishments, but surveyed with filial veneration by a very considerable proportion of the Higher and Distinguished Orders of Society of the present day." The remaining buildings of Harrow School form a somewhat motley assortment, varying greatly in merit, and include a few old houses. The High Street, on the top of the hill, is very much monopolized by the School, as is natural enough. It contains some old shops and an inn, the "King's Head," which boasts of an origin in 1533. Near the School cricket ground, in Lower Road, is an old weather-boarded house.

Headstone Manor stands within a moated enclosure about 300 feet square, and is said to be six centuries old. It has recently been acquired for the public together with 63 acres of land and the fine tithe-barn shown in the sketch, 150 feet by 30 feet, one of the largest remaining in Middlesex.

Pinner contains a charming old inn near the church, a number of old shops and houses in the High Street, and the old building known as Dear's Farm in Bridge Street, about to be demolished when my sketch was made. There are also many old farms round Pinner, including an interesting example with brick gables on the Uxbridge Road at Hatch End. "Pinner Fair" has been held regu-

HEADSTONE MANOR, NEAR HARROW
Showing Moat and Tithe Barn (fifteenth century)

larly since 1336, and took place in May 1934 as usual in the two principal old streets of the town. Great Stanmore used to contain a number of brick houses of the seventeenth and eighteenth centuries, but most of these have been altered for the worse during recent years. "The Pinnacles," one of the largest of them, was destroyed by fire in 1930, and the ruins have since been demolished. Near the church is Stanmore Park, a fine house apparently about a hundred years old, now used as a preparatory school for boys. The old manor-house of Fiddell's, now "Kingsdale" (and a cats' home), is ancient and picturesque but not of architectural importance. The new manor-house, a masterpiece of mock antiquity, was erected regardless of expense in 1901, and is for sale at the time of writing, twisted brick chimneys and all.

Bentley Priory, a really magnificent house on Stanmore Common, with extensive woods and a lake, has had a chequered career since Sir John Soane modernized it at the end of the eighteenth century. The Royal Air Force recently acquired the house as headquarters, but a large part of its 460 acres of park is to be utilized by the speculative builder. Little Stanmore, commonly called Edgware, provides one of the most depressing sights in Middlesex to anyone who has known it since childhood. Canons Park no longer contains the lordly mansion built by the Duke of Chandos in 1712–15 at a cost of about a quarter of a million sterling. In 1747 it was pulled down, the materials realizing only £11,000, and an upholsterer named John Hallet built a much smaller house on the site. This house was so extensively altered and modernized in 1911–13 as to lose its former appearance. In 1929 it was acquired by a well-known girls' school, together with some 10 acres of the fine formal gardens and a part of the park. A further 11 acres has been bought as a public open space, and negotiations are on foot for the acquisition of an additional open space of 35 or 40 acres. Thus 50 or 60 acres of Canons Park are likely to be preserved. The fate of the large lake (7 acres) is uncertain, as it has been purchased by a builder. The remainder of the park (originally about 400 acres in extent), is partially utilized as a golf course and partially for houses which are springing up in hundreds. The new Metropolitan Extension railway bisects the park. The old High Street of Edgware is disappearing visibly, and more of it will go within the next two years. Its most worthy ornament, the Chandos Arms, was a famous coaching hostelry, and up to five years ago or so was an attractive feature of the street. It is now a booking-office and service-station, and its shabby walls are defaced with over fifty yelling posters advising you where to go for a country excursion. The windows are broken, and the old hanging sign where the gorgeous heraldry of the Chandos Arms once appeared now bears the single magic word "Garage." The decrepit little hut where the

"Harmonious Blacksmith" inspired Handel has been replaced by a coal-agent's booth, and though that is admirably designed, and built of "genuine antique" materials, one sheds a tear for the vanished past, in spite of those who deride "fanatics interested in antiquities" (see page 143).

Pinner Fair is still held at Whitsuntide, the bounds of Great Stanmore parish are still beaten among the wilderness of villas, but there yet remains plenty of work for fanatics to do in preserving some of the charm of bygone days for posterity.

BOOKS ON LOCAL HISTORY AND TOPOGRAPHY

ARMSTRONG, B. J.	Some account of . . . Little Stanmore	Edgware	1895
BUSHELL, W. D.	Church of St. Mary, Harrow-on-the-Hill	Cambridge	1912
DAVENPORT, P.	Old Stanmore	Stanmore	1933
FOX, A. D.	Harrow (*Public School Life* series)	London	1910
GARDNER, S.	Harrow Church, Architectural History of	Harrow	1895
	Harrow: Some Notes on Historic Sites	Harrow	N.D.
HALLAM, G. H.	Official Guide to Harrow and Harrow School	London	1931
[HENDON R.D.C.]	Illustrated Report on Work of the Council, 1928–31	[Stanmore]	1931
HOWSON, E. W., and WARNER, G. T.	Harrow School	London	1898
KEESEY, W. M.	Harrow: a Sketch Book	London	1914
[*Pinner Observer*]	Historical Guide to St. John's, Pinner	Harrow	1921
RELF, T. J.	Ye Booke of Olde Edgware	Edgware	1924
RIMMER, A.	Rambles round Harrow	London	1882
SCOTT, E. J. L.	Records of the Grammar School founded by John Lyon	Harrow	1886
THORNTON, P. M.	Harrow School	London	1885
WILLIAMS, J. F.	Harrow (*Great Public Schools* series)	London	1901

Also:

Articles on "Canons Park," in *Country Life*, Vol. XL, pp. 518, 615.

CHAPTER XIII

WEMBLEY

INCLUDING ALPERTON, KINGSBURY, PRESTON, SUDBURY, TWYFORD
ABBEY; AND PART OF KENTON

THE large new district bearing this now familiar name has recently been formed by the amalgamation of the former urban districts of Wembley and Kingsbury. Wembley is by far the larger, both in area and population, but it is a mushroom growth, whereas Kingsbury has a history going back to Saxon times at least. One feels a good deal of sympathy with the inhabitants of Kingsbury who, after a corporate existence of more than thirty years, have had to sink their individuality in that of their *parvenu* neighbour, all for the sake of mere administrative convenience. The growth of the two townships has been so rapid that the new amalgamation will enable many municipal services to be strengthened, and among them will doubtless materialize a public library with a collection of documents and pictures to illustrate the history of the district and its quickly disappearing relics of the past. This is badly needed. Even the famous British Empire Exhibition of 1924–25, which is all that Wembley means to the average man, will soon become a matter of history.

"Wembley" appears to mean "Waemba's Field," and the name is found in the ninth century; "Alperton" indicates the "farm or enclosure of Ealhperht"; "Kenton" is explained as "the farm of the sons of Cena (or Coena)"; "Kingsbury," which occurs in the tenth century, is "the King's stronghold"; "Preston," a very common name, denotes "the priests' farm"; "Sudbury" of course means "the south stronghold"; and "Twyford," another place-name of frequent occurrence in England, is an Anglo-Saxon word signifying "the double ford."*

The new district of Wembley has an area of over 6,000 acres, or

* J. E. B. Gover, *Place-names of Middlesex* (1922).

about 10 square miles. Its shape is irregular. Its boundaries have been considerably "rationalized" to suit modern roads and railways, the playing-fields of Harrow School having been relinquished to Harrow, though "Ducker"—the school bathing-place—remains in Wembley.

The district has no striking natural features and no notable hills. The highest point is Barn Hill (282 feet), a beech-crowned knoll

KINGSBURY OLD CHURCH

which forms a prominent landmark for miles around and has been recently acquired as a public open space. Kingsbury Hill is now covered with houses, as is Wembley Hill (234 feet). The subsoil everywhere is clay, except at Kingsbury Church, where there is a curious layer of gravel and sand, and then the chalk. Up to a few years ago, the whole area consisted of pasture land, lightly wooded with elm- and oak-trees, and interspersed with occasional corn-fields and numerous "gentlemen's seats." The Wealdstone Brook traverses the district from north to south, and joins the Brent just below the "Welsh Harp," otherwise known as "Hendon Lake" or the "Brent Reservoir." The Kingsbury authorities have had the foresight to purchase the fields bordering on the lake as a public open space, where a community of sun-bathers with advanced ideas has recently caused them some perturbation.

Besides "Watling Street" and the Harrow Road, the old roads of the district include Blackbird Hill, Forty Lane, Wembley Hill Road, Kingsbury Road, Kenton Lane, Buck Lane, Church Lane, Stag Lane, Roe Green, Hay Lane, Salmon Street, Preston Road, and Woodcock Hill. In 1922 began a great road-widening campaign in view of the forthcoming exhibition, and several little winding lanes lost all their trees in the process of conversion into "Class A" motor highways. This was, in fact, the beginning of the end for Wembley of the old rural days. As for railway stations, there were twelve in Wembley alone before the recent extension of the Metropolitan line to Stanmore, and now there are two more in the Kingsbury area.

Although the Metropolitan Railway arrived on the scene so early as 1880 with its line to Harrow, the population did not begin to grow rapidly for many years. In 1901 the population of Wembley and Kingsbury together was not much more than 5,000. In 1911 Wembley had 10,696 inhabitants and Kingsbury only 821, being still an undiscovered village.* In 1921 the respective figures were 16,187 and 1,856; in 1931, 48,546 and 16,636. Thus in the decennium 1921–31, Wembley's population had trebled, while that of Kingsbury had multiplied nine times—a rate of growth surpassed by only one district in England. And this astounding increase seems to be continuing with unabated vigour throughout the district. In Kingsbury you are greeted with the slogan: "Eyes left for Houses of Artistry," and, after all, who can resist that appeal? Certainly not John Citizen or his wife.

With a population of over 65,000 in 1931, likely to rise to heaven-knows-what in 1941, there is a most urgent need for reserving an adequate provision of public open spaces, for Wembley

---

* But thirty years ago at least, long before anyone, except "fanatics interested in antiquities" and the countryside, had ever heard of Kingsbury, it possessed, close to the "Red Lion" in Kingsbury Lane, a terrace of small houses—still standing—which might be regarded as the ugliest thing in rural Middlesex.

could accommodate 300,000 people without undue crowding. Less than 200 acres had been acquired in 1932, but the local Council announced in their official guide published in that year that they hoped to double that amount shortly. The Stag Lane aerodrome at the corner of the district nearest to Edgware was sold for building in 1933: this means more houses and less open ground.

The district never contained many important historical monu-

JOHN LYON'S FARM AT PRESTON

ments, and among them there is only one old church, St. Andrew's, at Kingsbury. This building, however, contains Roman bricks, an authentic Saxon or very early Norman doorway, and a probably Saxon font shaped like a bowl. There are also some interesting brasses. The little wooden spire is said to be a copy of the original one. The church has suffered both neglect and over-drastic restoration at various times, and has lost—among other features—an old timber porch in the process. Its situation, on a little mound near the "Welsh Harp" reservoir, surrounded on three sides by villas, is still picturesque, but the suggestion that the banks round the square churchyard indicates a Roman camp is now discredited. The church

of St. Andrew's, Wells Street, London, is now being moved, stone
by stone, to a site adjoining St. Andrew's, Kingsbury, to serve the
needs of the increased population.

John Lyon's Farm at Preston still remains, but it has no architectural importance, and its survival seems to depend upon the
enthusiasm of Old Harrovians for the memory of their founder.*
Twyford Abbey has beautiful surroundings, but as a mock-Gothic
mansion of 1806 it may not long resist the encroachments of
industry on one side and suburban domesticity on the other. It is
now a Roman Catholic institution providing for the welfare of
"gentlemen-boarders." Two cottages at Kingsbury are rare specimens of the weather-boarded buildings, which were once common
in Middlesex and inspired the first homes of the Pilgrim Fathers in
New England.† The Plough Inn on Kingsbury Green was
another charming member of the same family, but was demolished
a few years ago to make way for an excellently designed modern
hotel. The "Green Man" at Wembley is a work of the same
talented architect. The farms which once were sparsely scattered
over the district are rapidly disappearing: few of them had artistic
merit of the first order, but nearly every one of them formed a
charming group with great barns, their roofs tiled and their sides
boarded. At the time of writing, a few still remain in Salmon
Street, but their days are numbered. Oakington Manor Farm,
near the Brent and close to the Stadium, has a long history rather
than an architectural interest. Its fields are now nearly covered
with the advancing sea of villas, and within a year or two at most
it will be engulfed. Near Kingsbury is the charming housing-scheme
built at Roe Green for munition-workers in the early years of the
war. It is perhaps too consciously picturesque, but one can forgive
that in view of many of the neighbouring developments.

As for Wembley Park, that now devastated and depressing area
was formerly the seat of one John Gray, who rebuilt the old manor-

---

* It is announced (February 1934) that "the remaining 146 acres of the
Lyon Farm Estate have been sold for the building of about 1,500 houses."

† See my book, *The Homes of the Pilgrim Fathers in England and America*
(1932).

house in 1810. The following description of the estate is so recent as 1887:

> Wembley Park, the seat of the lord of the manor, consists of some 250 acres, beautifully wooded, chiefly on high ground, but undulating to a branch of the River Brent, which runs through it.*

Some forty years ago the property was bought by a company, which began the erection of an enormous tower which was intended to exceed the height of the Eiffel Tower by 175 feet. About

TWYFORD ABBEY

100 acres of the park was used as a pleasure ground, and the remainder sold for building. Although large numbers of visitors patronized the place, the tower was never completed, and eventually its huge base was demolished. Then came the British Empire Exhibition of 1924–25; an artistic triumph, and a masterpiece of organization. To children it must have seemed a veritable fairyland, and even to middle-aged parents it was an experience never to be forgotten. Of all its glories, only the massive Stadium remains intact, serving to accommodate occasionally a mammoth crowd for a football match, and several times a week an audience of dog-

* H. J. Foley, *Our Lanes and Meadow Paths*, p. 59.

watchers. In more senses than one, Wembley has gone to the dogs. The vast Exhibition site has been farmed out to a host of small industrial firms, who carry out their various enterprises amid the tawdry ruins of Burmese palaces and African fortresses. Even the "Restaurant Lucullus" has shared the general fate. *Sic transit gloria mundi !*

BOOKS ON LOCAL HISTORY AND TOPOGRAPHY

[BRITISH EMPIRE EXHIBITION]	Official Guide	London	1924
POTTER, S.	Old Kingsbury Church (2nd edition)	London	1928
[WEMBLEY U.D.C.]	Wembley : Official Guide	London	1932

CHAPTER XIV

WILLESDEN

INCLUDING BRONDESBURY, DOLLIS HILL, DUDDEN HILL, HAR-
LESDEN, KENSAL GREEN, KILBURN, NEASDEN, AND STONE-
BRIDGE

IT might appear at first sight that there is very little to say about
Willesden: as a matter of fact, Willesden is full of historical
interest and local patriotism. The fine "Ball Collection" in the
public library at Willesden Green is an evidence of that, though
the paintings and drawings of bygone scenes have a pathos of their
own in these days. Moreover, Willesden has inspired one of the
best, if not the very best, of all local histories of Middlesex
townships.*

"Willesden," which was spelt "Wilsdon" up to recent times,
appears as "Wellesdune" in the tenth century and means "Wille's
hill"; "Brondesbury" is probably "Brand's fortress"; and "Dollis
Hill" probably recalls the name of some man, Dolley or Dalley or
Dollison. "Kilburn" commemorates the existence of a now concealed stream which flowed into the West Bourne; the name
appears as "Kyneburna" and "Cuneburna" in the twelfth century,
so presumably signifies "the stream of Cyna." "Kensal Green,"
once spelt "Kellsell Grene," is probably derived from a man's
name. "Harlesden," which appears as "Herulvestune" in Domesday, means "Herewulf's farm"; whereas "Neasden," almost always
spelt with a final "-don" or "-dune" in old documents, seems to
mean "the hill like a nose" [cf. "naze"].† Finally, the name of
Stonebridge is easily explained by the recently rebuilt little stone
bridge over which the Harrow Road crossed the river Brent.

The borough of Willesden, which for some unaccountable
reason did not claim or obtain municipal powers until 1933,
corresponds almost exactly with the ancient parish, and the

* S. Potter, *The Story of Willesden*, 1926.   † J. E. B. Gover, *op. cit.*

apparently senseless irregularity of its frontier with London is thus explained. Its other main boundaries, Watling Street and the river Brent, are obvious enough, and the curious salient which includes Park Royal is the survival of a medieval manor. The area of the district is just over seven square miles.

Willesden has a clay floor, with a small patch of pebbly gravel in the Brent Valley and a deposit of brick-earth on Mount Pleasant, where the brickworks have recently been closed. This is the highest

THE "WELSH HARP," OR BRENT RESERVOIR
From the Edgware Road

point (248 feet) in the district, Dollis Hill being a few feet lower. The ground is generally undulating, its variations being accounted for by the various small streams which exist, partly concealed to-day, in the area. The Brent itself is the principal watercourse, and is fed by a little rivulet known as the Slade or Mitchell's Brook which takes its rise on the slope of Shoot Up Hill, runs past Sherrick Green, and under Mulgrave Road, thence near Neasden Station, past the Isolation Hospital, and under the North Circular Road joining the Brent near the Harrow Road. For part of its course it is now buried in a sewer.

The "Kilburn" is a completely hidden stream which rose near

West Hampstead and crossed Watling Street at Kilburn Bridge, thence flowing south as the "West Bourne" to the Serpentine and so to the Thames. The east boundary of Willesden ran along Watling Street from the centre of Kilburn Bridge (over the Kilburn) to the centre of Brent Bridge (at the "Welsh Harp") and still does so to-day. Kilburn Wells, a great resort of the fashionable a century ago, were originally valued for their medicinal properties, but became a place for tea-drinking and similar dissipations in the

DOLLIS HILL FARM IN 1932

Regency period. The site is marked by a tablet on the Kilburn branch of Barclays Bank (No. 42, High Road). Willesden owns the southern part and foreshore of the "Welsh Harp" or Kingsbury Reservoir, constructed in 1835–9, and missed a great chance in recent years by allowing a large part of the land between the new North Circular Road and the lake to be sold for industrial buildings. But for this unfortunate error and the sordid patch at West Hendon, the whole margin of the reservoir would have been preserved as a recreation ground in the three districts of Kingsbury, Hendon, and Willesden.

Watling Street has often been mentioned in this book as a Roman road. The historian of Willesden tells us that excavations have proved that it was 24 feet wide, and formed of large black flints, weighing 4 to 7 pounds each, laid on a bed of gravel reinforced by cross-walls of gravel concrete. Besides Harrow Road, the following were the principal old roads, their modern names being given in brackets: Bowers Lane (Dollis Hill Lane), Neasden Lane, Mapes Lane (Willesden Lane), Walm Lane, Petticoat Stile Lane (Pound Lane), and Brand's Causeway (approximately Brondesbury Park). The construction of the North Circular Road through Willesden has completely altered the topography of the district. In canalizing the Brent at Stonebridge, the authorities encountered a rebellious spirit in that rigorously chastened stream, for it rose up in its wrath one fine morning a few years ago, and flooded their nice new housing scheme; since when, appropriate measures have been taken for the future.

Willesden contains an inordinate and bewildering jungle of railway lines. "The London and Birmingham" arrived first, in 1837, but did not trouble to construct a station until 1842, near Harlesden. It had a staff of one man, and three trains a day from Euston. Then came a host of other lines, the most important from the point of view of Willesden's growth being the Metropolitan which arrived in 1880 at Willesden Green. Curiously enough, the spur line which used to carry Midland expresses through Harlesden to various south-coast ports and watering-places was closed for passenger traffic many years ago.

The growth of Willesden occurred far earlier than that of Harrow or Wembley or Hendon, and was the result of railway extension* as the following figures prove. The population in 1801 was 751, of whom more than a quarter were "agricultural." The numbers grew slowly to 2,957 in 1841, 2,960 in 1851, and 3,871 in 1861. Then there comes a rapid rise: 15,861 in 1871; 27,632 in 1881; 61,266 in 1891; 114,811 in 1901; 154,214 in 1911; 165,674 in 1921; and finally 184,410 in 1931. The pace has slowed down, but there has been a great deal of building, mostly of a prosperous type, on Dollis Hill and Mount Pleasant since 1931, so

* Perhaps one should ascribe some credit to the trams, which arrived in 1901.

that 1941 will probably show a further increase, but it is unlikely that the population will ever rise much beyond 200,000.

By 1941 there will be very little building land left, and much of the recent development between Dollis Hill and Neasden has only been made possible because the Neasden Golf Club sold its fine links for building. It is to be hoped that the beautiful bit of Dollis Lane between Dollis Hill House (now Gladstone Park) and

MAPESBURY WINDMILL, c. 1860
Drawn from an old photo

Dollis Hill Farm will not be sacrificed, for it is the only fragment of rural Willesden now surviving.* Gladstone Park, with its noble trees and attractive lake, is a great acquisition, but part of its charm is due to its rustic hinterland. The Council has made the most of Roundwood Park and its other recreation grounds, but Dollis Hill is in an altogether different category: it is a lonely relic of the period when Willesden was a village and motors were unknown.

Once upon a time there was a priory at Kilburn, as various

* Some of the trees were cut down in September 1933, and building is beginning.

street names testify. It was a small establishment, of the Augustinian Order. The old parish church of Willesden is the only ancient building in all this large district, and has been so frequently enlarged and restored that only fragments of the original structure remain. This was evidently Norman, and there is a good late Norman font, a thirteenth-century arcade in the nave, and some very interesting

DOLLIS HILL LANE IN 1932

brasses. The church provides a welcome oasis in the midst of mean surroundings.

The windmill at Mapesbury, near Brondesbury, was demolished many years ago. Mapesbury Manor House, a fine old building near the site of the windmill, was destroyed in 1925, and the original Willesden Manor House, near Kilburn Bridge, exactly a century earlier. Brondesbury Manor House is a large and shabby-looking building, to which has been added a bright red chapel, presumably to brighten it up; it certainly needs it, especially as it is now a boarding school for young ladies. But the grounds are large and contain very fine old trees. They ought certainly to be scheduled for a future public open space, Willesden's provision of parks being somewhat inadequate.* Neasden Manor House still survives, but has been converted into flats and is (therefore) now known as "Neasden Court." The neighbouring Spotted Dog Inn has been rebuilt in the Tudor manner on a most lavish scale. Near it are The Grange, The Grove, The Cottage, and Elmsted, all pleasant country houses fifty years ago, but now awaiting the end.

There are a few other old houses at Neasden, doubtless doomed to early destruction, some fragments of the old farm at Oxgate, a timber cottage next to the post office in Grange Road at Willesden Green, The Grange itself adjoining it, and the charming old house known as Dollis Hill Farm. Then there is Dollis Hill House itself, a pleasant but somewhat ordinary building erected in 1825 and still standing in Gladstone Park. It is chiefly noted as the home of Lord Aberdeen, who frequently entertained Gladstone here in his palmiest days, when his every move was a royal progress. But Willesden is now a great industrial town, and the remaining traces of its former charms as a country retreat for jaded statesmen are hard to find.

* As this book goes to press, it is announced that the site has been sold to a builder, but that a portion is to be reserved for a new Town Hall. Half a loaf is better than no bread, but it is only half a loaf!

BOOKS ON LOCAL HISTORY AND TOPOGRAPHY

BRIDGES, J. S.	Dollis Hill House	——	1920
POTTER, S.	The Story of Willesden	London	1926
SLATER, E. T.	Dollis Hill and its Memories of Gladstone	——	1906
[WILLESDEN U.D.C.]	Willesden Past and Present	London	N.D.

CHAPTER XV

ACTON

T HE crowded borough of Acton, incorporated in 1921, does not appear at first sight to offer much of interest to a student of topography. Even in its rustic state a century ago it was summarily dismissed by a writer in a few lines, beginning with these disparaging words: "Acton is a village about five miles from London; it displays little to engage attention."* Yet this apparently mediocre and suburban township, nowadays bustling with industry, possesses a keen civic sense, and it provides a story of rapid growth which has a very definite lesson for the inhabitants of districts not yet "developed."

The very name of Acton recalls its all too recently lost country surroundings. It means simply a farm or enclosure among oak-trees. On its eastern side is a road with a charming rustic name, "Old Oak Common Lane." It is true that part of the common survives, though levelled to form a treeless and featureless emergency landing-ground for aircraft. But part of the lane is lined with high corrugated iron fences, beyond which extends on either side a wilderness of railway sidings and sheds. The present borough has an area of over 2,300 acres, about $3\frac{1}{2}$ square miles, with a length from north to south of about 3 miles and an average breadth of a mile and a half. It is smaller in area than any of the newly constituted administrative districts of Middlesex except Wood Green and Friern Barnet. Its population a century ago was about 2,000; in 1851 it was only 2,582; and even in 1861, some years after its first two railway stations had been opened, only 3,151. The Census figures then begin to show a rapid increase: 8,306 in 1871, 17,126 in 1881, 24,206 in 1891, 37,744 in 1901, 57,497 in 1911,

* *The History and Topography of Middlesex* (Pinnock's County Histories), 1824, p. 36.

61,299 in 1921, and 70,523 in 1931, with a density of 30·2 persons per acre. It might be inferred from this last figure that Acton is capable of accommodating another 30,000 people or more, on the basis of 50 persons or 12 houses per acre. But that is most unlikely, because a very large part of the district is occupied by railways and industrial works, while very little agricultural land remains available for the erection of further dwellings. It is improbable that the population will exceed 80,000 at any future census, in these days of limited families. In fact, Acton has nearly stopped growing.

Some of the secrets of that remarkable growth may be deciphered in the curious boundaries of the modern borough, corresponding as they do fairly accurately with the ancient parish boundaries, the beating of which was carried out annually within recent memory. At first glance these boundaries appear quite irrational as they are depicted on an up-to-date map. They seem to follow no natural features, and no main roads. For instance, the line separating Acton from the County of London on the east zigzags across a waste of railway sidings and then across Old Oak Common in an inexplicable way, afterwards maintaining a more regular but still rather uncertain southward course along Old Oak Common Lane to the London–Uxbridge road. It then vacillates west and south alternately to a point near N.N.W. of Stamford Brook Station, and turns nearly due south till it reaches the line of the Bath Road, which itself follows the line of the ancient Roman highway from Londinium along Oxford Street, Bayswater Road, and Goldhawk Road to Brentford, Staines, and Silchester. A century ago, workmen excavating in Goldhawk Road discovered the Roman causeway, 10 feet below the present street level.

It needs only a little acumen to divine the origin of Acton's east boundary: it was, of course, a stream now carefully concealed underground. But there are traces of it at the foot of the railway bank north of Old Oak Common, and there is a hint of it on Rocque's map of 1741–5, though not on Cary's atlas of 1800. It does, however, appear on larger maps of more recent date. Somewhere near the present Acton Sewage works it flowed into a larger stream, the Stamford Brook, which from this point to the Thames formed the boundary between London and Middlesex. The exit of that now hidden rivulet is quite easy to find, for it lies almost opposite the eastern tip of Chiswick Ait, and is marked by a small indentation or dock where Hammersmith Terrace in London jostles Chiswick Mall in Middlesex. Its upward course leads one along British Grove to King Street, then to "Stamford Brook" Station, and then to the point where it picked up the brook from Old Oak Common. Next it turned west through Acton, keeping south of Birkbeck Road and the Priory Club (where "Brookfield Road" affords a clue), and crossed the Uxbridge Road at a water-splash near the Steyne, thence following a north-westerly direction to its source.

Not far away from the Stamford Brook where it crossed the Uxbridge Road was another and even more insignificant stream, the Bollo or Bollar Brook, which once formed the curiously irregular west boundary of Acton south of the Uxbridge Road. It has given its name to Bollo Road, but it is now wholly or mainly covered. However, it is still justified by its works, for it feeds the ornamental water in the beautiful grounds of Chiswick House (see page 252).

This brief excursion into amateur deductive topography has enabled us to account for the queer boundary between London and Middlesex in the Acton sector, and also for a large part of the boundaries of the present borough. Let us now attempt to recall the aspect of Acton a century ago, when it was still an insignificant village on the Uxbridge Road, with several detached hamlets north and south of that famous highway. The traveller on the Oxford coach on his westward journey from Tyburn reached the conduit at Old Oak Common Lane in less than four miles. Here was perfect peace, with fields and oak-trees all round him, and indeed this was country even fifty years ago. Soon he came to the end of East Acton Lane which led to a green, even to-day preserving some of its charm; and there was the "Great House," or, as it was sometimes called, the "Manor House." Now the road rose gently towards Acton Church, and on the left was the wall enclosing the large grounds of Berrymead Priory. Here came a cluster of houses and, near the church, the entrance to Horn Lane, a picturesque winding road overhung by trees, leading to remote Willesden. The church stood at the top of a steep little hill, where the main road, often in a state of disgraceful mud, dropped sharply to a watersplash over the Stamford Brook, and then rose rapidly, passing Bank House (now demolished) and "The Elms" (still standing). Between "The Elms" and the Ealing boundary was a large pond on the right (now a public garden) and a large house, "The Woodlands," on the left. This house has been demolished, but its grounds have been preserved, and a part of them forms the playing-fields of the County School. There were at least two windmills in Acton: a very picturesque one in the present park, south-east of Churchfield Road Station, and another, which gave its name to Mill Hill Park, near the watersplash.

North of the Uxbridge Road were Acton House and Derwentwater House, large mansions at the corner of Horn Lane and the present Churchfield Road. Much farther north lay a small group of houses known as Friars' Place, one of which is incorporated into the Infectious Hospital, and farther still were the Assembly Rooms of "Acton Wells," a resort so fashionable in the eighteenth century that it earned the nickname of "The Devil's Orchard"; though, as a matter of fact, it belonged to the Duke of Devonshire. There were three wells, the water being saline and having medicinal properties. But even so long ago as 1795, Lysons wrote that "The wells have long since lost their celebrity, fashion and novelty having given a preference to springs of the same nature at a greater distance from the metropolis. . . . The assembly room, being nearly in ruins, is now about to be converted into two tenements." Since then, all trace of the wells seems to have been obliterated, though "Wales Farm Road" recalls their situation. The extensive stabling of Friars' Place Farm stands derelict at the corner of Western Avenue and Willesden Lane, bearing a board advertising it as a "Desirable Building Site."

The only other inhabited part of Acton parish a century ago was a cluster of houses at Acton Green (now bisected by the District

Railway) and an example of what we now call "ribbon development" on the Chiswick High Road. Such was Acton a century ago, and so it remained until the sixties of last century, when its phenomenal growth began, so that the population doubled itself in two successive decades. Evidently the railway was the first cause of this. Yet, curiously enough, though the Great Western line through Acton was opened so early as 1838, it was not until 1858 that a station was built on that railway; whereas the present "Acton Central" Station on the L.M.S. was opened in 1853. It was in the sixties that the area south of the Uxbridge Road was built up, and in this area the local council—not foreseeing the extraordinary growth that was coming—later made a great mistake. The lovely and historic grounds of Berrymead Priory, extending from the Uxbridge Road, with magnificent trees and a large lake, would have formed a perfect setting for a Town Hall in the very centre of the community. But the authorities lost their chance, acquired some of the property, covered it with municipal buildings of various kinds, and let all the rest—except the Priory itself (see page 175)— go into the capacious maw of the speculative builder. Had they secured the whole property, as they could have done in those days at a reasonable price, Acton would now possess a civic centre to be proud of.

South Acton was the first section of the district to be built up; then came Bedford Park, a very different story. This estate is commonly regarded as the first "Garden Suburb" in England, and was laid out in 1876, most of the houses being designed by the late Norman Shaw, R.A. Although to modern eyes they may appear old-fashioned, they are at least attractive to look upon, and the spacious lay-out of the pleasant tree-lined roads affords a welcome contrast to the previous fashion for crowded rows of villas. If Acton at that early date had had the foresight to prepare a town-plan for its whole area, it would be a more comely town to-day, and the drab streets of its southern quarters would never have been built. The Old Oak Common Estate of the London County Council was admirably planned just before the war in the east part of Acton, and is a model of municipal housing. Still more recent are Acton's own housing scheme, and the charming "Garden Village" of the Great Western Railway, designed by Mr. Alwyn Lloyd. The excellence of these various schemes makes one wish that more artistic sense, and indeed more common sense, had been exercised in developing other parts of the borough. It will soon be necessary to widen Horn Lane at vast expense, and to deal with the congested corners round The Steyne, where the old narrow lanes are quite unfit for modern traffic.

THE LAST OF OLD ACTON: EAST ACTON LANE IN 1933

Residents in those districts of Middlesex which are not yet built up are apt to consider themselves inviolate from the relentless march of progress, but the sequence of development can be foretold with clockwork regularity. The series of paintings and prints in the collections at the Acton Public Library and Gunnersbury Park make it clear, even to those who did not know Acton fifty years ago, that at least the northern half of the district was then completely rural, dotted with oak-trees and farmhouses, and inter-sected by quiet and narrow tree-lined lanes. The Park Royal district in the north of the borough was acquired as a permanent show-ground by the Royal Agricultural Society in 1901–2. But the venture was not a success, and the area was then offered for sale as building sites. Most of it lies within the boundaries of Willesden, but taken as a whole it has recently become one of the most important industrial areas in the south of England, and some twenty thousand workers are said to be employed in its numerous factories, which include some of the most striking recent buildings of the kind and are increasing in number almost monthly. The absence of smoke, due to the general use of electric power, is a point in their favour.

Much of the development of Acton, as well as many of the difficulties in its planning, is due to the network of railways—with vast areas of sidings—which cover the district. There are more than a dozen stations in the borough, the latest serving the extended Central London Railway. More recently the great arterial road known as Western Avenue has been driven across its hitherto almost rural northern districts, and in a year or two every building site will be covered.

The total area of public open spaces which have been saved from the wreck amounts to about 95 acres. These include the attractive Acton Park, with beautiful trees, another small park known as "Woodlands" where some trees have survived, and other recreation grounds of the ordinary suburban kind. By its purchase (jointly with Ealing, Brentford, and Chiswick) of the beautiful Gunnersbury Park (186 acres), which lies entirely outside its boundaries in the borough of Brentford–Chiswick, Acton may consider that it has done its duty in this matter, and the latest municipal townplanning scheme (1933) contains no proposal for further reservations. Possibly the sports grounds of the Gas Light and Coke Company in West Acton may be worth protecting, but they have no natural features. Very different is the case of the extensive and beautiful grounds of the former East Acton Manor House, magnificently timbered, and now used in part by various private associations for games. This land, the property of the Goldsmiths' Company, is surely deserving of preservation as a permanent open space. The "Great House" or Manor House, a building of the seventeenth and eighteenth century, which recently formed its centrepiece, was demolished for no particular reason (the site is still vacant) in 1911, and thus Acton lost its one noteworthy historical building. It is cold consolation that drawings and photographs of the house were made just before its demolition, and subsequently published (see Bibliography overleaf). The house contained a good staircase and had a beautiful doorway. It was probably remodelled by the Duchess of Hamilton (widow of that nobleman who fell in a duel with Lord Mohun, as described in Thackeray's *Esmond*) in 1712.

Acton Parish Church is modern, but contains some interesting tombs and relics. Berrymead Priory (now the Priory Constitutional Club), is said to owe its present castellated exterior to an owner of 1802–6, but the whole building is an architectural conundrum. It appears to include numerous fragments, some embellishments, and perhaps considerable structural portions of the medieval religious foundation. It was once occupied by Lord Lytton, the author. "The Elms," on the Uxbridge Road, is a dignified Georgian house still standing in its own grounds, and was purchased in 1755 by one Samuel Wegg, a great benefactor to Acton, whose descendants occupied it for nearly a century. In Churchfield Road East is a row of almshouses, standing back behind some fine cedar-trees and facing Acton Park. These, rebuilt in 1811, are the property of the Goldsmiths' Company, who own all the neighbouring land already mentioned, bequeathed to them by John Perryn, an Alderman and Prime Warden of the Company, at his death in 1656. He died at Acton in the "Great House," or its predecessor, and his memory is commemorated in the name of one of Acton's schools.

BOOKS ON LOCAL HISTORY AND TOPOGRAPHY

[ACTON TOWN COUNCIL]	Acton: Official Guide	London	N.D.
BAKER, W. KING	Acton	Acton	1912
COMMITTEE FOR SURVEY OF MONUMENTS OF GREATER LONDON	East Acton Manor House	London	1921
JOLLIFFE, P.	Acton and its History	Ealing	1910
LUSH, J. E.	History of Berrymead Priory	Acton	N.D.
MITCHELL, H.	Records and Recollections of Acton	Ealing	1913

CHAPTER XVI

EALING

INCLUDING GREENFORD, HANWELL, NORTHOLT, PERIVALE, AND
PART OF TWYFORD

In many ways Ealing presents a striking contrast to Acton, described in the last chapter. Its area is nearly four times as great, it includes large tracts of agricultural land in the Northolt district, and it has not yet begun to develop industrially except round Greenford, whereas Acton may almost be regarded nowadays as an industrial town. There was a time, not long ago, when Ealing claimed to be *par excellence* the suburban home of the retired colonial servant. Why this should ever have been so is far from clear, but somebody must have started a fashion which was followed by gregarious *sahibs*. One still sees them strolling aimlessly along the Broadway, twirling cheroots, but they must find it difficult to-day to leaven a lump which consists of nearly 130,000 people. Such is the modern borough of Ealing, certainly an attractive suburb as suburbs go, but not altogether different from several already described in this book, and certainly not immune from the various evils which we have met in other parts of Middlesex.

The official guide-book for once meets the case in characterizing Ealing with a notable economy of words. "Ealing," writes its anonymous and municipally inspired author, "popularly known as 'Queen of the Suburbs,' is a town of comparatively modern growth. Sixty years ago it was little more than a village, and the main road ran through cornfields." It became a borough so long ago as 1901, but has since trebled its total area by swallowing Hanwell and Greenford in 1926, and Northolt two years later.

The name of Ealing itself is not as ancient as many which we have previously encountered. Between the twelfth and sixteenth centuries it appears as "Illing," "Gilling," "Yilling," "Yellynge," "Tylling"; then "Elyng" in 1521, "Yelling" in 1535; and, at last, "Ealing al. Yealing" in 1622. Mr. Gover* explains this as "Place of the Gillingas"; but most of the local historians prefer to accept the far more amusing theory of Professor Skeat, that Yella was "one who yelled or shouted," and that Ealing was a settlement of the Yellings. Greenford's name goes back unaltered to the ninth century, and needs no explanation here. Hanwell appears in the tenth century (A.D. 959) as "Hanewelle," and is derived by Mr. Gover from the Anglo-Saxon *Hanan welle* (= "well or spring of Hana"). "Northolt" in its present form is found on a map of 1610, but from the fourteenth century back to the tenth —where it first occurs—it is spelled "Northall" or "Northale" (Domesday). This is "North Hale," as opposed to "South Hale" (i.e. modern Southall), and "hale," as we have already found, means "nook," "corner," "retreat." Perivale, known until the fifteenth century as "Greenford Parva" or "Little Greenford," may have derived its name from pear-trees; and Twyford means "a double ford."

The borough of Ealing consists of a group of ancient parishes, none of which was more than a village a century ago, while both Northolt and Greenford were remote and peaceful hamlets before the war. The total area, after revising the boundaries under the recent Middlesex scheme (which assigns most of Twyford parish to Wembley), is rather less than 9,000 acres, i.e. about $13\frac{1}{2}$ square miles. In order to understand how Ealing has grown to its present shape and size, it is necessary to cast back our imagination a century or more. Pinnock's miniature *History and Topography of Middlesex* (1824) says that: "Ealing, situated a little to the south of the road, seven miles from London, is a rural and retired village, in the neighbourhood of which are many elegant mansions." The ensuing descriptions, with a fine flavour of royalty, leave one in no doubt that in 1824 Ealing was in fact the home of *pukka sahibs*.

Almost a century ago, a local resident, Mr. James Hayles, wrote an account of Ealing as it was in 1832, which has been freely quoted by local historians. At that time the population of Ealing was 7,783, but the parish then extended to the Thames and included

* J. E. B. Gover, *Place-names of Middlesex*, pp. 23–4.

Old Brentford, where, in fact, most of the inhabitants lived. The Uxbridge Road, from the Acton boundary at the old house known as "Fordhook" on the east to the Hanwell boundary at the Old Hats Inn on the west, was a narrow and ill-kept highway with hardly any houses and only a few inns: the "Feathers," the "Coach and Horses," the "Bell," the "Royal Oak," the "Anchor," the "Green Man," and the "Old Hats." Ealing itself consisted of a

THE CANAL BRIDGE AT PERIVALE
Horsendon Hill in background

row of large houses and a few cottages on either side of the Green which continued, as St. Mary's Road, to the old parish church of St. Mary, since rebuilt. There was a small group of houses near the bridge at Hanwell, another little group—consisting of Ealing Park, Rochester House, and a few cottages (mostly surviving)—at "Little Ealing"; and mere hamlets at Northolt, Greenford, and Perivale. These rural conditions still prevailed up to 1863, when the Ealing Local Board was formed and Old Brentford was detached, leaving a total population of about 5,000 in the new district of Ealing. The Ordnance Map of 1867 shows that little development had taken place. There were a few new villas on the Castlebar Estate, and a few more in the Uxbridge Road west of Christ Church, erected in 1852; also some houses south of St. Mary's Church. The High Street was built up, but the island site between Uxbridge Road and the Green was otherwise practically open, save for Ashton House, a large mansion facing south down the Green. Hanwell had just begun to grow, the population of that parish being 1,547 in 1851, 2,687 in 1861, and 3,766 in 1871. It was unfortunate for Hanwell that the huge County Lunatic Asylum, for 2,500 patients, established in 1831 across the Brent in the adjoining parish of Norwood, was given the name of "Hanwell" although outside the area. Humorists soon rendered the word as offensive in the neighbourhood as "Colney Hatch" had become in Friern Barnet (see page 119), and an attempt was unsuccessfully made by the inhabitants to rechristen their parish "Elthorne," a name which, though perhaps not so old as Hanwell, does occur in Domesday and recalls one of the Saxon "hundreds" which still maintain a shadowy existence even when Middlesex is rapidly turning itself into a federation of county boroughs and urban districts. Elthorne appears as the name of a public park, and also on the boards of "Hanwell and Elthorne" railway station.

The present borough of Ealing has grown up from such a variety of civil parishes and has had its boundaries changed so frequently in the process of amalgamation that its growth is difficult to trace accurately; but it appears that the combined population of the four districts (Ealing, Hanwell, Greenford, and Northolt), which compose the borough to-day, amounted to about 45,000 in 1901. In Ealing especially, in Hanwell to a less degree, this total was the result of rapid and steady growth for fifty years, but even in 1901 Greenford and Northolt together—in spite of their large area—accounted for only 1,236 of the whole, and remained obstinately rural. In the next decade the total population leaped up to 81,972, in 1921 to 90,433, at the 1931 census it reached 117,688, and at the time of writing is estimated to be nearly 130,000. Ealing itself and Hanwell are nearly built up, but there is room for a vast population in the Greenford and

Northolt districts, and if the whole borough were to be covered with buildings at the rate of twelve houses to the acre, Ealing could eventually accommodate 450,000 people, a horrible and unlikely prospect.

But the erection of small houses is still proceeding at a great pace and it cannot be denied that the extension of "Western Avenue," now in progress, from its present terminus at Greenford

PERIVALE CHURCH

across the unpopulated fields of Northolt, will result in further developments on a large scale. This splendid highway has already completely destroyed the rustic isolation of Perivale and is already partly lined with some of the finest modern factories in England, being only surpassed in that respect by the Great West Road, which runs a few hundred yards from Ealing's southern boundary. The new Greenford Road gives access to a growing industrial district and the new North Circular Road, completed at long last, is another fine thoroughfare which has followed, in part, the line of one of Ealing's oldest roads, Hanger Hill Lane. (The Anglo-Saxon word *hangra* means "a wood situated on a hill slope," hence "a

hanging wood," and occurs again in Ealing in the name "Pits-
hanger" or "Pitzhanger"; see below). It is only in very recent years
that the narrow, winding elm-clad lanes round Northolt and
Greenford have begun to give way to the clamant demands of the
motorist, and for more than a century the Grand Union Canal
has wound sleepily through quiet meadows.

The scenery of the district can never have been very exciting;
and the nearest approach to a dramatic landscape effect is the view
of Hanwell Church on its knoll above a bend of the Brent. This
view, well seen from the Great Western viaduct, itself an admirable
design, is the more remarkable because Hanwell Church has no
great architectural merit, and stands only 140 feet above sea-level.
The prospect from Horsendon Hill (256 feet) is extensive rather
than exhilarating, and the outlook from Hanger Hill (200 feet), the
only remaining eminence in Ealing, no longer retains any of its
former attraction. Writing in 1754, Fielding, the novelist, who
lived in Ealing at a house called "Fordhook" (now demolished),
said that the air there was the best "in the whole kingdom, and
far superior to that of Kensington Gravel-pits; for the gravel here
is much wider and deeper, and placed higher and more open
towards the south, whilst it is guarded from the north by a ridge of
hills, and from the smells and smoak of London by its distance."
A map of surface-utilization, prepared for the Board of Agriculture
in 1794, shows that in those days about half the area of the present
borough was arable land, the remainder meadow and pasture.
Apparently there were few market-gardens or waste lands then.
though Ealing Common is an ancient green and there is still a
charming village green at Northolt. A sentence in the accom-
panying report, though not referring to Ealing, explains the origin
of "Lammas Lands," and hence the name of Ealing's "Lammas
Park." Such lands, we are told, are divided up in strips among
different proprietors, the average holding being from 2 to 3 acres.
"They are laid up to be mowed every year on the 5th of April,
and after the hay is cut, and taken off, are opened again for com-
monage on the 12th of August: and this is what is called 'Lammas
Tenure.' Every inhabitant of the respective parishes claims and

exercises a right of turning into these meadows what stock he pleases; there being no stint to this right of common."*

According to modern and generous ideas of town-planning, 10 per cent. of any urban area should be reserved for public open spaces, and at that rate Ealing's share should be 900 acres. Thanks to wise purchases in recent years, the area acquired for this purpose amounts to 568 acres, excluding allotments, cemeteries, and the

NORTHOLT CHURCH

borough's part share in Gunnersbury Park (186 acres, see page 252), which lies just outside the borough boundary: say 650 acres in all. Several of the open spaces—Walpole Park, with its magnificent trees, Lammas Park, Churchfields and Brent Lodge at Hanwell, Pitzhanger Park at Perivale, Islip Manor at Northolt, and even the more sophisticated Ealing Common—are really charming; while Horsendon Hill and Wood (228 acres), with its extensive view and its ancient name ("Horsa's down"), will preserve for

* Peter Foot, *The Agriculture of the County of Middlesex* (London, 1794), p. 69.

future generations a fragment of the pleasant English landscape which once was Middlesex. In view of these extensive and expensive purchases, it may seem churlish to suggest that Ealing has not yet made adequate provision for open spaces in the years ahead. But it appears fairly clear that Greenford and Northolt will soon become as populous as Ealing and Hanwell already are. In that case, some further reservation of ground in Northolt is desirable, preferably in the West End corner. Besides the actual acquisitions of open spaces, the town-planning scheme provides for the reservation of practically the whole of the land on either side of the winding Brent, of which some 90 acres have been scheduled as public open spaces; and the Selborne Society's bird-sanctuary in Perivale Wood (19 acres) has been scheduled as a private open space.

The borough of Ealing possesses comparatively few historical buildings. By far the most ancient and interesting are the three quaint little churches at Perivale, Northolt, and Greenford. All are very small, and all have timber spires covered with boarding. The tiny church of Perivale, formerly Greenford Parva, is the smallest in Middlesex and is said to date from the mid-twelfth century, though only a doorway of that period remains. It contains other Gothic features and a picturesque Jacobean porch, but was drastically restored in 1875. The population of the parish was only 28 in 1801 and only 34 in 1881. Thus, although the inhabitants numbered 60 in 1901, the church was adequate in size up to recent times. St. Mary's Church at Northolt is somewhat larger, and is charmingly situated on rising ground above the village green. The church at Greenford* resembles it in being something of an architectural patchwork, severely restored, but also contains an interesting wall-monument and a font with carved cover, both given by members of the Coston family (whose name is recalled in Coston Lane and Coston School). The parish church of Ealing itself, St. Mary's, is a large and hideous structure erected in 1866–73, incorporating some of the fabric of an earlier church of 1735, which in turn replaced a medieval building of stone. It contains

* Described by Mr. Heales in the *Transactions of the London and Middlesex Archaeological Society*, Vol. IV (1871).

some monuments. Hanwell Church, which forms an attractive
feature in distant views, but does not impress one so favourably at
close quarters, was the earliest church built by Sir Gilbert Scott
(the elder), in 1841. Eleven years later he designed Christ Church,
a striking building with a beautiful spire, on the Uxbridge Road in
the centre of Ealing.

THE PUBLIC LIBRARY, EALING
Formerly Pitzhanger Manor, the home of Sir John Soane

The present Ealing Public Library, on Ealing Green, formerly
known as Pitzhanger Manor, is the most interesting old house in
the borough. It was originally built in 1770 by George Dance, the
architect, for a prosperous Quaker named Thomas Gurnell, whose
daughter Dance prudently married two years later. In Dance's
employment at that time, as office boy or in some junior capacity,
was a lad of fifteen, John Soane, who afterwards became architect
to the Bank of England and Professor of Architecture at the Royal
Academy. But it was not until 1800 that he was in a position to
buy Pitzhanger Manor with 28 acres of land. He then pulled down

the central part of Dance's building, leaving the two beautiful rooms now used as a reference library and a reading-room. Soane's new central block reminds us of his house in Lincoln's Inn Fields in the studied elegance of its internal planning and decoration. The little domed vestibule at the entrance is typical of Soane's taste. As for the east front, illustrated on my drawing, one needs to have a great admiration for Soane's peculiarities to be able to appreciate that; it is a curious medley of late-Roman or Baroque design clothed with Greek detail. North of the central block, where now the Lending Library stands, Soane laid out a curious group of "ruins" approached through a colonnaded court, and within his house he had a "Monk's Parlour" like that in his town house in Lincoln's Inn Fields, now a museum. But ten years after he bought Pitzhanger Manor he sold it again, for though brilliantly successful in his profession he was a disappointed man in his family relationships, and his associations with Ealing had become painful.

There are two or three other houses of interest on Ealing Green, one now converted into a telephone exchange, while Westfield House, near St. Mary's Church, has become the South Ealing Conservative Club; and there are also a few old cottages in the same district. At Little Ealing still stands a very large house known in the past as Place House, afterwards as Ealing Park, and now as St. Anne's Convent High School. Hideous additions mar its appearance on one side, standardized villas have surrounded its sadly diminished grounds on two other sides, and the large block of farm buildings which formerly lay to the north of it have been swept away. Nevertheless, its long low front, with a colonnaded porch, retains some dignity, and a few fine trees remain to recall the days of the eighteenth century, when it was owned by several noble lords in succession, and when Alexander Pope visited it frequently. Nearly a century ago its gardens and grounds extended over a hundred acres, and were renowned. More recently, Queen Victoria was a guest here, and even up to the end of the century it was a famous seat.

Opposite to Ealing Park is another school, the Convent of the Sacred Heart, which occupies the fine brick building known as

"Rochester House," built by Thomas Pearce, who died here in 1752 and may have commenced it in Queen Anne's reign. It contains some features of interest and still possesses a garden of respectable size.

Brent Lodge at Hanwell has no great architectural merit, and if anything of interest remains at Greenford or Northolt the tide of suburbia will soon have removed all traces of it. A few farms survive, some dismantled and obviously waiting for the end, others carrying on a hand-to-mouth existence until their turn comes to be announced as "Eligible Building Sites." The days when Ealing could regard itself as the refined home of retired Indian civil servants has gone for ever; no community of 127,000 people can make such pretensions. But Ealing is a borough with some sense of civic pride, it has long possessed citizens sufficiently interested to trace its history and preserve some records of its past, and it may therefore be trusted to exercise wisdom in its future development.

BOOKS ON LOCAL HISTORY AND TOPOGRAPHY

BOLTON, A. T.	Pitzhanger Manor (Soane Museum Publication)	London	N.D.
BROWN, J. A.	Chronicles of Greenford Parva	London	1898
COCHRANE-HOLROYD, K.	History of Northolt Parish Church	——	1930
[EALING BOROUGH COUNCIL]	Ealing: Official Guide	London	1933
FAULKNER, T.	Brentford, Ealing, and Chiswick	London	N.D. [c. 1846]
[HANWELL U.D.C.]	Hanwell: Official Guide	London	N.D.
HEALES, A.	Greenford Church (London and Middlesex Archaeological Society, Vol. IV)	London	1871
HOLMES, MRS. BASIL	The Home of the Ealing Free Library	Ealing	1902
JACKSON, EDITH	Annals of Ealing	London	1898

JONES, C.	Ealing: Forty Years of Municipal Life	Ealing	N.D.
	A Decade of Progress (1901–11) . . . in Ealing	Ealing	N.D.
NEAVES, C. M.	History of Greater Ealing (2nd edition)	Brentford	1931
SHARPE, SIR MONTAGU	Bygone Hanwell	Brentford	1924
SYKES, D. F. E.	Ealing and its vicinity	Ealing	N.D. [c. 1905]

CHAPTER XVII

RUISLIP AND NORTHWOOD

THIS urban district with a clumsy, double-barrelled name, contains some of the most charming, unspoiled rural scenery in Middlesex, and, what is almost equally important nowadays, its inhabitants have had the foresight to safeguard its beauties for posterity, so far as is reasonably possible. The district obtained urban powers in 1904, when its total population was under 4,000, but it was one of the first in England to adopt the provisions of the Town Planning Act of 1909, and ten years later the "Ruislip Association" was formed "to discuss and take action upon local matters affecting the proper development of the district and, in particular, the preservation of its amenities." In 1931 this body published *A Short History of Ruislip*, which is a model of its kind. It is therefore due to the vision and the civic sense of a small group of intelligent people that Ruislip has not gone the way of most of suburban Middlesex, and has not yet succumbed entirely to the strident propaganda that has vulgarized so much of "Metroland."

Ruislip (pronounced "Rӯslip") starts with the advantage of an ancient and euphonious name, which is spelt "Rislepe" in Domesday and has undergone a number of variations since. The prefix, writes Mr. Gover,* is an Anglo-Saxon word meaning "rush," and the suffix is another Anglo-Saxon word "hlyp," "hlep" (= a leaping-place, hence the place where one jumps over the little rush-lined river Pinn, or Pin, a tributary of the Colne). Not far away, in the modern borough of Ealing, is Islip Manor at Northolt, formerly called "Ryslippe Place" (in 1489), and first built by John Ryslippe about 1374. The latest historian of Ealing† suggests that this John may have taken his name from Ruislip village, but also notes that,

---

* J. E. B. Gover, *The Place-names of Middlesex.*
† C. M. Neaves, *A History of Greater Ealing* (1931), pp. 183-4.

while the Manor of Northolt (including Islip Manor) was the property of Westminster Abbey, there was an abbot of Westminster named John Islip, who took an active part in the decoration of Henry VII's chapel besides building the other chapel there which still bears his name. It may be added that there is a village of Islip near Oxford, and a seaside town similarly named near New York. The local history of Ruislip offers two more suggested derivations of its name: "rhy" or "hry" (= a thorn), "slap" or "slepe," a slope or declivity; and "the enclosure by the marshes," a derivation favoured by Sir Montagu Sharpe. The name of Northwood is such plain English that no explanation is needed, except to remark that it was so-called because the wood lay north of Ruislip. Eastcote, which appears as "Estcote" in the thirteenth century and "Ascot" in the sixteenth, means "east dwelling or house," i.e. east of Ruislip. All this proves that Ruislip itself was the centre and chief place of the district; indeed, Northwood is by comparison a mushroom town, which only became a separate parish about 1854, when the present church was built.

The total area of the district is 6,584 acres (about $10\frac{1}{4}$ square miles) and has been hardly affected by the recent reorganization of Middlesex boundaries. The present boundaries are practically identical with those of the old parish of Ruislip, and on the north are coterminous with the county boundary.

The population of this comparatively large parish was only 1,012 in 1801, 1,392 in 1851, and 1,836 in 1891. It then began to grow, at first round Northwood Station, increasing to 3,566 in 1901 and 6,217 in 1911. In the next decade Ruislip followed suit, and the total population of the area rose to 9,112. But between 1921 and 1931 the Eastcote area began to play its part, and the figures show a population of 16,038 in 1931, with an increase of 76 per cent. over the previous census! This growth is remarkable even in Middlesex, and would be phenomenal anywhere else. A perambulation of the area to-day reveals an enormous activity in building, especially in the southern part of the district. In 1911 each inhabitant had an acre of ground to his share; at the present moment there must be three inhabitants to the acre. But if the maximum permissible density were to be achieved by the blandishments of "Metroland," then the Urban District of Ruislip–Northwood would be truly urban, with a population of about 320,000, packed in at fifty to the acre. That is unlikely, even impossible, thanks to the precautions already mentioned.

It is quite easy to divide the modern district into three zones, differentiated by natural features as well as by social characteristics. There is, first of all, the small area north of the main London–

RUISLIP VILLAGE

Rickmansworth road. This is Northwood proper, a typical suburban growth which commenced towards the end of the nineties and is slowly approaching saturation point. To a mere outsider it appears conventional, prosperous, and ordinary, with a strong bias towards golf; except in its eastern quarter, where bread-and-butter is probably a more vital question. Northwood has no history, its sylvan glades have given way to shady, villa-lined roads, and its shops and streets are exactly like all others built near London at the same time.

The south part of the district, that is, south of the District Railway, is completely different. It is an area almost square in shape, measuring nearly two miles in each direction, and is practically barren of natural charms. Its contours are negligible, its trees scarce, and the few farms and barns which still survive are not of outstanding interest. A large aerodrome, with its characteristically "useful" buildings, occupies part of the ground, the main Great Western–L.N.E.R. line to High Wycombe and the Midlands bisects it diagonally, and soon the extension of Western Avenue will cross the south-western corner. Already a squalid colony of huts and shacks has grown up round Northolt Junction, signs of intense activity are evident elsewhere, and the tide of "Distinctive Homes" is beginning to sweep relentlessly southwards from the District Railway, which has already opened an additional station to cope with the hundreds of misguided folk who think that they are going to live in the country. It is true that even an occasional plough-man can be seen at work in this district, but the few remaining cultivated fields have not long to live, and he knows it. The district is awaiting the glad time when every acre will carry its full quota of twelve "Baronial Halls." This tract of roughly four square miles seems certain to be built up, and as it has no natural features or perceptible contours, it will be a depressing district unless some really imaginative plan of lay-out be adopted. It is true that a considerable part of the rather dreary banks of the Yeading Brook has been acquired as an open space, but neither that reservation nor the recreation grounds also bought are very stimulating to the lover of beautiful landscape. They will provide space in which to breathe and to play games: that is all.

But the central part of the urban district, the part which contains Ruislip village, Eastcote village, Ruislip Reservoir, and its girdle of woods, is so beautiful that the council has done well to concentrate its resources on preserving as much as possible from obliteration. There is already a great deal of building between the District Railway and the Eastcote–Ruislip–Ickenham road, but much of it is excellently designed and practically all of it is well laid out. This part of the parish is pleasantly undulating, rising to 300 feet at Haste Hill on one side of the reservoir, and slightly more at Copse Hill on the other side, the water-level of the reservoir being nearly 170 feet above the sea. This fine expanse of water, with an area of some 80 acres, is, of course, artificial, and belongs to the Grand Union Canal Company, but it approaches the appearance of a natural lake as nearly as any reservoir can do, and the low embankment at the south end is hardly noticeable. It is beautiful at any time of year, especially on a quiet winter afternoon when summer visitors are not making merry on the lake and when the flocks of wildfowl are undisturbed. There must be a great

THE MANOR FARM, RUISLIP

variety of birds on this lake, swans among them. It is to be hoped that it will never be vulgarized by speed-boats, which have spoiled the county's other "lake," the Welsh Harp (see pages 133–4). Pylons carrying the "grid" transmission-wires somewhat mar the view looking south, but in Middlesex one cannot avoid these things. There is a group of modern cottages near the south end, but, like most other buildings in this enlightened neighbourhood, they are designed with taste and restraint.

East of the reservoir a magnificent tract of open space has been secured for ever, acquired by degrees during the past few years. This consists of the Haste Hill golf course, the adjoining Northwood recreation ground, and the lovely sylvan stretch known as Park Wood, purchased in 1933. This is an authentic fragment of the forest of Middlesex which once stretched from Lea to Colne, and was originally a famous hunting park, mentioned in Domesday as "a park of wild beasts of the forest" (*ferarum silvaticarum*). Its trees are mainly oaks and silver birches. Across the reservoir is the "Poor's Field," with an area of 30 acres, scheduled in the Town-Planning Scheme as a private open space. The total extent of this protected area, including the reservoir itself, amounts to nearly 480 acres, and the remaining open spaces acquired or scheduled comprise some 260 acres, making about 740 acres in all. This is considerably more than a tenth of the total area of the urban district, and therefore more than the ideal minimum laid down by modern town-planners.

That being so, it is probably futile to ask for more. Yet the view of Ruislip Reservoir is now so perfect that one longs to see the woods on its western side secured as successfully as has been done on the east. If houses were to be built all over Copse Wood, down to the Poor's Field, and quite near to the margin of the lake, that lovely vista would be lost. To preserve it would involve the purchase of at least a hundred acres of Copse Wood. To the objection that the proposal is fantastic, it may be rejoined that this is undoubtedly one of the most beautiful spots remaining in the county— indeed, one of the few places left where the ancient charm of Middlesex landscape, hardly altered since the Middle Ages, still remains.

There is not much to be said about the remaining open spaces. Most of the picturesque banks of the little River Pin are protected, as well as those of the less attractive Yeading Brook, already mentioned; though one of the "grid" pylons has been placed plumb in the middle of a charming meadow by the Pin at Eastcote. It seems probable that the area will develop as a dormitory district, though possibly industry may appear near Northolt Junction, and the large depots of the Royal Air Force, at Ruislip as well as at Northolt, vary the prevailing character of domestic building. Inevitably the busy road from Pinner through Eastcote and Ruislip to Uxbridge will be widened, and widening has already begun on

the Ruislip–Hayes road. The electric railways are showing great
enterprise in the area, and have recently opened another station on
the District line. The latest improvement in transport facilities, by
which Tube trains from Cockfosters and Enfield run through
the heart of London to Eastcote, Ruislip, and Uxbridge, cannot
fail to encourage the already active state of building development
in the district.

"THE BARNS," EASTCOTE

Historical buildings in the area, except for scattered farms and
barns, are entirely confined to the two old villages of Ruislip and
Eastcote. The ancient church of St. Martin (an unusual dedication
in Middlesex) was the only parish church in the whole district
until Northwood became a separate parish in 1854 or thereabouts.
It is a large building with nave, chancel, aisles, and a fine tower;
and it contains many features of interest. It was somewhat drastically
restored in 1869–72 by Sir Gilbert Scott, but, in this case as in
many others, too much has been made of his thoroughness. It is

true that nowadays the restoration of old buildings is undertaken more cautiously, but critics are apt to forget that Sir Gilbert Scott's knowledge of Gothic church architecture was as profound as his admiration of it was fervent, and that while he certainly was over-zealous in his restorations, he preserved from collapse and destruction innumerable old churches large and small. Possibly because one of his first commissions was a new church at Hanwell (see page 185), he was frequently employed in restoring old churches in the west of Middlesex. The church at Ruislip, which is charmingly situated in the centre of the old village, was originally a monastic foundation attached to the famous abbey of Bec in Normandy and is mainly a structure of the thirteenth and fifteenth centuries. Scott, unfortunately, removed the dormer-windows in the roof, a detail characteristic of old Middlesex churches. There are several interesting grave-slabs and tombs, a remarkable carved bread-cupboard, a Jacobean pulpit, some pre-Reformation pews, and numerous medieval wall-paintings.

Near the church stands the old Manor Farm, an ancient building with two large barns, one of which is perhaps the second finest in the county, being only surpassed by that at Harmondsworth (page 218), though the example at Headstone Manor (page 151) is a worthy rival. The great oak posts which divide this noble building into "bays" are a foot square. Near the farm, and forming part of the property, is a group of brick cottages of the Wren period, one of which was, until recently, the village post office. The whole of this interesting property was presented to the local council by King's College, Cambridge (the previous owners), when Park Wood was acquired. Thus Ruislip will continue to preserve, almost unimpaired, the greater part of the old hunting park of some 350 acres, together with the "hall" or manor house.* The original Saxon boundary of the park, forming a distorted circle, followed the line of the Ruislip–Eastcote road and of the curving line of Bury Street, and was traceable up to recent times.

* As this book goes to press, it is announced that "H.M. Office of Works has decided to list Ruislip Motte and Bailey, the remnants of the Norman castle at Manor Farm, Ruislip, as an ancient monument."

Other old houses in the village include the charming group separating the churchyard from the High Street, purchased with a view to preservation by the Ruislip Village Trust, the Bell Inn, and the Swan Inn. There are several in the hamlet of Eastcote, which incidentally boasts an inn with the queer sign "The Case is Altered." But the district also contains a number of really charming half-timbered farms and barns, the former mainly with white-washed brick filling and tiled roofs, the latter with tarred weather-

WOODMAN'S FARM, RUISLIP

boarding and thatched or tiled roofs. Among them may be mentioned Woodman's Farm in Bury Street, Hill Farm, Shirley's Farm, Green Farm, Mill Farm, and "The Barns" at Eastcote.

As already remarked, the standard of new building in Ruislip is far above the average, thanks to wise direction and artistic taste. Even the modern shops along the High Street are less blatant than usual, and the new post office is charming. As regards dwelling-houses, there is one in Bury Street, at the corner of Meadway, which is an examplar for architects of the way to build in an old village, for it shows that modern needs can be satisfied without insulting a settled landscape.

BOOKS ON LOCAL HISTORY AND TOPOGRAPHY

ANDERSON, A. H.	Northwood (*Homeland Handy Guides*)	London	1913
[ANONYMOUS]	Descriptive Guide to Ruislip	Ruislip [N.D., *c.*1913]	
HOOPER, J. (editor) *See also:*	A Short History of Ruislip	Ruislip	1931
BRAUN, H. S.	Earliest Ruislip (in *Middlesex Schools' Gazette*)	London	1933–4
FENDICK, G.	Park Wood, Ruislip (in *Middlesex Schools' Gazette*)	London	1933

CHAPTER XVIII

UXBRIDGE

INCLUDING COLHAM GREEN, COWLEY, HAREFIELD, HILLINGDON, AND ICKENHAM

THE large urban district of Uxbridge is one of the most important in Middlesex from the point of view of size, scenic attractions, and historical associations. The old market-town of Uxbridge itself lies at the point where the London–Oxford road crosses the River Colne, and still retains some of the aspect which it presented to our great-grandfathers in the busy coaching days. But the agricultural districts of Hillingdon and Ickenham are rapidly transforming themselves into residential suburbs, thereby following the prevailing and apparently inevitable trend of things in the county.

The name of Uxbridge puzzles the philologists. The tempting and obvious explanation is "Ox-bridge," and some old forms of the name do encourage that supposition. But the careful Mr. Gover* gives us good reasons for discarding this, as also another derivation, *wysc-bridge* (= water-bridge) on the grounds that *wysc* is Celtic, and therefore unlikely here in Middlesex. He favours Wuxa's or Wusca's Bridge, assuming the existence of an unknown Anglo-Saxon personal name, which may also explain Uxendon Farm, near Wembley. Colham Green may mean "the enclosure of Cola," and the name of the River Colne may be a "back-formation" from it, or may be of separate Celtic origin. Cowley, on the other hand, is defined by Mr. Gover as "the pasture or clearing of Cūfa." It is a very old name, occurring long before Domesday, where it appears as "Covelei." Harefield, which figures in Domesday as "Herefelle," may be a relic of the Danish invasions, "an open space where the army (Anglo-Saxon *here*) was encamped. Hillingdon may be "the down of the hill dwellers," or "Hilla's down."

* J. E. B. Gover, *The Place-names of Middlesex*.

In either case, it may be noted that this part of the district is almost dead level! And lastly Ickenham, which occurs in Domesday as "Ticheham," is explained by Mr. Gover as "Ticca's home," a delightful and unexpected derivation.

The urban district of Uxbridge, as we now know it, is a very recent creation. It is built up of various parishes—Cowley, Ickenham, Harefield, Hillingdon East, Hillingdon West, and

UXBRIDGE HIGH STREET

Uxbridge itself—in the Hundred of Elthorne. The Saxon town of Uxbridge had an area of some 87 acres, and was a fortified *burh* surrounded by a ditch. The modern parish of Uxbridge represents this ancient settlement, and has an identical area. It was not until 1849 that Uxbridge became an urban district, by which time the parish of Hillingdon West, with an area of 781 acres, had been amalgamated with it. The "Rural District of Uxbridge," abolished in 1929, consisted of Hillingdon East, Harefield, Cowley, Northolt, and West Drayton. The last-named parish was handed over to Yiewsley (see next chapter) in 1929, Northolt had been transferred to Ealing in the previous year, and now the new urban district of

Uxbridge absorbed the remaining four parishes of the former rural district. Its area became 6,585 acres (10¼ square miles), one of the largest in the county.

It is difficult to trace the growth of population in the present urban area with absolute precision, owing to the successive changes in the grouping of parishes already described. If one takes the sum of the inhabitants of the old parishes of Cowley, Harefield, the

HAREFIELD CHURCH

two Hillingdons, Ickenham, and Uxbridge, it appears that the total population was 5,272 in 1801, 11,794 in 1851, 13,047 in 1861, 14,057 in 1871, 15,018 in 1881, 16,436 in 1891, and 17,833 in 1901. It will be noticed that, up to this point, the population grew steadily at an even rate of about 1,000 a year. Thereafter the population rose from 17,292 in 1911 to 20,626 in 1921 and to 31,866 in 1931. Judging by appearances, there is every prospect that the wild leap from the 1921 figure to that of 1931 will be repeated at the next census, for building is proceeding apace. It is curious, and indeed significant, that the population of the crowded little old parish of Uxbridge, which was 2,111 in

1801 and 3,043 in 1831, rose only slightly during the next fifty years, and then actually dropped back to 3,063 in 1901. This fact shows that the rapid development of the district is occurring outside rather than inside the town. It may also be observed that if the whole district were to be populated as densely as the old parish is, that is about thirty-five persons to the acre, it would have some 350,000 inhabitants. This appalling prospect, however, is not likely to be realized.

By far the most important natural feature in the Uxbridge district is the River Colne with its picturesque valley. This valley is not on the grand scale, for the river bridge at Uxbridge is 120 feet above the sea, and the low hills on either hand nowhere reach 300 feet. But near Harefield their sides are steep, the valley narrows, and this produces a type of scenery not found elsewhere in Middlesex. For here the chalk of the Chilterns appears on both sides of the river, this and South Mimms being the only places in the county where it shows on the surface. There is an almost precipitous little sunken lane north-west of Harefield which is more like Devonshire than anything in Middlesex. The Colne on the west of the county resembles the Lea on the east in consisting of numerous channels, but on its passage through the Uxbridge district its course is fairly clear, though it bifurcates into the Colne proper and the tributary or channel known as the "Frays Water" which supplies the motive power for the old Uxbridge mills. For part of its length this channel forms the county boundary. The Colne is a beautiful stream, clear and rush-lined. It has always served industry along its banks, so one cannot grumble that the town-planners have seen fit to schedule a large part of the valley floor for "industrial purposes." But they have wisely confined this recommendation to the land immediately adjoining the Grand Union (formerly Grand Junction) Canal, already partly utilized for factories, reserving the actual riverside strip as an open space in collaboration with the Buckinghamshire scheme. The whole canal was opened in 1805, twelve years after it was authorized, but as early as 1801 a regular service of packet-boats had been established between Uxbridge and London. It was not a success—

the distance of 23 miles (by water) proving too lengthy—so it was soon abandoned; but the Packet Boat Inn at Cowley preserves its memory. In spite of the existence of factories beside part of its course through the Uxbridge district, there are other parts (notably near Denham Lock) where a walk along the towing-path is very pleasant, and a few places where the views are really charming. The courses of the Yeading Brook and the River Pin through

ALMSHOUSES AT HAREFIELD

the district are far less picturesque and attractive, the adjoining country being almost flat and the foliage somewhat scanty, but most of the banks are preserved under the regional and local town-planning schemes.

Long before the canal was made there was the famous road from London through Oxford to distant Milford Haven. At one time, no earlier than the end of the eighteenth century, it was in a shocking state of repair, for Middleton wrote thus of its condition in the winter of 1797–8:

There was but one passable track on this road; that was less than six feet wide, and it was eight inches deep in fluid sludge. All the rest of the road was from a foot to eighteen inches deep in adhesive mud. This track was thronged with waggons (many of them drawn by ten horses and most of them having broad wheels, even to sixteen inches wide) and farmers' six-inch wheel carts which occupied almost the whole of this confined space. It was, therefore, with great difficulty and some danger that horsemen and light carriages could pass.

It was during the eighteenth century that highwaymen operated on Hillingdon Heath, but their exploits were less notorious there than on Hounslow Heath, and need not detain us. Later came the great days of coaching, when the distance from Oxford to London or vice versa was covered at an average speed of 14 miles an hour while one coach was actually driven from High Wycombe to London, 29 miles along a hilly road, in the incredible time of 100 minutes. It was at this period, about the time of William IV, that the numerous inns in Uxbridge High Street must have attained their greatest prosperity. Most of them have been wholly or partially remodelled, but many of the inn-yards still remain together with a charming row of old brick houses, behind which are long gardens shaded with cedars, extending down to the margin of the Frays River.

There is just a chance that this delightful bit of street scenery may survive, but everything depends upon the time taken to complete Western Avenue from its present terminus at Greenford to the point near the "Red Hill" where it is planned to join the old Oxford Road. If that occurs within three years, old Uxbridge may again revert to comparatively peaceful conditions. Otherwise the appalling congestion of traffic, aggravated by the existence of tramlines which actually arrived here in 1904, may involve drastic widening,* and may render life in the stately old houses insupportable, even if their foundations are capable of resisting the vibration. The daily procession of new Morris cars from Oxford has not added to the peace of the town. Traffic north and south, from Reading and Slough to Rickmansworth, the Great North Road, and Hertford, has recently been diverted to the new orbital road

---

* At the time of writing, a group of old houses in the centre of the very picturesque village of Hillingdon is being demolished for the same reason. (Cf. p. 211.)

which runs along the west side of the Colne Valley, and therefore in Buckinghamshire; but it seems likely that traffic from Harefield through Uxbridge to Cowley and West Drayton will soon involve the widening of the tortuous and narrow road that now exists. Certainly, Uxbridge High Street is the most crowded thoroughfare in Middlesex. One may hope that the promised relief afforded by the bypass roads just mentioned will obviate the need of rebuilding the old bridge over the Colne at Uxbridge built in 1770. The views from this bridge, looking up or down the river, are very attractive.

Railway development in the district has been continuous,* and the recent extension of the Tube from Cockfosters and Finsbury Park to Uxbridge enables one to travel from Central London without a change. The position of the Great Western station, or rather one of the Great Western stations, near the bridge is unfortunate; and there seems to be no reason why an ugly dead-end should have been contrived in such a place. The designers of the new Cockfosters extension railway stations would have done better than that.

All these improved methods of getting to Uxbridge as fast as possible lead one to wonder whether the district will soon be worth living in, twenty years hence, when the house-builders and the road-builders have completed their task. The author of *Rural Nooks round London*,† writing in 1907, says: "Uxbridge up to now has resolutely refused to be modernized," and describes Hillingdon End as "a pleasant flat suburban interlude" with "a pretty expanse of nursery grounds"; while Mr. Walter Jerrold, in *Highways and Byways in Middlesex*‡ (1909), speaks of Ickenham as "a small, quiet village" and of the Harefield district as "one of the most beautifully rural bits that the county has left to show." Only twenty-five years ago, yet how much has happened since

---

* The Great Western main line was originally planned to pass through Uxbridge. As the inhabitants objected, it was diverted through West Drayton and opened in 1835, the spur-line to Uxbridge being opened in 1838.

† C. G. Harper, *Rural Nooks round London*, p. 114.

‡ Walter Jerrold, *Highways and Byways in Middlesex*, pp. 218, 226.

then! The "quiet village" of Ickenham is now disturbed by a constant thunder of builders' lorries. Opposite the village church you can get a permanent wave or buy gramophone records, or even imbibe "morning coffee." Hillingdon is no less sophisticated and Harefield is rapidly following suit.

But the city fathers of Uxbridge appear to be fully alive to the situation, and during the last few years they have made generous provision for the safeguarding of large tracts of their still inviolate beauty spots. These reservations include the greater part of the actual banks of the Colne and the Yeading Brook, as already mentioned; also part of the banks of the River Pin at Ickenham. In Uxbridge itself there are the Fassnidge Recreation Ground, the Manor Way Recreation Ground, the Rockingham Recreation Ground (14 acres), and Uxbridge Common (15 acres); at Harefield there are Mount Pleasant (6 acres), Taylor's Meadow (12½ acres), The Grove (5 acres), and Watts' Common (5 acres); in Cowley there is Cowley Hall Recreation Ground (14 acres); in Hillingdon there are Hillingdon House Farm (137 acres), Hillingdon Court (56 acres), Colney Green (10 acres), and several smaller open spaces, besides nearly 80 acres of the Yeading Brook reservation; while at Ickenham some 14 acres have been purchased, and part of the Swakeleys estate (32 acres) has also been acquired. In all, these open spaces actually acquired amount to over 500 acres, to which must be added Ickenham Marsh (41 acres), leased to the Council by the Lord of the Manor. Besides all this, a further area of 158 acres has been scheduled for additional public spaces, and the extensive reservations in the Colne Valley and elsewhere bring the total area of land protected from future building to more than 1,200 acres in all. When one remembers that Uxbridge also contains large areas occupied by the Royal Air Force, of which at least a portion is unlikely to be built upon, one may congratulate the authorities on having done their best to preserve for posterity a substantial fragment of Middlesex scenery, and upon having exceeded the bare minimum of open spaces usually stated as a percentage of the area of any district.

Uxbridge and its constituent parishes contain several historical buildings, of which the most ancient are the five old churches at Cowley, Ickenham, Harefield, Hillingdon, and Uxbridge itself. All these have been described in detail elsewhere, some in great detail; and brief notes will suffice here.

The little church of St. Laurence at Cowley is a quaint and interesting flint building with a timber belfry covered with boarding and a small lead-covered spire above. It is considered to be an indisputable Saxon foundation, but most of the structure is of the

ICKENHAM CHURCH

thirteenth and fourteenth centuries. One of the roof-trusses is of unusual form, the space between tie-beam and rafters being filled with arcading. This arcading is thought to have been a continuation of the former rood-screen below, since removed. The parish church of St. Giles at Ickenham has many features in common with that at Cowley, as with the little churches at Greenford, Northolt, and Perivale. It has a boarded belfry of timber, crowned by a small spire. Here again the walls are of flint and stone, and the date of building appears to lie in the late fourteenth century, though the wooden porch is considerably later. As at Cowley, and formerly at Ruislip, there are dormer-windows in the roof. The church contains some interesting monuments. It was restored by Sir Gilbert Scott, and again—more gently—by Messrs. Johnson and Forsyth in 1921. St. Mary's Church at Harefield, beautifully situated below the village, though comparatively small is of a very different type, with a squat embattled tower at the west end of the north aisle. It is a fourteenth-century structure, but was so drastically restored about 1840 that not much of the original architecture has been left untouched. But the little building is a perfect museum of brasses and sculptured memorials to the Newdigate family (who founded the famous prize at Oxford), a Countess of Derby (1637), and other local residents, from the fifteenth century onwards. The church also contains a "three-decker" pulpit, old-fashioned pews, and many other unusual features. One of the sculptured memorials (to Lady Mary Newdigate) is by Grinling Gibbons, whose account for the work is still preserved. Hillingdon Church (St. John Baptist) was very considerably altered and enlarged by Sir Gilbert Scott in 1847–8, when a new chancel and transept were added. It is a fine and imposing building, with a striking tower capped by a cupola, but so much of the fabric is modern that historical interest is chiefly limited to the sixteenth-century brasses and the later monuments. The parish church of St. Margaret at Uxbridge, though an old building, was a mere chapel-of-ease to Hillingdon Parish Church up to 1842. It stands on a cramped and very noisy site behind the Market House, close to the High Street, and a complete outfit of stained-glass windows makes it pitch dark on a winter day. However, that does not matter much, because Sir Gilbert Scott dealt very faithfully with it in 1872, and in any case its monuments are of slight importance. It may be added that the same ubiquitous Sir Gilbert provided Uxbridge in 1865 with the large new church of St. Andrew, graced with one of the noble spires which he could design so admirably.

Coming now to secular buildings, the finest historical house in Middlesex—Hampton Court always excepted—is the mansion of Swakeleys, between Ickenham and Uxbridge. This has been fully described elsewhere, yet, in spite of its reputation, it seems to have had a narrow escape from demolition a few years ago. Originally built in or about 1638* by Edmund Wright, who purchased the property in 1629 and became Lord Mayor of London in 1641, it stands on the site of an earlier house, some parts of which are said to be incorporated in the later work. The estate passed to Wright's daughter, who sold it in 1665 to Sir Robert Vyner. On September 7,

SWAKELEYS, NEAR UXBRIDGE

1666, it was visited by Samuel Pepys, who gives this characteristic and amusing account of the occasion:

Thence to Branford [Brentford], reading *The Villaine*, a pretty good play, all the way. There a coach of Mr. Povy's stood ready for me, and he at his house ready to come in, and so we together merrily to Swakely, to Sir R. Viner's, a very pleasant place, bought by him of Sir J. Harrington's lady. He took us up and down with great respect, and showed us all his house and grounds; and it is a place not very moderne in the garden nor house, but the most uniform in all that I ever saw; and some things to excess. Pretty to see over the screene of the hall, put up by Sir J. Harrington, a Long Parliament-man, the King's head, and my Lord of Essex on one side, and Fairfax on the other; and, upon the other side of the screene, the parson of the parish, and the lord of the

---

* Swakeleys, though an unusual design, is curiously similar to Broome Park, near Dover, built 1635-8, and for many years the home of Lord Kitchener.

O

manor and his sisters. The window-cases, door-cases, and chimneys of all the house are marble. He showed me a black boy that he had, that died of a consumption; and, being dead, he caused him to be dried in an oven, and lies there entire in a box. By and by to dinner. . . . After dinner, Sir Robert led us up to his long gallery, very fine, above stairs, and better, or such furniture I never did see. A most pleasant journey we had back.

In 1750 Swakeleys was bought by Mr. Thomas Clarke, and remained until recent times in the possession of his family, whose tombs are to be seen in Ickenham Church. The last private owner disposed of it a few years ago as a country club to the Foreign Office Sports Association, remaining as their tenant in occupation of the beautiful rooms on the first floor. The fine marble screen in the hall, with the heads mentioned by Pepys, the huge marble fire-places, and a certain amount of old panelling are still to be seen on the ground floor. The house suffered greatly by the removal, many years ago, of the original leaded lights, but these are gradually being replaced as funds permit: and indeed, an effort is being made to restore the house to its former state. The walled garden has been used to enclose a series of hard tennis courts, but some of the old ironwork remains, and the surrounding park contains a number of magnificent trees and a lake. North of the house is the spacious and picturesque stable court, worthy of comparison with those at Cranford and Osterley. It appears that Swakeleys has now escaped its very imminent peril of demolition, and that though rows of "Tudor Homes" are creeping up to it from all sides, the house itself with its stable-court, gardens, immediate surroundings, and lake—some 28 acres in all—is saved for posterity. Considering the enormous area of still virgin land around it, there seems to be no reason why such a splendid mansion should ever have been in danger, but it was so. Some land-grabbers seem to have the mentality of a small boy with a catapult.

At Harefield there is a picturesque group of brick almshouses, built early in the seventeenth century by the Countess of Derby. It is a pity that some of the windows have been blocked up. The so-called "Treaty House" at Uxbridge, near the river, still remains in part, but its original brickwork is nearly concealed by modern stucco, and the beautiful panelling of the historic room,* where the abortive "Peace Conference" between Royalists and Roundheads was held in 1645, was unfortunately sold to an American purchaser in 1929.

Uxbridge, Hillingdon, Cowley, and Harefield all contain large brick houses of the Queen Anne and Georgian periods, notably in Uxbridge High Street. On the north-east side of the street the mansion known as Frays House, with its large garden, is now advertised as a building site. The Cedar House at Hillingdon, in the main road nearly opposite the church, is a gabled brick building, apparently of the mid-seventeenth century, which contains fine panelled rooms and chimneypieces, a little heraldic glass, some remarkably fine smith's work on window-shutters, an iron gate to the main road, a magnificent cedar-tree, and beautiful formal gardens. Unfortunately, its garden will suffer from the road-widening now in progress.

The Market House at Uxbridge (1788) has a long frontage on to the High Street, and is a stark building made picturesque by the open colonnade beneath it. The district does not possess many striking examples of modern architecture, the new flats in the park at Swakeleys being perhaps the most remarkable specimens.

* Illustrated on page 81 of G. F. Bosworth's *Middlesex* (Cambridge, 1913).

BOOKS ON LOCAL HISTORY AND TOPOGRAPHY

COCHRAN, REV. C. S.	St. Mary's, Harefield, Description of the Monuments	Rickmansworth	1926
	More about Harefield Church and Parish	Rickmansworth	1927
GODFREY, W. H.	Swakeleys (*London Survey Committee*)	London N.D. [1934]	
HUGO, THOMAS	History of Moor Hall, Harefield	London	1866
KING, J.	Guide to Picturesque Uxbridge	Uxbridge	1904

REDFORD, G., and RICHES, T. H.	History of Uxbridge (2nd edition)	Uxbridge	1885
SALIS, R. DE	Hillingdon through Eleven Centuries	Uxbridge	1926
SPRINGALL, S.	Country Rambles round Uxbridge	London	1907
[UXBRIDGE U.D.C.]	Uxbridge: Official Guide	London	N.D
	Directional Guide-Map of Uxbridge	London	N.D.
VERNON, W. F.	Notes on the Parish of Harefield	London	1872

Also article by:

| TIPPING, H. A. | Swakeleys (in *English Homes*, Vol. II, pp. 407–14) | London | 1927 |

CHAPTER XIX

YIEWSLEY AND WEST DRAYTON

INCLUDING HARMONDSWORTH, HEATHROW, LONGFORD, AND SIPSON

THERE are not many residents in other parts of Middlesex who even know where Yiewsley is, and very few who could say much about it. This is excusable, for Yiewsley is comparatively a mushroom-growth and has only recently blossomed into urban maturity with a smart new town hall (which, by the way, is still lacking in the ancient market-town of Uxbridge). Nobody has ever written a local history of Yiewsley, but the "town" has just converted a small derelict chapel into a county library, so who knows when the idea may not occur to one of its inhabitants to exercise his literary ability in that direction? Nevertheless, the district can claim to be unique in the county in several respects. Yiewsley itself, for instance, has a floating school maintained by the Middlesex Education Committee for the children of canal-boat employees; Harmondsworth, besides possessing one of the finest timber barns in all England, is still the scene of the annual ploughing-match of the Middlesex Agricultural Society; and West Drayton last summer entertained the "British Fly and Bait Casting Association," which held its third annual tournament at Thorney Weir in that parish. There is also a large private aerodrome in the district.

Its name is a modern variant of the form "Wyveslee" in which it first appears in the fourteenth century, and means "the clearing of Wīf" (or *Wīfel*); it might even mean "the wife's clearing." "Drayton" is believed to mean a "hidden homestead or farm"; Heathrow means a line of houses or a hamlet on (Hounslow) Heath; Longford needs no explanation, because the name exactly describes the village strung along the Bath Road which crosses several arms of the Colne; Sipson (according to Mr. Gover,* from whom these

* J. E. B. Gover, *The Place-names of Middlesex.*

derivations are taken) means "Sibbe's Farm"; while Harmonds-worth, spelt "Hermodesworde" in Domesday and now pronounced "Harmsworth" locally, means "the farm of Heremod."

The modern urban district of Yiewsley and West Drayton is a composite affair, comprising the former urban district of Yiewsley (which was taken out of Hillingdon Parish to form a civil parish in 1895), the parish of West Drayton which was transferred to it from the rural district of Uxbridge in 1929, and the parish of Harmondsworth transferred from the rural district of Staines in 1930. The areas of the three parishes are 1,091, 878, and 3,308 acres respectively, making a total area of 5,277 acres; that is, about 8¼ square miles.

The population of this large district was very sparse up to recent times, and even at the turn of the century cannot have greatly exceeded one person per acre. So recently as 1931 there was less than this density in the large parish of Harmondsworth, which contained only 3,084 persons; while there were 7,126 in Yiewsley and 2,856 in West Drayton. The total population was 8,033 in 1911, 9,163 in 1921, and 13,066 in 1931. It is thus still a small community as Middlesex districts go, but the growth of nearly 50 per cent in the decennium 1921–31 is significant.

What is likely to be the future of this extensive area, capable of accommodating a quarter of a million people on a moderate estimate; and how is the welfare of so large a district to be safe-guarded by the recently created authority of a comparatively small population? To answer these questions we must briefly survey the natural and artificial features of the locality. Foremost among these features is the River Colne, here a considerable waterway, widening out almost to a lake below the mills at West Drayton, and running as several streams all its way to the Thames. The "Colne Brook," one of the largest of these tributaries, leaves the parent stream near Harefield and passes through Buckinghamshire for the remainder of its course, except where it crosses a corner of Middlesex near Poyle. The Frays River, which we have met before, rejoins the Colne near West Drayton. Other streams are the Wyrardisbury River, the Bigley Ditch, and the "Duke of

Northumberland's River"—an artificial stream which crosses the
Bath Road at Longford, and is described in Chapter XXIV. The
flat country lying between these streams, a veritable Middlesex
Mesopotamia, is an angler's paradise, and is studded with the
willow-trees which are the most distinctive feature of the landscape.
Most of the area is very lonely, though here and there are old mills,
and round West Drayton Station a number of modern factories.

THE GATEHOUSE, WEST DRAYTON

There are also great lagoons where gravel has been excavated, and
near Yiewsley there is a large and unpleasant refuse-dump. The
rest of the district is dead level, and the large areas unbuilt upon
are about equally divided between arable land and orchards, while
a considerable tract of wild common—almost the only surviving
portion of the famous Hounslow Heath—occupies the south-east
corner.

The Grand Union Canal enters the district near Dawley, runs
close to the Great Western Railway to a point near West Drayton
Station, and then turns north on its way to Uxbridge, Watford,
and Northamptonshire. It still retains some evidence of activity,

but not the bustle it once displayed when huge quantities of brick-earth were excavated and burnt all round West Drayton. The tree-planted square now known as "Royal Avenue" was formerly "Otter Dock," a basin, now filled in, where bricks were loaded on to barges for London and elsewhere. It must have been this industry, coupled with the existence of a railway junction, that created the little town of Yiewsley during the latter half of the nineteenth century, and its somewhat dreary older streets prove it. The Bath Road, busy as it is, had led to no building activity up to a few years ago, and the Colnbrook Bypass has diverted most of the through traffic from Longford. Where the new Great West Road crosses the corner of the district, at New Bedfont, signs of "life" are beginning to appear.

It might be thought that the urban council of so small a community would not have been able to achieve much progress in town-planning and rural preservation: on the contrary, an excellent scheme has already been adopted. Some credit for this must be ascribed to the regional town-planning scheme for West Middlesex, in which it was proposed to reserve as a public open space practically the whole of this part of the Colne Valley, in collaboration with Buckinghamshire, which is similarly protecting the west side. The share of the Yiewsley and West Drayton Urban District in this reservation amounts to 230 acres. It is a beautiful bit of country, traversed by broad, clear winding streams, dotted with willows, and furnished with pleasant riverside walks. The fact that it is unsuitable for building sites is an additional argument for its use as a public space, and it is to be hoped that the refuse-dumps and gravel-pits which mar portions of the area will be rendered less objectionable in the future. Besides this, some 80 acres have been acquired for various recreation grounds in different parts of the district. In West Drayton there is the Avenue and the Green (28 acres in all); in Yiewsley there is Royal Avenue, the recreation ground in Falling Lane, and some open spaces in the housing scheme (12½ acres in all); in Harmondsworth there is the village recreation ground, Magpie Meadows, and the War Memorial Recreation Ground near Sipson (27 acres in all); while in Uxbridge district is Clark's Meadow (13 acres) belonging to Yiewsley. This total of 310 acres of public open spaces, acquired or reserved, amounts to considerably less than the usual minimum of 10 per cent. of the total acreage of the district (5,277 acres) which is usually aimed at nowadays, but the Great West Aerodrome at Heathrow, belonging to the Fairey Aviation Company (180 acres), might usefully be acquired or reserved as a *private* open space in order

HARMONDSWORTH

to increase the allowance. It can hardly be said that the enormous area reserved for the new Sludge Disposal Works of the County Council at Perry Oaks, south of the Bath Road (250 acres), can be regarded as a permanent place of recreation!

The historical buildings of the district include two small but very interesting old parish churches at Harmondsworth and West Drayton. The former, restored in 1853, consists of an aisled nave and chancel with a squat tower of brick and stone. There is a very fine late Norman south doorway elaborately carved, and some Norman work in one of the nave arcades. The other aisle is of the thirteenth century, the chancel of the fifteenth century. There is an old marble font, a good hammer-beam roof, and some original Gothic pews—a rare survival. The church of St. Martin at West Drayton has a fine clerestoried nave of the fifteenth century, a chancel, and a picturesque tower with a turret but sadly smothered in ivy—the delight of pottering spinsters and the enemy of architecture. The church suffered from a severe restoration in 1852, when its pulpit and Gothic seating, several of its tombs, and some of its stained glass were sacrificed to a perverse desire for neatness, but a very fine Gothic font and some brasses have survived.

Among secular buildings there is the brick gatehouse of the destroyed manor-house of the Pagets (afterwards Earls of Uxbridge), lords of the manor of West Drayton, recalling the architecture of Hampton Court. This gatehouse, built c. 1550, has recently been purchased by the Middlesex County Council, and thus saved for posterity at a moment when it was threatened with demolition. At Harmondsworth there is a charming half-timbered house, but the glory of the village is the wonderful medieval barn which lies near the church and was formerly the tithe-barn of a priory which stood here. Its age is uncertain, but must be considerable. As it now stands, it is 191 feet long and 38 feet wide. The construction is of massive oak posts and beams, with weather-boarded sides and a tiled roof "hipped" at the gables. It was formerly L-shaped, but one side of the "L," 128 feet long and 38 feet wide, was taken down and re-erected at Heathrow in 1774, when the adjoining manor-house was demolished, but it was afterwards blown down. It is most important that the Harmondsworth Barn, the finest in Middlesex, should be preserved.

There is a thatched cottage at Heathrow of no architectural pretensions, but one of the few surviving examples of thatching in the county. The craft is now practically dead in Middlesex, and it is difficult to find any man capable of executing repairs. Longford contains a few old houses and farms, as does Sipson, but nothing of outstanding interest; while Yiewsley, except for an old cottage or two on the Cowley Road, is a rather sordid little town clustering round the railway junction, trying to improve on a not very satisfactory heritage from the nineteenth century.

BOOKS ON LOCAL HISTORY AND TOPOGRAPHY

NIL.

CHAPTER XX

HAYES AND HARLINGTON

INCLUDING BOTWELL, CRANFORD, DAWLEY, AND YEADING

ONLY twenty-five years ago a critical and observant writer could say with justice that Hayes "is still one of the most rural villages in this remarkably rural county of Middlesex. Hayes is beautiful. The surrounding country is flat, and was until quite recent times an uncultivated waste, where the highwayman and the footpad lurked; but its flatness is now masked by many an acre of orchards and market-gardens, with intervening homesteads. In the centre of the parish stands the hoary church, one of the oldest and most interesting in the rural villages round London."[*] It would be difficult to better this description. My own first recollections of the place date from a few years later when, pausing on the narrow railway bridge which has since become perhaps the most dangerous "bottle-neck" in the county, I looked over endless acres of white and pink blossom stretching to the horizon.

And now? The population of the district has multiplied five times in the intervening years. Round the station rises the largest group of modern factories in Middlesex, one firm alone employing some fifteen thousand hands—in spite of a marvellous installation of labour-saving machinery. The straggling main road north and south is a seething mass of cosmopolitan humanity and becomes almost impassable when the midday and evening whistles release an army of workers on bicycles. Huge cinemas and brand-new multiple shops line this thoroughfare. A large housing scheme, one of the best designed in Greater London, lies in the angle between this road and the great highway from London to Uxbridge, and another "model village" for the Great Western Railway, the work of Mr. Alwyn Lloyd, is about to occupy the opposite corner. By way of contrast, the hamlet of Yeading includes an untidy settle-

---

[*] C. G. Harper, *Rural Nooks round London* (1907), pp. 105–6.

ment of shacks and caravans, where obsolete tramcars and motor-buses* are inhabited by unfortunate families who do their best with lace curtains tied up with pink bows; and Yeading also contains the largest and most offensive of the numerous refuse-dumps in the county. Yet in spite of these evidences of modernity, the neighbourhood of Cranford remains delightfully rural, and there is still an authentic water-splash over the River Crane. Cranford is

BRIDGE OVER THE CRANE, CRANFORD

not the locale of Mrs. Gaskell's famous novel, the scene of which is laid at Knutsford in Cheshire, but the Middlesex Cranford could have provided an equally appropriate setting with its great mansion and park, its peaceful winding stream, its noble elms, and its dignified Georgian houses, not yet marred by the relentless sweep of suburbanism and industrial progress, though villas are appearing round the corner.

The names of the five old villages included in the new urban district of Hayes and Harlington are all at least as ancient as Domesday, and some are earlier still. Hayes, for example, occurs

* One of which is appropriately labelled "Old Bill."

as *linganhese* in 793, as *hæse* in 831, and as "Hesa" in Domesday. This means "land covered with brushwood," but Mr. Gover, from whose book* these derivations are quoted, says he cannot explain *lingan*, though "ling" (= heather) is of Norse origin. Harlington appears as *hygereding tun* in 825 and 969, and as "Herdintone" in Domesday, i.e. "farm of the sons of Hygered." Its modern form, which occurs in 1535, gave its name to the peerage of Arlington by a curious slip, the H having been accidentally omitted by the clerk who made out the patent to Henry Bennet, who owned land in the village. This is confirmed by Pepys, who writes in his *Diary* for September 8, 1665: "He showed me my Lord Arlington's house that he was born in, in a towne called Harlington." Cranford is spelt "Cranforde" in Domesday, and is explained by Mr. Gover as "ford frequented by cranes" or "ford over which a crane could wade," while the name of the River Crane is assumed by him to be "a back formation." Dawley (an obscure hamlet associated with several important people, including Bolingbroke, Pope, Swift, and Voltaire) appears in Domesday as "Dallega," and seems to have an affinity with our overworked word "dole," in this case meaning perhaps land parcelled out to various owners. Yeading, pronounced "Yedding" and so spelt from the fourteenth century up to recent times, occurs in the eighth century as "Geddinges," signifying "the place of the sons of Gedd (or Geddi)." Botwell is almost as old, and means "the well or spring of Bota or Boda."

The new urban district of Hayes and Harlington is, like Uxbridge and some other neighbouring townships, an artificial union of several old parishes; in this case Hayes, Harlington, and Cranford, united so recently as 1930, when Harlington and Cranford were taken from the Staines Rural District. Of these, Hayes was much the largest in area, and Cranford much the smallest. The new district has a total area of 5,513 acres, that is, about 8½ square miles.

In 1801 the combined population of Hayes, Harlington, and Cranford was 1,601, and in 1851 it reached 3,385, thus having just doubled in fifty years. During the next half-century very little growth took place, and in 1901 the figure was only 4,772, or less

* J. E. B. Gover, *The Place-names of Middlesex*.

than one person per acre. The 1911 census recorded 7,250, the following one 9,705, but then came a sudden upward leap, and in 1931 the population had reached 23,649, an increase of 144 per cent on the figure for 1921. This sensational growth, though surpassed in Middlesex by Kingsbury and Wembley, is startling even in this record-breaking county; and, as building is still

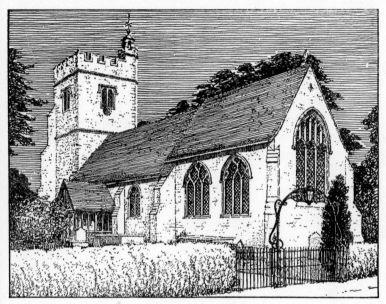

HARLINGTON CHURCH

proceeding frantically in several parts of the district, it is likely to be followed by more hideous revelations in 1941. At all events, no one can now be in any doubt as to the future of Hayes and Harlington: it is bound to become a large town with an industrial centre, and contains space to house 200,000 or 250,000 people with ease.

The general question of industrial expansion in West Middlesex will be touched upon in the next chapter, and the topic of disappearing agriculture in the one following, but something must be said here of the natural geography of the Hayes district. The land is very nearly flat. Its sole natural watercourse is the River Crane, known in its upper reaches as the Yeading Brook, a somewhat prosaic stream north of the Great Western Railway, but very attractive as it passes through Cranford Park. Here it has been artificially widened, and is well wooded. There is a charming ornamental bridge in the park, another of the hump-backed type near Cranford Village, and a "water-splash" between Cranford and Hayes. The Grand Union Canal traverses the district from east to west, and must have played some part in its industrial expansion. It is strange that this now busy area with its hordes of workers contains less than 2 miles of railway and only one station, over which the crowded highway from Twickenham and Feltham to Harrow and the North is constricted on a narrow bridge which, in these days, is a disgrace to all concerned. From Hayes to Yeading this important road has already been widened, and a bypass has been constructed round that ugly little village. But the southern part will certainly need early attention to cope with the now heavy traffic that roars past Harlington Church. The main London–Oxford Road and the Bath Road through Cranford have already been widened and straightened, their bridges over the Crane rebuilt, and the greater part of their elms cut down. Ribbon development has made great strides here, with long lines of blatant hoardings and screaming petrol-pumps to vary the monotony of "Distinctive Homes" and builders' advertisements. There is a glaring contrast between the Uxbridge Road at Hayes, with its cinemas and its canned music, on the one hand, and the surroundings of the old church, not half a mile away, on the other. The urban council occupies the former country home of some eminent (or at any rate prosperous) Victorian, formerly known as Barra Hall, a curious name for such a dwelling, and probably—like most things in modern Hayes—an importation. It has charming and well-kept gardens.

Harlington and Cranford are beginning to feel the squeeze of suburbia, but the surroundings of Cranford Park are still the most attractive and rural corner of the whole district. This brings us to the very important question of public open spaces and reservations

under the Town Planning Acts. In this respect credit must be
given to the local authorities for great foresight and an admirable
scheme, worthy of attention by more backward districts. In spite
of the few existing defects already mentioned—the refuse-dump
and the caravan-settlement at Yeading, and the dangerous railway
bridge at Hayes—the whole area has been planned out for future
development on sound lines, and provision has been made for open
spaces on a scale that will satisfy even the idealists. The land

HAYES CHURCH, THE PORCH

actually acquired includes Cranford Park with the old mansion
(148 acres), part of the Yeading Brook reservation (137 acres),
the recreation grounds at Barra Hall and Cranford, and Wood End
Green—some 345 acres in all, excluding allotment grounds. To
these must be added two large reservations under the town-planning
scheme, viz. the remainder of the Yeading Brook strip (125 acres),
Botwell Common (9 acres), and some land near the town hall.
Thus the district has acquired or reserved a total area of 490 acres
for public open spaces, and this includes those parts which contain
the most attractive survivals of its former rural scenery.

The town still lacks a public library. When that comes, it should contain a collection of records and illustrations of the old buildings and vanished beauties of the district. The three parish churches still remain, and are not likely to be disturbed. St. Mary's at Hayes, restored by Sir Gilbert Scott in 1873, is a large flint building with a thirteenth-century chancel, an aisled nave of the sixteenth century with a fine wooden roof, a sturdy tower, and a beautiful timbered south porch closely resembling that at Harlington. The interior contains an interesting medieval wall-painting, a piscina, three sedilia, a pulpit of 1726, and several noteworthy sculptured monuments and brasses. The remarkable lych-gate outside is so like that at Heston that it seems probable that the same craftsman was employed. Hayes Church is mentioned several times in John Wesley's *Journals* (1750–4).

Harlington Church (St. Peter and St. Paul) is another building of great artistic merit and interest, and is in excellent preservation, except the tower, which is in need of attention. It was restored in 1880. Here the nave is Norman, since altered, and the chancel Decorated. There is a fine carved Norman doorway, protected by the charming south porch (*c.* 1500) mentioned above. Other features of note are the Norman font, a fine Easter sepulchre in the chancel, and a number of interesting monuments and brasses.

Cranford Church (St. Dunstan) is small and is mainly a building of Queen Anne's time, but contains portions of a much older structure and a remarkable collection of large monuments, including one to Thomas Fuller, the historian, formerly rector of the parish. The adjoining mansion in Cranford Park is a depressing block of no obvious interest, erected in the middle of the eighteenth century, but the adjoining stables compete in magnificence with those at Osterley and Swakeleys. The whole of this extensive property now belongs to the town, and it will be interesting to see what happens to the buildings. For the rest, the district is not rich in old houses, and the only remains of Dawley Court, the famous house where Lord Bolingbroke entertained Pope and Swift and Voltaire in great splendour from 1726 to 1735, are said to be preserved in the steward's house which "may be seen between the railway and the canal on the road from Harlington to Hillingdon."* The Manor House (formerly the Rectory) at Hayes has a long history, and Cranmer once lived there, but it is difficult nowadays to ascertain how much of its fabric is original, so much has it been restored. It has recently been bought, with its beautiful grounds, by the Middlesex County Council as a site for a secondary school.

* J. B. Firth, *Middlesex*, p. 129.

BOOKS ON LOCAL HISTORY AND TOPOGRAPHY

[HAYES U.D.C.]	Hayes, Harlington, and Cranford: Official Guide	London	N.D.
MILLS, T.	History of Parish of Hayes	London	1874
WILSON, REV. H.	Eight Hundred Years of Harling ton Parish Church	Uxbridge	1909

CHAPTER XXI

SOUTHALL–NORWOOD

THIS busy urban district, now humming with industry, has changed greatly during the last century, when it was thus described in a miniature geography of Middlesex*:

> Southall is a small village on the Uxbridge Road, famous for its large cattle market, which is held every Wednesday. At Norwood, in the vicinity, are some alms-houses and other charitable institutions.

The cattle market still continues, on a much smaller scale, but otherwise the above description no longer holds good. Writing so far back as 1909, Mr. Walter Jerrold† dismisses Southall in one line as a "new, tram-made suburb" in a district which "is flat and has no particular claims to beauty"; while Mr. C. G. Harper,‡ writing two years earlier, is still more uncomplimentary:

> Southall, although it possesses a quaint and interesting old manor-house . . . has become in these latter days a crowded and rather grim and striving place, with great gasworks and manufactories of margarine, and its ancient manor-house stands in what is now a mean street of crowded traffic.

These descriptions are only too true to-day, though other important industries have to be added to gas and margarine, and Southall now covers a far larger area than it did twenty-five years ago. But it is only fair to add that both the writers quoted have pleasant things to say about Norwood Green, which still retains some part of the dignity and charm which it had in the past, and that the north portion of the Osterley Park Estate, described in Chapter XXIV, lies within the Southall–Norwood boundary, on the south side of Norwood Green. Southall itself is completely suburban and utterly modern. A development company with a Hebraic name is blotting

* The History and Topography of Middlesex (Pinnock's County Histories), 1824, p. 38.

† W. Jerrold, Highways and Byways in Middlesex, p. 122.

‡ C. G. Harper, Rural Nooks round London, p. 98.

out the only field remaining near its centre, while the usual cinemas and multiple shops line the busy pavements thronged with immigrants from all parts of Britain, who live in depressing streets built in the nineties or in more imaginative "housing schemes" of our own day. Southall is not devoid of distinctive characteristics, for—besides Norwood Green and the old Manor House—it has gasworks of appalling magnitude, a huge mental hospital, and two sections of the Grand Union Canal. The largest gasholder, nearly

NORWOOD GREEN

280 feet high and over 200 feet in diameter, is politely described by one writer as "a landmark for miles around"; that description is surely euphemistic, and one hopes that science will devise some means of eliminating these abortions or rendering them invisible.

In such a mushroom-town, with only a sprinkling of inhabitants born within its boundaries, there is a need that some effort should be made to collect and preserve some records of the past before the combined assault of industry and suburbia has trampled every vestige of antiquity out of existence. Southall is ahead of some districts of Middlesex in having a small public library where this work has been begun, but the only attempt at a local history

is a small and unambitious booklet which has long been unobtainable.

Southall has an old name, which first occurs, early in the
thirteenth century, as "Sudhale," meaning "South nook or corner,"
as opposed to Northolt ("Northale"). But it was a mere hamlet in
the parish of Norwood up to modern times. The derivation of
Norwood is obvious, and it appears as "Northwode" in 1294.*
A far more interesting name is "Chevy Chace," so spelt on
Cruchley's map of 1840. It appears as "Chivoy Chace" on Cary's
map of 1800, and as "Cheaffey Chace" on Rocque's map of
1741–5. The name refers to the short length of the main London–
Oxford Road from Hanwell Bridge (over the Brent) to Windmill
Lane. Having hitherto associated it only with the famous ballad
describing the fight of Chevy Chase near Otterburn, in the Cheviots,
in 1388, it was a complete surprise to me to find the name inscribed
on maps of Middlesex, and I am unable to offer any explanation
of its meaning. The cheerful suggestion of a local author,† that
here "no doubt Edward the Confessor used to meet when he came
to Norwood to hunt the wild boar," is picturesque but not con-
vincing, and he gives no authority for his idea. As for "Mount
Pleasant," which appears on all the three maps mentioned, that
name has long lost its previous significance, the site being a trifling
elevation and pleasant no more.

The modern urban district of Southall–Norwood has an area
of 2,575 acres, or about 4 square miles.

The population of the old parish of Norwood, corresponding
with the modern urban district of Southall–Norwood, was only
697 in 1801. It rose to 2,693 in 1851, 4,484 in 1861, 5,882 in
1871, 6,681 in 1881, 7,627 in 1891, 12,499 in 1901, 26,323 in
1911, 30,287 in 1921, and 38,932 in 1931. Building is proceeding
rapidly in several parts of the district, and the population must
considerably exceed 40,000 to-day. The density (14·7 persons per
acre in 1931) is not high, and at fifty persons per acre there is
ample room for 135,000 inhabitants. But it is very unlikely that

---

* J. E. B. Gover, *The Place-names of Middlesex*.
† S. G. Short, *Southall and its Environs* (1910), p. 11.

so large a figure will ever be reached. The area occupied by the asylum, the gasworks, and the factories already erected is already very extensive; and, after deducting other areas purchased or reserved for open spaces, it appears that Southall need not anticipate a total population of more than 80,000 even if all available land be built over.

The area actually acquired for public open spaces, excluding

SOUTHALL MANOR HOUSE

allotments, amounts to 116 acres, and includes Southall Park and Norwood Green as well as three somewhat depressing recreation grounds. On the basis of 10 per cent of the total acreage, this allowance is meagre, but there is also a large area reserved, between the Brent and the Greenford Road, which will improve the position. Unfortunately, only a small part of the land now occupied by the West Middlesex Golf Club is reserved under the town-planning scheme.

Except for Norwood Green itself, it cannot be pretended that Southall includes much natural scenery worthy of preservation, and the filling in of the beautiful pond on Norwood Green in order to widen the busy road to Heston and Hounslow is a regrettable loss to that charming corner. Further road-widening is inevitable, and the narrowness of the railway bridge at Southall Station, if not so dangerous as that at Hayes, will soon require alteration. The canals in the district are picturesque and comparatively busy. The chalybeate springs which gave the name to Dormer's Wells Farm, the quaint wooden water-mill in Windmill Lane, the medieval bridge over the Brent, the stocks near the Co-operative Stores, and the blacksmith's forge at the corner of South Road and High Street, have all disappeared in recent times, together with many old houses and cottages.

Of the few old houses still remaining, the Manor House is by far the most important. It is dated 1581, and is now public property, but it was restored drastically in 1847–8 (an unfortunate period), and looks it. The modern additions made then or at some subsequent date betray a heavy hand, and have detracted from the appearance of the old part of the building which is shown in my sketch. In Southall High Street there is Grove House, while the "Red Lion" and the "George and Dragon" still retain some old features, though the "White Hart" has just been demolished. Bridge House on Norwood Green is another old building, with excellent iron gates. Near the church is a curious old school, still in use, bearing the inscription: "A FREE SCHOOL, ERECTED BY E.B., 1767." Norwood Church, an old foundation rebuilt in 1439, has been so drastically restored, in 1864 and 1896, that its aspect has been completely changed. Surviving medieval features include the south doorway, the font, a few windows, and some of the timber-framing of the former belfry. Originally it had the small wooden turret and the dormer-windows characteristic of Middlesex. It is illustrated by Lysons (*Environs of London*, III, 322).

Southall shares with Hayes, Acton, Willesden, and part of the Lea Valley the distinction of being a prominent industrial district of changing Middlesex. Regret for this change is quite futile; it has come to stay, and we must accept it. Its effects are not so disastrous as in some of the northern strongholds of nineteenth-century industrialism, because electric power has largely eliminated smoke, and most modern factories, designed to produce a large output from contented workers, are a great advance on those which made England prosperous fifty years ago. But this sudden industrial expansion in West Middlesex, spreading a huge population of immigrants over a district hitherto engrossed in market-gardening and occasional brickmaking, has found the authorities in some cases unprepared; and has certainly proved the need for attention to the various problems which are now generally described as "town-planning."

BOOKS ON LOCAL HISTORY AND TOPOGRAPHY

SHORT, S. G.   Southall and its Environs   London   1910
[SOUTHALL U.D.C.]   Southall and Norwood: Official   London   N.D.
                       Guide

CHAPTER XXII

FELTHAM

INCLUDING EAST BEDFONT, HANWORTH, AND HATTON

IF the more intelligent inhabitants of Middlesex were required to answer an examination question somewhat on these lines—"State all you know of the town of Feltham, its imports, exports, and geographical features"—it is certain that a large number of blank papers would be received and that the number of high marks awarded would be very few. Yet Feltham has a much larger population than the city of Durham, or the town of Warwick, or many others of historical importance. Its principal exports are fire extinguishers, mushrooms, gravel, lettuces, reformed boys from the Borstal School, and firearms. Its principal imports are juvenile "criminals" (the raw material of the Borstal Schools), building materials, and human beings from all over England who presumably come to live in Feltham because the house agents tell them to do so, no other very obvious explanation being apparent. Feltham is full of "strangers," of people who have just arrived and have not yet found their feet. Other outstanding features of Feltham include an incredible number of "Ideal Homesteads by Britain's Best and Biggest Builders," or so they say; the enormous marshalling yards of the Southern Railway with 25 miles of sidings; the altogether hideous depot of the Army Service Corps; the large reservoirs at Hanworth; and the Hanworth Air Park with its curious types of aircraft. Feltham has established its Council Offices in a Victorian house with a charming garden, near the station, but it has not yet obtained a public library of its own, nor has it occurred to anyone to write a local history book.

The four names at the head of this chapter all occur in Domesday. Feltham is older still, and appears precisely in its present form as early as 969. Its origin seems to have something to do with "felt," which is an Anglo-Saxon word. Bedfont is spelt

"Bedefunt" in Domesday, and means "the well or spring of Beda."
Hanworth figures as "Haneworde" in Domesday: that is, "the
farm of Hana"; while Hatton ("Hattone" in Domesday) is
probably "the farm on the heath."[*] Yet, in spite of its old name,
Feltham is another of the Middlesex mushroom towns. The parish
became an urban district in 1903, with an area of only 1,798 acres
and a population of about 5,000. In 1930 the adjoining parishes
of East Bedfont and Hanworth were added, increasing the total
area to 5,089 acres, about 8 square miles.

The recent proposals of the County Council for the redistribution
of districts in Middlesex do not materially affect the area or
boundaries of Feltham, some 27 acres being transferred to adjoining
districts. The population of this large area is even now comparatively
sparse, with a density of only 3·2 persons per acre. In 1801 the
total population of its three component parishes was only 1,410,
and fifty years later only 2,934. The growth then proceeded very
gradually until it reached 8,824 in 1901, 9,749 in 1911, and
11,567 in 1921. Then came the sudden spurt which affected so
much of West Middlesex during the last decade, and between 1921
and 1931 the number of inhabitants jumped to 16,316, an increase
of 41 per cent in ten years. Judging by the rate at which "Ideal
Homesteads" are being rushed up, and knowing that a thousand
houses of various types have been erected during the past year, it
is safe to assume that the present population of Feltham exceeds
20,000, and will soon be far more. The existence of the great
marshalling yards, the reservoirs, the Air Force Depot, and the
Borstal institution will prevent the whole district being closely
built up, and thus carrying its quota of a quarter of a million people
at fifty persons per acre.

But it can and almost certainly will carry a far larger population
than it has at present, so that due precautions should already have
been taken to deal with such an eventuality. To an impartial
observer it appears that this provision has not been made, and that
unless it is made at once the chance will have gone and Feltham
will become, as it now tends to become, a thoroughly undis-

[*] J. E. B. Gover, *The Place-names of Middlesex*.

tinguished and eventually even a squalid suburban area. Town-planning does not consist simply in cutting down trees and widening roads; in those respects Feltham has made great strides. It involves vision and preparation for the future. The regional report of the West Middlesex Regional Town Planning Committee observed, even in 1924, that "there is a good opportunity in Feltham of creating a fine civic centre adjoining the station," and that is a point that should be borne in mind so that, looking ahead, suitable sites may be reserved for municipal and commercial buildings. More immediately urgent is the provision or reservation of public open spaces. The amount of land actually acquired in this very large area is less than 30 acres, whereas according to modern ideas of town-planning it ought to be at least 500 acres. One can sympathize with the difficulties of a small local authority which has to cope with a population increasing by leaps and bounds, so rapidly that the existing machinery of government has constantly to be extended and modified, and the rateable value of the district is an uncertain quantity. Less than thirty years ago Feltham was an overgrown village: now it is having to face heavy municipal commitments.

Yet it remains true that 30 acres of open spaces is a ridiculously inadequate allowance for a large town, and that the price of land in Feltham is rocketing upwards at an absurd rate: so that market-gardens worth £80 an acre not long ago are now being sold as building land for three or four times that price. They will then be cut up into small slices and resold at an enhanced profit, until perhaps agricultural land in Feltham will rise in price—as it has risen in my own district—to £800 or £1,000 an acre on a main road. How is it possible, objectors may ask, for a small authority with limited resources, to reserve Hanworth Park Aerodrome for an open space, as recommended by the West Middlesex Committee, when the cost of its 200 acres is becoming annually more pro-hibitive—and indeed, why reserve it at all when it is an aerodrome? Taking the last objection first, the answer is easy: a private aerodrome to-day may be building land to-morrow, and this has already happened to the aerodromes at Stag Lane and at Cricklewood. And the answer to the first point is the secret of all town-planning reservation in this county of Middlesex: if you do not acquire land for open spaces many years ahead of present needs, when you can reserve it before it becomes potential building land, you will find that, in popular jargon, you have "missed the bus." Suburban growth in Middlesex is so relentless, so inexorable, that it can be foretold now with almost mathematical accuracy, and the county provides innumerable examples. There is already a

LOWER FELTHAM IN 1933

girdle of "Ideal Homesteads" round most of Hanworth Park, and the hideous A.S.C. dump has occupied its western end, but if Hanworth Park cannot now be considered, for financial reasons, then some other provision should be made. Nothing appears to have been done to acquire the other land recommended as an open space by the West Middlesex Committee in 1924, viz. the strip along the banks of the Yeading Brook, and here again early action is desirable. Another detail of town-planning that will arise is the future of the large areas where gravel has been excavated, now forming shallow lagoons. Are these to be filled with rat-ridden refuse, reinforced with bits of discarded motors and rusty fruit tins, and then to be offered to eager brides as sites for "Ideal Home-steads"? Or will they eventually become the only playground of Young Feltham a generation hence?

Mention of canned fruit suggests another line of thought. It has long seemed to me deplorable that agricultural districts such as Feltham, Hayes, and Heston, where market-gardening has become a fine art and where expensive delicacies such as mushrooms and lettuce are grown close to the great consuming population of London, should be given over to suburban dwellers who cheerfully order their vegetables from abroad and so diminish our trade balance. If a green girdle round north-west Middlesex has been judged necessary for purposes of recreation and scenic enjoyment, surely a girdle of market-gardens in south-west Middlesex is equally important for other and more obviously practical reasons? Yet here again we have "missed the bus," and the patient labours of centuries are being thoughtlessly swept away. Acres of glass-houses, of orchards, and of intensively cultivated lettuce-beds, mushroom-beds, and the like are disappearing almost daily. When the Board of Agriculture in 1793 instituted a county survey of Middlesex,* they learned that southern Middlesex "may be reckoned the great garden, to the north of the Thames, for the supply of London," and they severely censured those lax landlords who allowed any part of their land to remain uncultivated, with such a market available. Hounslow Heath extended up to Feltham, but south and west of that village the whole area was arable land. Since then market-gardening has spread all over this part of Middlesex, and it is only in recent years that any serious diminution of the highly cultivated area has taken place, as also in the Lea Valley at the other end of the county.

The Feltham district contains few important historical buildings. Feltham Parish Church was entirely rebuilt in 1802 and enlarged in 1856. The brick tower has some dignity and even charm for an austere taste, though it does not please all critics. Hanworth Church

---

* *General View of the Agriculture of the County of Middlesex*, by Thomas Baird (1793); *General View of the Agriculture of the County of Middlesex*, by Peter Foot (1794).

was rebuilt in 1865 in an extremely orthodox and correct Gothic style, but a considerable part of the fourteenth-century fabric is said to be embodied in the present structure. East Bedfont, however, possesses an old church of real interest in a beautiful setting on a practically unspoiled village green near to the London–Staines Road. The quaintly cut yew-trees outside the church are over two hundred years old. There is a Norman south door, a low Norman chancel arch, some original Gothic windows, and some medieval wall-paintings, but the rather freakish spire is modern and ugly.

Apart from a few old houses at Old Feltham, Hatton, and East Bedfont, the only domestic building of historical interest is "Tudor Court" at Hanworth, formerly known as "Queen Elizabeth's Stables," and now divided into flats. Parts of this perplexing structure—such as the huge brick fireplaces and the two terra-cotta busts of Roman emperors—are certainly Tudor work, approximately coeval with the older portions of Hampton Court. But their precise relation to the adjoining relics (including a moat) of Henry VIII's royal residence of Hanworth, subsequently favoured by Queen Elizabeth, is very obscure; and a cursory inspection of "Tudor Court" leaves one in doubt on the whole problem of its history. Obviously it contains fragments of the past, perhaps substantial fragments, but as obviously it has been greatly altered and enlarged within the past hundred years.

Among modern buildings, Feltham possesses a splendid church tower (St. Catherine's) near the station, built in 1898 and forming a landmark for miles round: an admirably designed factory belonging to the Minimax Company, on the London–Staines road; an interesting Roman Catholic church on the Green; and some good modern design in the latest buildings at the Hanworth Waterworks.

BOOKS ON LOCAL HISTORY AND TOPOGRAPHY

FELTHAM U.D.C.   Feltham: Official Guide   London   N.D.

CHAPTER XXIII

BRENTFORD AND CHISWICK

THE last six chapters of this book describe the Thames-side districts, perhaps the part of Middlesex that is best known to the average person, and the part that may be regarded as London's most important playground. Some of the ground is covered by the West Middlesex Regional Town Planning Report published in 1924, but that report excludes the districts of Twickenham, Teddington, Hampton Wick, and Hampton. Another regional report, *The Thames from Putney to Staines*, published in 1930, is only concerned with the portions of these districts which border on the river, and takes no account of the hinterland. My own method of treatment continues the process followed in previous chapters, and describes each of the new boroughs and urban districts as a separate entity, attempting to create a sense of local interest, civic consciousness, and responsibility which is only too often lacking in communities composed largely of an immigrant population with no roots in the soil.

The two towns of Brentford and Chiswick were amalgamated into a single urban district in 1927, and obtained a charter of incorporation as a municipal borough in 1932. This artificial union was presumably made for purposes of administrative convenience, but in many ways it is regrettable. Both Brentford and Chiswick —unlike the groups of villages forming the nucleus of other new districts of Middlesex—were clearly defined communities of some importance; each with its administrative machinery, its long tradition, its history books, its library, and its collection of local antiquities. It is true that the chapelry of Old Brentford was only transferred from Ealing parish in 1863 (cf. page 179), but from those days up to 1927 the two Brentfords were sharply separated from the parish of Chiswick.

Brentford, the old capital of Middlesex, still retains its Petty Sessions, even its Custom House at the docks, but the administrative work of the county is now all concentrated at the Middlesex Guildhall in Westminster (which, as was pointed out at the beginning of this book, is not in Middlesex at all). Brentford, nevertheless, boasts the most notable record in all the county, thus

BRENTFORD: THE MOUTH OF THE BRENT
In background: Kew Gardens

inscribed on the four sides of a plain granite stone near the ferry steps:

B.C. 54. At this ancient fortified ford the British tribesmen under Cassivelaunus bravely opposed Julius Caesar on his march to Verulamium.

A.D. 1909. The identity of the place has been recently established by the discovery of lines of oak palisades extending both along this bank, and in the bed of the river, and brought to public notice by Montagu Sharpe, Esq., D.L., Chairman of Quarter Sessions and County Council of Middlesex.

A.D. 780–1. Near by Offa, King of Mercia, with his Queen, the bishops and principal officers, held a Council of the Church.

A.D. 1016. Here Edmund Ironside, king of England, drove Cnut and his defeated Danes across the Thames.

A.D. 1642. Close by was fought the battle of Brentford, between the forces of King Charles I and the Parliament.

Much later, in the eighteenth century, there was an extraordinary but apparently quite serious offer to the Government from the Jewish community in England to buy the whole town of Brentford for £500,000 and form a Zionist colony there. The rejection of that offer has thus deprived Middlesex of a New Jerusalem, and has allowed Brentford to develop the county's greatest and (with the possible exception of the Alexandra Palace and the gasholders at Harrow and Southall) its most hideous eyesore, in the huge and untidy mass of buildings for the Gas Company along the riverside, mercifully sheltered from Kew Gardens over the water by the trees and undergrowth of Brentford Ait.

Chiswick is as different from Brentford as cheese is from chalk. One's first reaction to the name is a thought of artists, printing presses, and the Boat Race. A little reflection recalls the memory of Pope and Hogarth and Burlington, of Zoffany at Strand-on-the-Green, of Becky Sharp at school, of Beerbohm Tree returning late at night to Walpole House from histrionic impersonations of Shylock. If the swish of aristocratic and ghostly satin skirts is not quite so audible in Chiswick as in Twickenham, it still lingers in the stately apartments of Chiswick House and in the old houses along the Mall. In those cultured corners something of the storied past remains, but most of the district is now covered with suburban villas, traversed by a roaring flood of traffic, and includes the enormous repair shops of the London Transport Board.

The name of Brentford would seem to need no explanation, for, although in its earliest form, in A.D. 705, it appears as "Breguntford," the name of the River Brent itself was once "Braegenta," probably a Celtic or pre-Celtic word according to Mr. Gover.* However, one may still speculate as to the origin of "Braegenta," variously explained as the name of one *Brigantios*—a Celtic chief—a clan *Brigantia*, or even *Brennius*, son of the reputed British chief of the Trinobantes. Brentford contains many very old names: "Troy Town," "Old England," "Half Acre," "The Butts," and "Town Meadow"—now a little slum. Chiswick, originally "Chesewyk," is confidently defined by Mr. Gover as

* J. E. B. Gover, *The Place-names of Middlesex*.

"cheese farm or dwelling," and he adds that "the flat meadow lands in the neighbourhood were doubtless early recognized as rich pasture grounds." However, Miss Gilbert, the latest local historian, is prepared to break a lance with him, and prefers the derivation suggested many years ago by the Rev. F. W. Isaacs, "the *wic* or village by the stony landing place or beach. Such a stony landing place still exists at our ferry."* Gunnersbury, which appears in the fourteenth century as "Gunnyldesbury," is the stronghold of some chieftainess, "Gunhild" or "Gunilda." Strand-on-the-Green,

CHISWICK FROM THE SURREY SIDE

spelt "Stranda" in a document of 1219, has an obvious meaning of "margin" or "shore," because its little row of houses lies along the shore of the Thames. Turnham Green eludes the ingenious Mr. Gover, but Miss Gilbert says that "the name 'Turnham' is said to be derived from one of the older lessees or tenants of the manor, a Thomas Thornham."† The same writer explains that Bedford Park was so called after the arboretum formerly occupying the site, which was owned by Mr. Jonathan Carr, of Bedford House, Turnham Green.‡

The borough of Brentford and Chiswick, which comprises the

* M. Gilbert, *Chiswick Old and New* (London, 1932), p. 10.
† *Ibid.*, p. 14.   ‡ *Ibid.*, pp. 19–20.

ancient parishes of Old Brentford, New Brentford, and Chiswick, has an area of 2,341 acres, or nearly 4 square miles. Of this area Chiswick provides 1,250 acres (not 13,396, as Mr. Warwick Draper rashly asserts!).* The rectifications of boundary recently recommended by the County Council affect the total area very slightly and are based entirely on common sense, the tongue of Acton which now projects to Chiswick High Road being sheared off so that Chiswick will extend up to the District Railway line. The southern boundary of the borough is the Thames, the western boundary the Brent, and the eastern boundary (between Chiswick and London) marks the line of the now buried Stamford Brook.

It is difficult to disentangle the census figures of the three component parishes of the borough during the nineteenth century, because Old Brentford formed a part of Ealing parish up to 1863. Chiswick itself had a population of 3,235 in 1801, 6,303 in 1851, 6,505 in 1861, and 8,508 in 1871. Then came a rapid increase: 15,972 in 1881, 21,965 in 1891, and 29,804 in 1901. New Brentford had 1,443 inhabitants in 1801, 2,063 in 1851, and only 2,029 in 1901. The present century has seen the usual rapid growth characteristic of modern Middlesex, the population of the present borough area being 55,268 in 1911, 57,970 in 1921, and 62,617 in 1931. There is a good deal of building in progress near Grove Park and near the new Great West Road, so a considerable increase may still be expected, but it is most unlikely that the population will ever reach 100,000, as large areas are unavailable for housing development, either because they are in use for industrial purposes or because they have been acquired as public open spaces. The density of population in 1931 was twenty-seven persons per acre.

The district is almost dead level. The subsoil consists of gravel and sand, with patches of brick-earth. Up to quite recent times the greater part of the area was covered with orchards and market-gardens, fragments of which survive north of Brentford and near Gunnersbury Lane. Peter Foot, writing in 1794, reported to the Board of Agriculture that Chiswick barley was "distinguished for

* Warwick Draper, *Chiswick* (1923), p. 5.

its good quality, and has been much sought after for seed." For this reason, he deprecated the substitution of market-gardens for cornfields, a process then just beginning. A year earlier Thomas Baird, also reporting to the Board of Agriculture, had made the comment quoted in my last chapter (page 238). A few years later Lysons estimated that Chiswick contained 1,200 acres, of which 300 were corn land, 300 market-gardens, and 200 under grass,

HOGARTH HOUSE, CHISWICK

exclusive of parks, paddocks, and private pleasure grounds. Most of the area between Turnham Green, Duke's Avenue, and Barrowgate Road was occupied by the gardens of the Royal Horticultural Society from 1822 until 1904, when this popular resort of fashion was abandoned to the speculative builder.

Of the various streams which form the boundaries of the borough on three sides, the Thames is the most important. From Kew Bridge to the London frontier it encloses Chiswick in a generous bend and has an ample width. For half this distance one may walk along the bank, and the chief remaining task for the burgesses of Chiswick is to ensure that in the future the promenade may be continuous. From Kew Bridge to the mouth of the Brent, a matter of three-quarters of a mile, no such desirable objective can ever be reached, for there is an unbroken line of gasworks, docks, and wharves. But with inscrutable foresight, Providence has not only provided a screen of thickly wooded islands to shelter these hideosities from Kew Gardens on the other side, but has also thought fit to include them within the county of Surrey which, one may hope, will see that they are never built upon. Chiswick Ait or Eyot—a charming old name—is covered with muddy willows, and at low water can be reached from the Mall. It also should be prevented from ever becoming a building site. This portion of the Thames has none of the beauty of the upper reaches, but it has a charm of its own, enhanced by swans and barges, with the occasional added excitement of a racing "eight."

The Brent at Brentford Docks is quite a substantial stream, and where it passes Boston Manor Park—a little higher up—is positively attractive. The small tongue of land across the Brent, occupied by the Great Western Railway's warehouses, bears the significant name of "Old England," and has yielded such an amazing quantity of weapons and other relics, from the Neolithic period onwards, that it may be regarded as the cradle of Middlesex history. Of the Stamford Brook and the Bollo Brook, minor streams forming parts of the east and north boundaries of the district, enough has been said already (page 169). Then there is the Grand Union Canal, of which this section of the Brent forms a part, and at Brentford it always provides plenty of life.

The old Roman Road from London to Staines is still the chief artery of the district. It was cleverly aligned at a tangent to the Thames near Kew Bridge, but its original line from Shepherd's Bush to Kew is not now easy to follow. It may be traced westwards along Bath Road, whence the borough boundary (now to be altered) gives a straight line across Chiswick Common and the railway line to a small street significantly named "Chiswick Road." Then the present tram-ridden Chiswick High Road, past Gunnersbury Station, deviates slightly from the direct line, but through Brentford the line is almost straight. Tolls for the maintenance of this great coaching road were instituted in 1769, and abolished in 1864. The abundance of old inns (now for the most part rebuilt) in Chiswick, and still more in Brentford, testify to its importance. Even in Ben Jonson's time they were famous, and he makes one of his characters suggest a visit to Brentford to "tickle it at the Pigeons," referring to a celebrated hostelry, "The Three Pigeons," recently burned down. When the electric tramway lines were first

BOSTON HOUSE, BRENTFORD

opened in 1901, and extended to Hampton Court in 1903, the narrow High Street of Brentford, which even now is only 19 feet wide at one point, became so congested that some alternative had to be devised. Hence the magnificent Great West Road, recently opened: a paradise for scorching motorists, a great place for consequent casualties, and now lined with some of the most splendid new factory buildings in England. Then there is the New Chertsey Road, cutting diagonally across Old Chiswick; and Gunnersbury Lane, now widened to become part of the new North Circular Road.

Brentford Bridge, a thirteenth-century structure with a chapel

adjoining, was rebuilt in 1740 and again in 1824. The first bridge
at Kew was of wood and was opened in 1759. A fine new stone
bridge followed in 1789, but was demolished to make way for the
present excellent bridge, opened by King Edward VII in 1903.
Just thirty years later the long-promised new bridge at Chiswick,
on the New Chertsey Road, was opened in 1933 by the Prince
of Wales.

With eight railway stations serving the borough of Brentford–
Chiswick, it is obviously a place easy of access, and one naturally
inquires what provision has been made to preserve its undoubted
amenities. It is heartening to find a local authority so far-sighted
and generous in its provision of open spaces. The town-planner's
ideal allowance of 1 acre of public open spaces for every 10 acres
in a district has actually been far exceeded if one includes, in the
present provision, the area (187 acres) of Gunnersbury Park,
which, though situated wholly within the borough boundaries, was
acquired jointly by Acton, Ealing, and Brentford–Chiswick in
1925. Yet even without this really noble possession, the area of
public open spaces in the borough amounts to 325 acres and
includes nearly every reservation proposed by the West Middlesex
Regional Report in 1924. Foremost among these spaces is Chiswick
House, the former residence of the Duke of Devonshire, who
lived here in almost royal state, and indeed it was for a short time
occupied by King Edward VII when he was Prince of Wales.
The beautiful grounds include a small lake and some magnificent
trees, comparable with those in Gunnersbury Park. Fifty years
ago most of Chiswick still belonged to the Duke, as the names of
"Duke's Avenue" and "The Duke's Meadows" still testify, while
"Burlington Lane" recalls the name of that gifted amateur
architect, the Earl of Burlington, an ancestor of the Duke's, who
built the fine mansion or "villa" now used as a civic art gallery.
South of the park, in the bend of the river, lay "The Duke's
Meadows," a large level area of over 150 acres, now also owned
by the corporation and laid out as sports grounds. Second only to
these remarkable acquisitions is Boston House with its gardens and
park (41 acres) at the other end of the borough. As previously

mentioned, it now only remains for the corporation to round off their scheme of town-planning, if possible, by purchasing a strip of land behind the houses in Hartington Road to give a continuous riverside walk all the way from Chiswick Bridge to Strand-on-the-Green; and finally, if and when funds and circumstances permit, to improve the riverside view of the hideous works south of Chiswick Church. The banks of the Brent, from Boston House to the borough boundary, have been preserved under the town-planning scheme.

The number of interesting old buildings in the borough exceeds that of any district of Middlesex, in spite of all which have been demolished during recent years. Among the latter may be mentioned Grove House (demolished 1928), Corney House (demolished 1832), Heathfield House (demolished 1837), Sutton Court (demolished 1897), and the charming Manor Farm House (demolished 1896), all at Chiswick; the picturesque Malthouse at Strand-on-the-Green; Noy's House and the Old Vicarage at Brentford (demolished 1889), and Brent House at Brentford, where Nell Gwyn is said to have lived (demolished 1909).

The old parish church of St. Nicholas at Chiswick is the most important ecclesiastical building still surviving, but was almost entirely rebuilt in 1884, the embattled stone tower being the only substantial relic of the medieval structure. There are, however, some interesting monuments within the church, and still more outside. Here are the tombs of Hogarth, of Kent, the architect and painter, who designed Chiswick House, and of his patron the Earl of Burlington. Much more of a surprise is the imposing tomb of "Richard Wright, Bricklayer, late Inhabitant of this Parish," who died in 1734, aged sixty-two years.

The parish church of New Brentford, dedicated to St. Lawrence, and also retaining its fifteenth-century tower, is mainly a building of 1762, during the curacy of the celebrated Horne Tooke. It contains several old monuments, including sculptured memorials by Flaxman and Westmacott.

The oldest important domestic building in the borough is probably Boston House at Brentford, occupied continuously by the Clitherow family—benefactors of Brentford—from 1671 to 1924, when it was bought for the public with its surrounding land. It seems uncertain when it was built. The beautiful "State Drawing-Room," one of the finest apartments in the county, bears the initials "M.R., 1623," referring to Lady Reade, the widow of Sir William Reade, who inherited the house in 1598. The rain-water heads outside the house are lettered "M.R., 1622," but it seems probable that the building owes many of its features to its restoration by James Clitherow in 1671. The cedars in the grounds are said to have been planted in 1574.*

Hogarth House, Chiswick, was erected about 1700, and was inhabited by the great painter from 1749 till his death in 1764. From 1814 to 1826 it was the home of Cary, the translator of Dante. It is related that Hogarth used to spend much of his leisure in smoking a pipe beneath the fine mulberry-tree that figures in my sketch. In 1902 the house was purchased by Lieut.-Col. Shipway, a local resident, who presented it to the Middlesex County Council as a Hogarth museum. The rooms are all panelled, and contain much of Hogarth's furniture, together with a number of his works.

Chiswick also possesses a Boston House, in Chiswick Square, off Burlington Lane. This beautiful little backwater now lies open to the New Chertsey Road, and it is to be hoped that Boston House itself stands sufficiently far back from that roaring artery to escape being shaken to pieces by the vibration of traffic. It seems to have been built about two hundred years ago by Lord Boston, and is now used as a welfare centre by the Chiswick Products Company. There is a fine staircase with twisted balusters, a chimney-piece and ceiling in the Adam style, and a very pleasant garden with cedar-trees.

Of the charming houses on Chiswick Mall, the most notable is Walpole House, which disputes with Boston House at Chiswick the honour of being the place where Becky Sharp, in her school-days, threw a lexicon at Miss Pinkerton. The latest historian of Chiswick† favours Walpole House in this dispute, pointing out

---

* J. B. Firth, *Middlesex* (2nd edition, 1930), p. 62.

† M. Gilbert, *Chiswick Old and New*, pp. 65–7.

that Thackeray himself was once at school there and furnishing other evidence. The house is said to have been "rebuilt" by Charles II for the famous, or infamous, Barbara Villiers.* It contains a fine staircase of that period, and has some admirable wrought-iron gates. From 1904 to 1910 it was occupied by Sir Herbert Beerbohm Tree. The present owner, Mrs. Benson, has

CHISWICK HOUSE
"Lord Burlington's Villa"

laid out an attractive formal garden behind the house. Adjoining old houses on the Mall are Strawberry House and Morton House (both of the late eighteenth century), and the large brick mansion now divided into "Bedford House" and "Eynham House." Near the church is an old brick schoolroom (1707), and the charming timber-framed house which was formerly the Burlington Arms, a building of great age. Brampton House has a dignified Georgian façade.

* M. Gilbert, *Chiswick Old and New*, p. 65.

Lastly, there is Chiswick House itself, built for that enthusiastic patron of architecture, Richard Boyle, third Earl of Burlington, in 1730 by the famous painter-architect William Kent, on the site of a much larger Elizabethan mansion acquired by the first earl, with its beautiful surroundings, for £4,600 in 1702. The "villa" or house which he erected was modelled on Palladio's celebrated Villa Capra near Vicenza in Italy, and it now forms the central block of the present structure, used as a municipal art gallery, but also containing a most depressing municipal café. It is the most stately and most Italian piece of architecture in Middlesex, and it hardly merits the scathing remark of a contemporary wit, "too small to live in and too large to hang on a watch-chain." The interior of the house is sumptuously decorated. Its beautiful grounds contain, besides a wealth of fine and exotic trees, a small lake originally fed by a canal constructed at vast expense, a classical bridge of perfect proportions (designed in 1788 by Wyatt, who also added the side-wings to the house), statues of Palladio and Inigo Jones, and a gateway—designed by Inigo Jones for Beaufort House at Chelsea in 1621, and presented by Sir Hans Sloane to Lord Burlington in 1737.

At Strand-on-the-Green a few old houses still remain, but none of them is of architectural importance.

Gunnersbury Park has an immensely long history, going far back to the castle of that Gunhild or Gunilda who was niece of King Cnut, and lived there long before the Norman Conquest, so it is suggested. At any rate, it was the home of a troublesome but beautiful "girl friend" of Edward III in the fourteenth century, passed through a series of famous hands, was purchased by Princess Amelia (daughter of George II) in 1761 and occupied by her until 1786, was later acquired by two members of the Rothschild family, and finally was purchased in 1925 by the joint Councils of Acton, Ealing, and Brentford–Chiswick. The two mansions which stand near together in the park are of no great age. One of them contains a large and valuable collection of Middlesex antiquities. The "temple" is officially ascribed to the seventeenth-century architect, John Webb, and some of the other outbuildings to Princess Amelia's time.

Brentford possesses Clifden House in Windmill Road, a stately mansion of the eighteenth century formerly belonging to Lord Clifden, and containing fine ceilings and carved woodwork; several picturesque old Georgian houses on "The Butts," especially Beaufort House, Chatham House, Linden House, and Cobham House; and some very fine wrought-iron gates with handsome piers outside the Congregational Church.

BOOKS ON LOCAL HISTORY AND TOPOGRAPHY

[BRENTFORD-CHISWICK U.D.]	Official Souvenir of . . . Incorporation	Chiswick	1933
DALE, L. W. T.	Notes on Chiswick Church	——	1884
DRAPER, WARWICK	Chiswick	London	1923
FAULKNER, T.	History and Antiquities of Brentford, Ealing, and Chiswick	London	1845
GILBERT, M.	Chiswick: Old and New	London	1932
ISAACS, F. W.	Brief Notes on Chiswick Church	——	1919
JENKINS, REV. R.	Sketch of the History of Turnham Green	Turnham Green	1849
MAXWELL, D.	A Pilgrimage of the Thames (Chapter XVII)	London	1932
PHILLIMORE, W. P., and WHITEAR, W. J.	Historical Collections relating to Chiswick	London	1897
PEEL, F. W.	Hogarth and his House	London	N.D.
SANDERS, LLOYD C.	Old Kew, Chiswick, and Kensington	London	1910
TURNER, F.	History and Antiquities of Brentford	Brentford	1922
	Brentford: Literary and Historical Sketches	London	1898
	Brentford and Chiswick: Official Guide	London	1833
Also:			
TIPPING, H. A.	Articles on Boston House, Chiswick House, and Gunnersbury Park, in *Country Life*	London	--

CHAPTER XXIV

HESTON AND ISLEWORTH

INCLUDING HOUNSLOW, LAMPTON, OSTERLEY, ST. MARGARET'S,
SCRATTAGE, AND SUTTON

WHEN the Urban District of Heston and Isleworth became a borough in 1932, it is to be presumed that the authorities gave due consideration to the name which it should bear. At any rate, they decided that the names of the two ancient parishes which form the modern borough should be preserved as a clumsy double-barrelled title, and that the equally ancient and far more familiar name of Hounslow—the portion of the area which accounts for more than half the inhabitants—should not be substituted as a single convenient name for the whole. To the average man, whether a citizen of Middlesex or not, Hounslow Heath is a household word: it rightly recalls to him the absurdly overdrawn exploits of the "Knights of the Road." Heston has an interesting church, but was unknown till its smart little airport brought it into the newspapers; and Isleworth, the home of Pears' soap, is familiar to riverside loungers mainly because Syon House lies within its borders. Hounslow is a somewhat squalid town containing a hideous block of barracks; Heston was, up to recent years, a pretty village surrounded by orchards; and Isleworth a picturesque riverside settlement with great flour mills. Now they, and their satellite hamlets, are all bunched together to form a single sprawling and amorphous borough. Yet, in spite of all these accidents and obstacles of birth, "Heston and Isleworth" is becoming a recognizable entity. It has a public library, its local history has been written, it has carried out an excellent housing scheme, and it has taken steps towards formulating a scheme of town-planning which will be satisfactory enough if only it can be realized.

The names of its component villages are for the most part as old as Domesday, though Heston is not found until *c.* 1180, when it occurs as "Hestune," a name of doubtful significance, possibly cognate with "Hayes." Isleworth appears as Gistelesworde in Domesday, and means "the farm of Gistel." Hounslow is spelt "Honeslauu" in Domesday and signifies literally "dog's mound," but actually "the mound of Hund," Hund being here a personal name. Osterley again is uncertain, and seems to indicate a sheepfold. Lampton is probably "lamb farm," and Sutton certainly "south farm." "Scrattage" is apparently inexplicable to Mr. Gover, from

ISLEWORTH FROM THE SURREY SIDE
The land on the right is scheduled as an "industrial area"

whose book* these derivations are taken; but he explains the name of "Worton," near Hounslow, as, probably, "kitchen-garden." "St. Margaret's" and "Spring Grove" appear to be modern names.

The area of the borough is 6,851 acres, or about 10½ square miles. The population of the area was 6,128 in 1801, and 12,209 in 1851. During the latter half of the nineteenth century growth was gradual, rising to a total of 30,863 in 1901. There were 43,313 inhabitants in 1911, 46,664 in 1921, and 75,446 (showing the enormous increase of 61·7 per cent in ten years) in 1931. There

* J. E. B. Gover, *The Place-names of Middlesex.*

is no doubt whatever that this figure will be substantially increased in the future, for building is proceeding apace in many parts of the district, and there is ample space for an ultimate population of 350,000.

Nevertheless, one cannot help wondering what is the attraction which brings these hordes of people into the borough. It is true that there is a certain amount of local industry; and this is likely to increase, judging from the erection of several new and large factories of various kinds near the Great West Road. It seems inconceivable that many of the inhabitants are drawn to the district by its natural scenery, still less by its historical associations, so one arrives at the conclusion that the double lure is the enterprise of the electric railways and the astuteness of house builders. The first of these factors is likely to operate more powerfully than ever with the recent extension of through fast Tube trains to Hounslow West; and the second is partly due to the activity of the municipality, which had advanced over £3,000,000 up to the end of 1932, "under the Small Dwellings Acquisition Acts, to enable persons to purchase houses for their own occupation, and it is estimated that one-half the houses in the district are owned by their occupiers."*

A somewhat optimistic paragraph in the Council's *Official Guide*, published a few years ago, suggests that climate is an additional factor, for one can "at times detect the sea salt upon one's lips as brought direct from the English Channel by some brisk southerly breeze." Nor is this all, for "even thunderstorms appear to vent their fury upon distant hills, rushing across the Hounslow plateau at amazing speed unchecked by any natural obstacle." A grain of salt is certainly necessary here. "Plateau" is a euphemism for a dreary waste with an elevation of 50 or 60 feet above sea-level, and in fact the whole district is very flat, rising from about 25 feet above sea-level in Isleworth to about 100 feet near Heston and Osterley. Its former allocation to market-gardens and orchards has led to a shortage of trees in many parts, but at least three areas are splendidly wooded: Osterley Park, Syon Park, and the banks of

---

* *Heston–Isleworth Charter Celebrations Souvenir Programme* (1932), p. 34.

the Crane. For the rest, occasional elm-trees form the chief feature in the rapidly disappearing landscape.

The district is traversed by several first-class highways: the old Roman Road from London via Brentford to Staines, the Bath Road which forks from it in the middle of Hounslow, and the fine new Great West Road. The equally straight road from Hounslow to Hanworth is becoming important, also the formerly quiet country lane through Heston to Southall, while even Cranford

OSTERLEY PARK

Lane, which passes Heston Airport, is destined to have a busy future. There is only one bridge across the Thames within the borough boundaries, the so-called "Twickenham Bridge" at St. Margaret's, opened in 1933, but this will be included in Twickenham under the County Council's proposal for the re-distribution of districts.

Of the open spaces in the area, Hounslow Heath used to be by far the most important, and is said to have extended over 6,658 acres even so lately as 1754, when highway robbery was at its zenith. From Hounslow it stretched west to Stanwell and Harmondsworth, north to Heston, south to Twickenham and Teddington. Of this storied and dreaded waste, only two fragments remain, so far as I am aware: the small area of genuine common near Heathrow, and the depressing patch of some 250 acres used "for military purposes"—whatever they may be—near Hounslow itself, and owned by the War Office. The latter fragment still retains the name of "Hounslow Heath."

The worthy Mr. Baird, reporting to the Board of Agriculture in 1793, wrote of it thus:

> Almost the whole of the heath is sacrificed to a few farmers who live on the borders of it, and put on immense quantities of greyhound-like sheep, that hunt about for their food, and devour with avidity every pile of grass they can meet with. These, with a few cottagers who cut turf or fuel for sale, and keep a parcel of ragged, shabby horses, that are continually breaking into the neighbouring fields, and doing mischief to their neighbours, are the only persons who have any benefit by the commons lying in their present uncultivated state.

Elsewhere he laments over the fact that Middlesex, in 1793, "to the astonishment of every foreigner who visits us," still contains

> many thousands of acres, still in a state of nature; and, though within a few miles of the capital, as little improved by the labour of man, as if they belonged to the Cherokees, or any other tribe of American savages.[*]

But Hounslow Heath was chiefly famous as a highwayman's paradise. Claude Duval operated on its lonely roads in Stuart times, and throughout the eighteenth century the "Knights of the Road" were a terror to all travellers. It is said that "the road beyond Hounslow was literally lined with gibbets, on which were in irons the carcases of malefactors blackening in the sun." At that time the Bath Road and the Staines Road were mere mud-tracks across the waste. Then came tolls and turnpikes; so that, when Queen Victoria ascended the throne, five hundred stage coaches passed daily through Hounslow, which consisted largely of inns where 1,500 horses were stabled. Now motor-buses and electric trains have replaced the coaches, and house agents have supplanted the

[*] T. Baird, *General View of the Agriculture . . . of Middlesex* (1793), pp. 7, 23.

highwaymen. The roads are as busy as ever, but a new need for open spaces has arisen.

When the West Middlesex Regional Town Planning Report appeared in 1924, three major recommendations were made in regard to public open spaces in the Heston and Isleworth district. These involved the reservation and ultimate purchase of Osterley Park (313 acres), Syon Park (154 acres), and a riverside strip along the banks of the Crane (128 acres). All recommendations

THE STABLES AT OSTERLEY PARK

have been included in the local Council's preliminary scheme, together with other open spaces already acquired or scheduled, amounting in all to some 700 acres. This handsome provision slightly exceeds the ideal figure of 10 per cent of the total district area, already mentioned elsewhere in this book. Yet it does not include the 250 acres of Hounslow Heath, automatically excluded because it is War Office land, or the much smaller area of the Heston Airport, which is private property and therefore liable to be sold for building land, as has already happened in the case of the aerodromes at Stag Lane and Cricklewood. The Council has laid out recreation grounds at Lampton, Isleworth, Heston,

Carville Hall, Hounslow, and elsewhere, and has actually acquired about 50 acres of the Crane-side land. This last is well worth preserving, for it will form a beautiful promenade shaded by fine trees, and includes a bit of really charming scenery where the little river widens into shady pools near Baber Bridge on the Staines Road.

But the acquisition of the two "lordly seats" of Osterley Park and Syon Park, each with a huge mansion, is a serious matter for the corporation, with land at its present high cost. There is no question that these two magnificent parks are worth preserving, but it seems reasonable to suggest that Southall—which, as we have seen, is under-equipped with open spaces and would make full use of Osterley Park at its very door—should be asked to contribute to one, and Brentford—as well as Richmond, whose riverside amenities depend so much on the view of Syon Park—to the other. It may be added that local residents are fortunate in having unrestricted access to a road through Osterley Park and to a footpath across Syon Park. Also, that it is most regrettable that the corner of Syon Park near the riverside "temple" has been scheduled as an "industrial area." Surely wiser counsels will prevail, for this is a real gem of Thames-side scenery (see p. 255).

The historical buildings of the borough include two old parish churches, at Heston and at Isleworth. The former, except the fine fifteenth-century tower, was entirely destroyed and rebuilt in 1865, apparently without much justification. It contains an interesting brass, a font with a cover, and a holy-water stoup—all from the original building—but its most striking feature is the lych-gate (c. 1450). Isleworth Parish Church stands near the river, and has been described as "a painfully plain building of red brick . . . mistakenly described as the work of Sir Christopher Wren," though, as at Heston, the old stone tower (c. 1320) was left standing. It appears that Wren did furnish a design in 1701, but that shortage of funds caused the churchwardens to modify and mangle it when they proceeded with the building four years later. The church contains some eighteenth-century monuments. The borough contains two relics of monastic foundations. The neo-Gothic church of Holy Trinity at Hounslow stands on the site of a medieval chapel of the Order of the Holy Trinity, a French order of mendicant friars, and was founded in 1211. Suppressed at the Dissolution, about 1538, the chapel continued to be used for religious services until it was demolished in 1828 and replaced by the present church, which was enlarged in 1855. Only a few monuments remain from the old building.

HESTON CHURCH, THE LYCH-GATE

Syon Monastery, a much more important establishment, was founded in 1420 and dedicated to St. Saviour and St. Bridget. It was a double community of sixty nuns and twenty-four monks, whose buildings were entirely separate, being connected only by a gate in the chapel, and the arrangements for locking that gate were as elaborate as those adopted for a modern safe-deposit in the City. Nevertheless, the nature of the organization furnished an excellent excuse for scandal-mongering when the Dissolution came, and an income equivalent to £20,000 a year provided an incentive. At any rate, the monastery was suppressed in 1539, and seventy-two of its inhabitants were pensioned off. In 1604 James I gave the property to the Duke of Northumberland, to whose family it has belonged ever since. The abbess of Syon had possessed a water-mill at Isleworth, and had constructed a canal from the Colne to the Crane, and another from the Crane to the Thames to feed it. This latter canal, having been subsequently extended to feed the ponds in Syon Park, came to be known as the "Duke of Northumberland's River," a name which it bears to the present day, and it may still be seen passing under the Isleworth mills. The demesne of the old monastery consisted of the present park from the Thames up to the outer edge of the ponds, and the northern part of Isleworth Village including the mill and the church. The present Syon House is probably on the same lines as the original monastery, which was not completed so late as 1468, and was altered in 1546–62. Between 1604 and 1613 the Duke of Northumberland spent £9,000 on the house and gardens, and in 1632 Inigo Jones was commissioned to do some repairs there. It is held by the chief authorities that he may have designed the striking arcaded cloister on the river front. The fine Long Gallery upstairs (136 feet long) is almost certainly Elizabethan. But the whole interior was completely remodelled by Robert Adam, who began work in 1761, on a scale of magnificence hardly surpassed even at Ken Wood or at Osterley Park, his work including the furniture and some of the carpets. The remarkable screen and gateway on the main road are also Adam's work, but the beautiful little boathouse is probably by James Wyatt.

Osterley Park, the seat of the Earl of Jersey, was formerly a possession of the abbess of Syon. The first house on the site was commenced by Sir Thomas Gresham, the famous London merchant, about 1564, and had just been completed at his death in 1579. The charming stable-court illustrated presumably dates from Gresham's time, but has evidently been altered since. In 1713 Francis Child, the banker, obtained the property and began to rebuild it in the grand manner, his brother Robert completing the work, which was carried out by the famous architect Robert Adam, and finished in the third quarter of the century. The four angle-turrets of Gresham's building were retained; otherwise the whole building, including the internal decorations and furniture, is a magnificent monument of Adam's work. Horace Walpole described it as "the palace of palaces," but said of the park that it was "the ugliest spot of ground in the universe." That can hardly have been true in 1773, and certainly to-day Osterley Park with its lakes and its lovely trees is a thing of beauty. Except for these two famous houses, the borough of Heston and Isleworth contains few domestic buildings of historical interest. The London Apprentice Inn at Isleworth, a quaint old hostelry, appears on the left of my sketch on p. 255, and James Wyatt's boathouse in Syon Park on the right.

BOOKS ON LOCAL HISTORY AND TOPOGRAPHY

[ANONYMOUS]	Syon House: its Pictures, Galleries and Gardens	London	1851
AUNGIER, C. T.	History of Syon Monastery, Isleworth, and Hounslow	London	1840
BATE, G. E.	A History of . . . Heston and Isleworth	London	N.D.
	A History of the Priory and Church of Holy Trinity, Hounslow	Hounslow	1924
[HESTON–ISLEWORTH U.D.C.]	Heston–Isleworth Charter Celebrations Souvenir	Hounslow	1932
MARSHALL, A. C.	Hounslow, Heston, Isleworth, and District	[Hounslow]	N.D.
Also:			
TIPPING, H. A.	Articles on Osterley Park in *Country Life* (Vol. LX)	London	1926
	Articles on Syon Park in *Country Life* (Vols. V and XLVI)	London	—

CHAPTER XXV

TWICKENHAM

INCLUDING FULWELL PARK, STRAWBERRY HILL, AND WHITTON

THE borough of Twickenham, incorporated in 1926, differs from many of the newly arranged districts of Middlesex in the respect that it corresponds almost exactly with the old parish of the same name, one of the three parishes forming the ancient hundred of Isleworth. This division of Middlesex into "hundreds" (Ossulston, Edmonton, Gore, Elthorne, Spelthorne, and Isleworth) is a direct and continuous survival from Domesday, where these six names appear with slightly altered spelling, but the Saxon system of hundreds in Middlesex goes back to a far more remote period, and according to Sir Montagu Sharpe* perpetuates a Roman arrangement of local government.

The name of Twickenham, however, has a very different significance for our "governing class," to whom it primarily suggests Rugby football, college ties, and a comfortable feeling of athletic exclusiveness. The crowd which clogs the station platforms and the neighbouring roads periodically is far less democratic than the annual jostle on the towing-path from Chiswick to Putney. To some at least of that glad throng the reputation of Twickenham in the eighteenth century will be familiar, when Horace Walpole toyed with his mock-Gothic house at Strawberry Hill, when Pope lived at his famous villa not far away, and when Lady Mary Wortley-Montagu, Swift, Fielding, Colley Cibber, Gay, Sir Godfrey Kneller, Sir William Chambers, and a whole host of other notabilities were among its inhabitants. The eighteenth century was undoubtedly Twickenham's "Golden Age," but long before that time Francis Bacon's residence in the town had made it known. And then, much later, came its "Indian Summer,"

* Sir Montagu Sharpe, *Middlesex in British, Roman, and Saxon Times*, 2nd edition (1932), pp. 134–6.

when, for some obscure reason, it developed an attraction for dethroned monarchs and exiled aristocracy from abroad, a veritable Home of Lost Causes. From 1800 onwards there was a whole clan of French royalties and royalists in the neighbourhood: the Duc d'Orleans at Orleans House, the Comte de Paris at York House, the Prince de Joinville at Mount Lebanon, and the Duc de Nemours at Bushy Park not far away. Last of all came the exiled King Manoel of Portugal with his Queen in the present century to settle at Fulwell Park, where he died. His widow left Twickenham in December 1933 to live in Switzerland, and thanked its citizens for twenty years of happy life in the district. Dickens lived in Twickenham in 1838–9, while Tennyson and Turner also spent much of their working lives in the town.

Orleans House is practically demolished, Mount Lebanon has gone, Fulwell Park and Whitton Park are being covered with "Distinctive Homes," York House has been converted into a town hall, and few of the numerous old mansions for which Twickenham was once noted still survive. One has to be very imaginative and very well informed in order to recapture much of the famous literary and aristocratic atmosphere which once clung so palpably to its streets and gardens. Less than thirty years ago the approach from London by tramcar, through Isleworth, provided an enchanting panorama of orchards, a blaze of pink and white blossom, with a carpet of daffodils in the spring, followed by a glorious display of chestnut blooms with a background of high brick garden walls and dark cedars. Now it is becoming the complete suburb: rows and rows of "Houses of Artistry"—all just alike— forests of crazy wireless masts, acres of screaming hoardings, petrol pumps, and cinema posters, streets vulgar at worst and undistinguished at best. It is true that Twickenham has, in King Street, a really well-designed modern thoroughfare; that it possesses one of the most attractive cinemas near London; that its municipal officials are doing their best to preserve some of its amenities; and that the possession of the river and the neighbourhood of the Royal Parks and Marble Hill will prevent the town from ever becoming completely sordid. But when one reads the hypocritical appeal of a builder at Whitton to "Come and build your home in an orchard," one realizes the hopelessness of expecting a district to retain any of its rural charm. For the builder knows, as we all do who think about it, that nothing of that orchard will remain when he has completed his scheme except an occasional stunted tree here and there. The incredibly obtuse brides who answer his call will spend the residue of their married lives—after the first month or so—in admiring Mrs. Smith's washing and the wireless posts which have replaced the orchard that formed the lure only a few weeks before. Yet a girdle of real orchards might have been preserved all round London had the advice of town-planning enthusiasts been heeded thirty years ago.

In the eighteenth century the wits almost always spoke of "Twit'nam"; Heaven knows why. The name appears as "Twican hom" in 704, as "Tuicanhamme" in 793, and as "Twikenham" in the thirteenth century, and means "Twica's bend" (of the river), Twica being a personal name. Whitton means "white farm." The name of Fulwell does not appear in Mr. Gover's book,* whence these derivations are obtained, and Strawberry Hill is a comparatively modern name.

The area of the borough at present is 2,421 acres, about 3¾ square miles. But the rearrangement of administrative areas in Middlesex, mentioned often on several previous occasions in this book, may considerably extend this area. At the time of writing, the Council's original proposal to amalgamate Hampton Wick and Teddington as one district and Hampton and Sunbury as another has been superseded by a proposal to include the districts of Hampton Wick, Teddington, and Hampton in the borough of Twickenham. Should this proposal be approved, as now seems probable, it would have the effect of increasing the acreage of the borough to nearly 7,000 acres (nearly 11 square miles).

The population of the old parish and the later borough of Twickenham was only 3,138 in 1801, in spite of its considerable celebrity, and, like so many other districts of Middlesex, it doubled (6,254) in the next fifty years. From 1851 to 1901 there was a

* J. E. B. Gover, *The Place-names of Middlesex*.

regular increase of about 20 per cent each decennium, reaching
20,991 in 1901. Between 1901 and 1911 there was a tremendous
jump, the figure rising to 29,637. The last two censuses have
shown a less sensational growth (34,790 in 1921, 39,909 in 1931),
but large parts of the district—hitherto agricultural—are now
being rapidly developed, and it seems possible that the present
population of something over 40,000 may eventually be doubled

TWICKENHAM

within the existing boundaries, as most of the total area is available
for housing. But the proposed extension of the borough boundaries
just mentioned will, if adopted, double the present population and
greatly increase the prospects of growth.

There is not much to say about the natural features of
Twickenham, which is almost dead level and has been so intensively
cultivated that most of its trees are found in private parks and
gardens, where—as, for example, at Marble Hill—there are some
magnificent specimens. Cedars, as elsewhere in Middlesex, are
very plentiful in the old gardens. The Thames is, of course, the
outstanding natural feature of the district, and its amenities come

in for mention later in this chapter. The course of the little River Crane, which meanders right across the borough, varies from the beautiful to the ultra-sordid, and some effort is being made to preserve the more attractive portions of its length. Nothing need be said about the part of the Duke of Northumberland's River that lies in Twickenham.

There are no first-class roads in the borough, but the projected New Chertsey Road will cut diagonally across it from the so-called new "Twickenham" Bridge at St. Margaret's to a point near the bridge over the Crane at Sixth Cross Road. As a writer in *The Times* recently pointed out, the fine bridge designed by Mr. Maxwell Ayrton is in the St. Margaret's district and should be so described; the fact that another new bridge, in the heart of Twickenham itself, is included in the proposals of the regional town-planning scheme is a further argument against the present name. Richmond Bridge, completed in 1777, is one of the most beautiful on the Thames, and joins Richmond to the Middlesex shore. Mention of "Sixth Cross Road" calls for an explanation of its curious title. From Twickenham Green, where the roads to Staines and Hampton diverge, the cross-roads are numbered serially, American fashion. The sixth and last of them, "Sixth Cross Road," is rapidly becoming important as a traffic artery. Twickenham is one of the districts which has seen fit to substitute the "trolley-bus" for the tramcar on the route to Teddington. Another recent innovation is the opening of a new station at Whitton on the Southern Railway.

Of the public open spaces in the borough, much the largest is Marble Hill Park, but, strange to say, this belongs to the London County Council, which took the lead in its purchase in July 1902 when Middlesex was very much the "little brother" and had less than half its present population. Marble Hill is an invaluable possession for at least two reasons: firstly its own intrinsic beauty, and secondly the large share it occupies in the lovely view of the Thames from Richmond Hill where it constitutes the most important part of the foreground. The area of the park is 72 acres, and but for the timely action of the L.C.C. in 1902, when it was on the verge of being sold to builders, the whole estate would now be crammed with rows of little houses and most of its fine trees would have been felled. Something will be said of Marble Hill House later in this chapter.

The actual area of public open spaces owned by Twickenham is very small indeed, only about 50 acres. This includes the bare triangle of grass and asphalt known as Twickenham Green (7½ acres), formerly a part of Hounslow Heath, Kneller Gardens (12 acres), and Murray Park at Whitton (8¾ acres). A short length of the Crane banks, known as Moor Mead (12 acres) has been acquired; and a further length of the banks of that little stream, with an area of nearly 60 acres, has been reserved as recommended in the Thames Valley Regional Report, but, rather inexplicably, as a "private open space." The War Office owns the grounds of Kneller Hall, and also the considerable portion of Hounslow Heath that lies within the Twickenham boundary, but—as has been pointed out hitherto in this book—these areas are excluded from the town-planning schemes and there is no guarantee that they will not be sold for housing purposes at some future date. This being so, it is a question whether the borough of Twickenham has made adequate provision in this respect for the future needs of its rapidly growing population. Such a district should theoretically have 250 acres of open spaces. In fact, it has about 50 acres of its own, 72 acres of Marble Hill, and some 78 acres scheduled as "private" or public open spaces in its town-planning scheme, say 200 acres in all. However, the proximity of the immense areas of the royal parks of Bushy and Hampton Court may be held to constitute a sufficient reason for proceeding no further towards additional commitments.

Nevertheless, it is essential to the amenities of the district that the banks of the Thames should be preserved as far as possible. From the Richmond railway bridge to Richmond Bridge a continuous strip has been reserved; then comes Cambridge Gardens, already acquired. From Cambridge Gardens to Marble Hill Park another strip has been reserved, and from Marble Hill Park to Orleans Gardens and thence to the churchyard beyond York House

Gardens the river-bank is either acquired or reserved. Next comes a short length occupied by buildings, then the short but charming tree-planted quay known as the Embankment. Beyond this lies the long frontage of Poulett Lodge, a large ugly house recently demolished to make room for a block of flats. It is regrettable that the authorities have not found it practicable to acquire a strip of ground between this site and the river-bank, in order to extend the small riverside garden just mentioned.

Then comes a row of new houses whose gardens have been allowed to extend right down to the water's edge; then the private gardens of "Pope's Villa" (so called), Cross Deep Lodge, and some other houses; then Radnor House, now public property, with charming gardens on the river's brink; and finally a length of about a quarter of a mile to the Teddington boundary, where industrial premises and private houses occupy the foreshore. Altogether, about $1\frac{3}{4}$ miles of the total of 3 miles of river frontage in Twickenham has been acquired or reserved, and that is something to be thankful for. The extremities of Eel Pie Island or "Twickenham Ait" have also been bought for the public, so that the "end-on" view from the river is preserved in either direction. Boat-houses, bungalows, and a hotel stand on the Twickenham side of the island, as is inevitable, but they are fairly well shielded by trees and shrubs from the main channel of the Thames, and it is to be hoped that they will be prevented from spoiling it with blatant hoardings. The Surrey side of the river for all these 3 miles of frontage is entirely open except for a line of houses south of Richmond Bridge, and Ham House stands finely opposite Marble Hill, surrounded by meadows. From Twickenham's point of view, it would be a thousand pities if this noble prospect were to be replaced by a depressing vista of "Distinctive Homes." The beauty of the Thames Valley, London's playground, is something unique, and there is room in Middlesex for the whole population of London, even of Greater London, without trespassing on that sacred strip of waterway.

The historical monuments of Twickenham include only one old church, and that not of the first order. St. Mary's Parish

Church has a stone Gothic tower which is attributed, on insufficient evidence, to William of Wykeham; but the body of the building was erected in 1714 by the architect John James, working under the supervision of a zealous churchwarden, Sir Godfrey Kneller, the painter. It is not a romantic design, but there are interesting tombs, including those of Pope and of Kitty Clive, the actress.

Houses destroyed in recent years are very numerous, and include

FERRY HOUSE, TWICKENHAM

Twickenham Park, Whitton Park, and several mansions in or near King Street. Pope's villa, where the poet lived from 1719 until his death in 1761, was demolished early in the nineteenth century. The building now occupying the site is a convent, of no architectural merit whatever. Kneller Hall, now the Royal Military School of Music, was originally built by Sir Godfrey Kneller the painter in 1709–11, but during its tenancy by the "Council of Education" was so completely altered and enlarged by one George Mair, who took as his model the hideous Wollaton Hall in

Nottinghamshire—says one authority—that little, if any, of the old building now remains. A proper architectural survey might, however, reveal a different story.

Twickenham possesses two superb specimens of eighteenth-century street architecture in Montpellier Row (1720) and Sion Row (1721), perfectly illustrated by T. R. Way in his drawings of Twickenham and neighbourhood.* Tennyson inhabited Chapel House (now called Tennyson House) in Montpellier Row from 1851 to 1853. Orleans House was built in Queen Anne's reign by her Secretary of State for Scotland and afterwards intermittently occupied by a succession of expatriated royalties from 1800 to 1877, had a brief career as a club, and was recently demolished, the only surviving portion being the remarkable Octagon Room which was specially designed for the reception of Queen Caroline. Marble Hill House is another example of the period, having been begun in 1723. It is a noble and dignified Palladian design, almost certainly the work of the talented Twickenham architect, Robert Morris,† although Horace Walpole rashly ascribes it to Lord Pembroke. It contains a beautiful mahogany staircase, a finely decorated saloon, and other notable rooms. It was built for the Countess of Suffolk, who became mistress to the then Prince of Wales, according to Walpole, in consideration of £1,200 a year paid to a complacent and despicable husband. York House, now the municipal offices of the borough, is the largest and most historic mansion in Twickenham. It appears to be a work of the late seventeenth or early eighteenth century, and may derive its name from that Duke of York who became King James II in 1685, but the property was acquired by Lord Clarendon in 1660 and was known as Yorke's Farm a century earlier still. Subsequently it passed through several notable ownerships, and was finally bought by the Twickenham Council in 1924. It contains a local museum and some interesting decoration, while the gardens,

---

* See bibliography at end of this chapter.

† See the admirable article by D. S. MacColl in the *Architectural Review*, X, pp. 23–9 (1901); also Sir Reginald Blomfield's *Short History of Renaissance Architecture in England*, pp. 198–200 (1900).

with a surprising bevy of marble nymphs recalling Baroque Italy, enhance its attractions.

The most notorious house in Twickenham is, of course, Horace Walpole's ridiculous mock-Gothic villa of Strawberry Hill, which he began to manufacture in 1747 round an older house which formed its core. A great deal has been written about this architectural curiosity; here it is enough to say that it still survives, in constricted surroundings but nevertheless retaining a large area of ground, as St. Mary's Training College. Among surviving houses of the same century may be mentioned Fortescue House near the railway station; Heatham House close by it, and Crossdeep Lodge near the river, both with good ironwork; Cambridge House near Richmond Bridge; and Ferry House near Twickenham Ferry. Arragon House near the church is stated to contain fragments of Tudor building, and there are some quaint old houses of great age between Church Street and the river. Radnor House, a Victorian nightmare, is now shared between the British Legion and the Christadelphians—strange bedfellows!

BOOKS ON LOCAL HISTORY AND TOPOGRAPHY

[ANONYMOUS]	Principal Seats and Gardens ... about Twickenham	Twickenham	1760
COBBETT, R. S.	Memorials of Twickenham	London	1872
IRONSIDE, E.	A History of Twickenham	London	1797
[L.C.C.]	Marble Hill House	London	1930
TWICKENHAM BOROUGH COUNCIL	Twickenham: Official Guide	London	N.D.
	York House, Twickenham	London	N.D.
WAY, T. R., and CHAPMAN, F.	Architectural Remains of Richmond, Twickenham, etc.	London	1900
Also:			
TIPPING, H. A.	Articles on Marble Hill in *Country Life*, Vol. XXXIX	London	—
	Articles on Strawberry Hill in *Country Life*, Vol. LVI	London	—

CHAPTER XXVI

TEDDINGTON

A T the time of writing this chapter it seems probable, as already stated, that the existing separate urban districts of Teddington and Hampton Wick are likely to be absorbed into Twickenham, together with the district of Hampton. It was my intention, when planning this book, to treat each of the new administrative areas as a separate entity in a single chapter describing its growth from a nexus of villages, and thus to create a sense of civic consciousness that is apt to be lacking in communities whose boundaries are, of necessity, artificially determined. In the districts covered by this chapter and the next the final adjustment of boundaries still remains to be settled. But it appears likely that, whatever happens, Teddington and Hampton Wick will be linked together hereafter. There is some reason for this amalgamation. Hampton Wick "hamlet," as it used to be called, is a very small area of houses, which could be enclosed inside a square measuring half a mile each way, crowded together round the Middlesex end of Kingston Bridge. The remaining and greater part of its area consists of the royal parks of Bushy and Hampton Court (though a good deal of the former lies in the adjoining district of Hampton). Teddington, on the other hand, is now fairly closely populated over all except the western part of its area, and its houses have joined those of Hampton Wick. Hampton Wick, with only three thousand inhabitants in spite of its 1,300 acres, is too small a unit for economical and efficient local administration; hence the proposal to amalgamate it with one or more of its neighbours.

Few Middlesex people can be aware of these subtle administrative problems, but nearly everybody has heard of Teddington's famous lock, and has been told that Teddington means "Tide-end-town." Certainly I was so informed in my boyhood. But that was long before the days of Mr. Gover,* who has recently corrected all our childish and erroneous ideas on these things. "Teddington," he tells us, which occurs long before Domesday as "Tudingtun," means the "farm of the sons of Tuda" (or, more probably, "Tedda"); and he ignores all the schoolroom chatter about tides. In this he has common sense behind him, for the tide must have extended farther up the river before Teddington Lock was constructed in 1810. As for Hampton Wick (cf. "Hackney Wick"), that delightful old name means "the house in the enclosure at the river-bend"; and it is interesting to note that the "p" in "Hampton," still generally silent, does not appear until the thirteenth century, the earliest quotations cited by Mr. Gover being "Homtune" in 781, and "Hamntone" in Domesday (1086).

The present area of Hampton Wick is 1,306 acres, and of Teddington 1,214 acres, making a total of 2,520 acres, or nearly 4 square miles. It includes the extensive grounds of the National Physical Laboratory. That now gigantic complex of workshops and whatnots was originally started in 1900 on modest and academic lines in the beautiful old building known as Queen's Lodge or Bushy House, situated in Bushy Park and within the urban district of Hampton. Since then, and especially since 1914, it has spread over a large area into Teddington. It may be noted that something in the air of Teddington, or more probably the N.P.L. itself, has attracted other research laboratories to the neighbourhood. What with the river, the royal parks, the deer, and the hordes of scientists, this district is relieved of suburban mediocrity; and it also contains a magnificent half-church, "the cathedral of the Thames Valley" as it has been called, which still awaits its nave but is a really noble building.

The population of the two parishes of Hampton Wick and Teddington rose from 1,492 in 1801 to 2,814 in 1851, thus maintaining the tendency noted elsewhere in Middlesex to double itself in these fifty years. Up to 1871, when Teddington suddenly forged ahead, Hampton Wick had the larger population, and has only increased from 1,994 in 1861 to 2,957 in 1931. Teddington,

* J. E. B. Gover, *The Place-names of Middlesex.*

on the other hand, jumped from 1,183 in 1861 to 4,063 in 1871, then grew steadily and rapidly to 17,847 in 1911, since when it has slowed down, reaching 23,362 in 1931. It does not seem probable that the combined population of the two parishes, now 26,319, is ever likely to exceed 35,000, and it may not even exceed 30,000. This is far below the usual density for such an area, even after making due allowance for the royal parks, but the circumstances of the district are peculiar.

The planning of roads in the district is fairly sound and adequate, but there is a proposal to construct a new road-bridge in place of the present foot-bridge at Teddington Lock, connecting to a fine new road on the Surrey side. This bridge will be built over the site of the present Anglers' Hotel, and will involve the demolition of Weir House. Another bridge has been suggested at Surbiton. Kingston Bridge, opened in 1828, was widened in 1914, and is well designed. There seems to be no likelihood of further railway development in the region.

The natural beauty of the district is now confined to the riverside and the royal parks, Teddington itself being a built-up area with no scenic attractions; and the royal parks are more conveniently discussed as a whole in the next chapter. The public open spaces in Teddington are negligible, and at Hampton Wick nil. The Thames Valley Regional Report recommends the acquisition of the grounds of Weir House as a public open space; also the islands at Teddington Lock, but these are in Surrey. Trowlock Island and a small area near it, screening the Teddington Sewage Works from the river, have already been acquired or scheduled. The surroundings of Teddington Lock on both sides of the river are certainly worth preserving, and development on the banks—which so far has been fairly satisfactory—should be watched with care. The large gravel-pit between Sandy Lane and the railway, now a watery mere, presents a problem for future development. At present it is very picturesque, but one wonders whether eventually it is to be filled with refuse as a building site for "Ideal Homes."

Neither Teddington nor Hampton Wick is rich in historical buildings. The old parish church of Teddington has been so largely rebuilt that little of the sixteenth-century structure remains, but there are monuments of interest, including one to "Margaret Woffington, spinster" (d. 1760), the famous "Peg Woffington" immortalized by Charles Reade, and others to Sir Orlando Bridgman, John Walter, the founder of *The Times* (d. 1812), and Flitcroft, the architect (d. 1769). The poor little building is

TEDDINGTON LOCK

completely overshadowed by the great new church of St. Alban across the road.

Most of the old houses in the district, including Bridgman House in the High Street and the charming gabled "Queen Elizabeth's Hunting Box" at the corner of High Street and Udney Park Road, have been demolished. The chief survivor is the dignified Georgian building known as Elmfield House, now used as offices by the Urban District Council of Teddington. It contains a fine carved staircase and other internal features of interest. In the adjoining Public Library is a small collection of photographs and prints of bygone Teddington.

BOOKS ON LOCAL HISTORY AND TOPOGRAPHY

[HAMPTON WICK U.D.C.]	Hampton Wick: Official Guide	Hampton Wick	N.D.
INGRAM, KENNETH	A Short History of Teddington	Teddington	1909
[Teddington U.D.C.]	Teddington: Official Guide	London	N.D.

(For Hampton-on-Thames, Hampton Court, and Bushy Park, *see* Bibliography at end of next chapter.)

CHAPTER XXVII

HAMPTON AND SUNBURY

INCLUDING UPPER AND LOWER HALLIFORD, HAMPTON COURT,
HAMPTON HILL, KEMPTON PARK, LITTLETON, AND SHEPPERTON

As explained at the beginning of the previous chapter, it seems probable that Hampton, together with Hampton Wick and Teddington, will shortly be incorporated in the borough of Twickenham. With that prospect in view, an endeavour will be made in this chapter to keep separate the interests of Hampton and Sunbury as far as possible.

We have now reached a part of Middlesex that has hitherto been known as a peaceful pleasure-ground rather than as one of London's dormitories. Except for the vast reservoirs of the Metropolitan Water Board, industry has not penetrated this charming corner of the county, and though the "bungalow menace" has made its appearance in places, it has not spread far, and we may postpone consideration of its effects until the final chapter. Rows of villas have begun to sprout here and there, but on the whole the riverside is still given up to boating parties, while the hinterland remains agricultural. Littleton Park has become a "sound city" with film studios, Kempton Park draws thousands for its races, and when sketching in the formerly quiet surroundings of Shepperton Church one summer Sunday I found that there was a never-ending procession of cars, with a petrol station, behind me, and beach pyjamas (not shown in my drawing) in the foreground. The church bell certainly had to compete with a good deal. Nevertheless, things have not changed here so much as in other districts, and Hampton Court is still the most beautiful place in all the county of Middlesex. The swans on the river are getting used to gramophones, and at any time of year except summer Saturdays and Sundays, or even at those times after dusk, the banks of the Thames retain much of their restful beauty.

Beginning with the old names of the villages in this district, we find that Sunbury has nothing to do with the sun, but means "Sunna's stronghold," and was spelt "Sunnanbyrg" in 962. Halliford, which occurs as "Halgeford" at the same date, is "the saint's ford." Hampton was explained in the previous chapter. Kempton Park, which figures as "Cheneton" in Domesday, recalls "the farm of Cena's sons." Littleton is, obviously, "little farm." Shepperton suggests "sheep farm," but philologists are cautious

HAMPTON COURT FROM THE NEW BRIDGE

people, and Mr. Gover, from whose book* these derivations are taken, says that "shepherd's farm" is probable, though doubtful.

The area of the existing Hampton district is 2,045 acres, while that of Sunbury is 5,463 acres. Of the total area, a very large amount (say 2 square miles) must be water, for the Littleton reservoir alone extends over 745 acres; and more than another square mile is accounted for by the portion of Bushy Park which lies in Hampton. Thus it appears that not more than 5,000 acres are available for building.

To trace the growth of population in the Sunbury section, one

* J. E. B. Gover, *Place-names of Middlesex.*

has to add together the figures for the old parishes of Sunbury, Littleton, and Shepperton. The result shows that the number of inhabitants grew from 2,325 in 1801 to 2,989 in 1851, rose to 5,708 in 1881, dropped back to 5,497 in 1891, rose rapidly to 9,829 in 1921, and still more rapidly to 13,329 in 1931. The population of Littleton, a tiny village that was partially obliterated when the huge reservoir was constructed there a few years ago,

HAMPTON FROM THE SURREY SIDE
Garrick's "Temple" on the right

shows some curious ups and downs. It was 147 in 1801, 106 in 1851, 111 in 1861, 165 in 1871, 126 in 1881, only 99 in 1891, 320 in 1901, and is now only 434.

Hampton shows a very regular growth from 1,722 in 1801 and 3,134 in 1851 (thus practically doubling itself in fifty years, in the old-fashioned Middlesex way) to 10,675 in 1921 and 13,053 in 1931. Any forecast as to the future population of this area would be rash. The number of visitors which throngs the banks of the Thames here on a fine summer Sunday is prodigious, but the bulk of them are day-trippers who return home to sleep. Every layer of society is represented, from the ultra-superior people in Rolls-Royces and fur coats down to stolid matrons of the Skipton Women's Liberal Association packed perspiringly into charabancs, or a deputation of the Ancient Order of Buffaloes from Wigan. These parties do indeed travel enormous distances, and their comments on places and people are worth hearing. But the really exclusive (and publicity-provoking) method of arriving at Hampton Court is by coach. The boats on the river, the deer in the parks, the daffodils under the trees in early spring, and the blaze of colour in the Long Border a little later, all have a charm. But for a real thrill down one's spine give me the four horses of that coach taking the turn into the forecourt of the "Mitre," the conductor tooting his horn, and the plutocratic passengers in Ascot toppers descending from their lofty perch at the end of their long drive from London. Such a spectacle makes even the Rolls-Royces and the fur coats look cheap, and the passengers know it.

Returning to the real business of this book, we have next to consider what can be done to preserve as much as possible of the undoubted beauty and gaiety of this delightful riverside neighbourhood. Ignoring minor twists and turns, the course of the Thames included in Hampton and Sunbury amounts to about $7\frac{1}{2}$ miles, and of that length some 6 miles of the Middlesex bank is private property, built upon already or liable to be built upon in the near future. Only the frontage of the Palace itself and the Hampton property of the Water Board, with its prosaic embankments and utilitarian buildings, can be regarded as immune. The regional plan for the Thames Valley recommends the preservation of a narrow strip of river-bank about half a mile long east of Sunbury, a meadow on either side of Shepperton Village, and a meadow near Chertsey Bridge, possibly 2 miles in all, with an area of rather more than 60 acres.* Considering that much of the land is liable to flooding, that provision seems no more than a reasonable

---

* Near Shepperton lies the spot known as "Coway Stakes." Sir Montagu Sharpe has effectively exploded the legend that Caesar crossed the Thames here and argues that it was merely a ford or "cow-way" across the river.

minimum. It is further recommended that the various islands be scheduled as "private open spaces," another reasonable precaution. The field known as War Close, at Shepperton, commemorates a battle between our forefathers and the Danes under Olaf King of Norway, who sailed up the Thames in a fleet of ninety-three ships in 993–4. This field also is suggested as a private open space.

Farther back lies the immense stretch of Bushy Park, which, with the adjoining Hampton Court Home Park (in the

THE ROYAL MEWS, HAMPTON COURT

Teddington–Hampton Wick district), covers nearly 1,750 acres, but this magnificent reservation does not affect the riverside problem, and one could wish that at least another mile of open river frontage between Sunbury and Shepperton could be controlled to the extent of requiring that houses should be set back a short distance from the water's edge. With the river so near, and Bushy Park in the background, the need for public open spaces in the hinterland is not so urgent as in less favoured districts, and some provision has been made. The 400 acres of the racecourse at Kempton Park are not scheduled as an open space, and are therefore liable to be built over whenever the owners decide that houses are more profitable than horses. But the fact that money is now being spent freely on grandstands appears to dispel this as an immediate risk.

Hampton has no town-planning scheme at present. Sunbury has formulated a scheme, but has not yet accepted the proposals of the regional report for the acquisition of the riverside meadows, and only owns some 50 acres of public open spaces, exclusive of allotments. This is a meagre allowance for so large an area, and does not safeguard the banks of the Thames. One has to remember that things change rapidly in Middlesex, and that, without some measure of foresight and artistic judgment, a patch of really hideous development, such as one can see at Sunbury Common near the station, may spring up at any moment in these Elysian fields. It has been suggested that the New Chertsey Road might be planned as a "parkway," a suggestion so admirable that it is hardly likely to be adopted.

Judging by examples farther down-stream, notably at Hampton Court, there seems no cause to fear an ugly bridge where this projected highway crosses the Thames below Chertsey. The new Hampton Court Bridge is indeed a great improvement upon its predecessor, and harmonizes admirably with its superb surroundings.

The Palace of Hampton Court, with its appendages and surroundings, is by far the most important historical building in the extra-metropolitan area of Middlesex, so important indeed that it would be futile to attempt any description of it here. Its history has been worthily told in several books by Mr. Ernest Law, and these are mentioned in the bibliography at the end of this chapter. The palace was originally founded in 1515 by Cardinal Wolsey as a private house, where he lived in great magnificence, attended by a household of five hundred persons. Ten years later he presented the whole property, furniture and all, to the king. On Wolsey's fall in 1529 Henry VIII entered into possession, and made several important alterations and additions. Many of these were demolished by Sir Christopher Wren, but the Great Hall, the Great Kitchen, the Tennis Court, and some other features remain. The remarkable

canal or aqueduct, 11 miles long, which supplies the palace and
its gardens with water from the Colne was constructed by Charles I,
and is known as "Longford River," or "The Cardinal's River."
Wren was commissioned by William III to pull down the old
palace and build a new one. This scheme he might have achieved
but for the king's sudden death in 1702. But though that event
curtailed the vast project, much of the beautiful decorative work
in the State Apartments was carried out in Queen Anne's reign.

SUNBURY PARISH CHURCH

It is curious that the battlemented Banqueting House on the river-
bank, which is not open to the public, is one of Wren's works,
and not a part of the Tudor buildings as appears at first glance,
until one notices the great sash windows.

It may seem presumptuous to summarize the special features of
importance in this gigantic architectural complex in a few lines,
but no one will deny that it is universally acclaimed as one of the
finest specimens of Tudor building, and one of the greatest
monuments of Wren's genius, in all England. It is also a perfect
museum of craftsmanship of both periods, in woodwork, ironwork,

plasterwork, and masonry. It contains a thousand rooms, and the happy idea which has made it a sort of almshouse or haven of refuge, for those who have earned the gratitude of the Court or the State, prevents it from becoming a mere museum-piece and gives it a semblance of usefulness. Compared with its vast and pompous rival at Versailles, it is more colourful, more homely, and more English. But above all it stands out as the greatest English example of "garden architecture" on the grand scale. Vast as would have been the ultimate palace planned by Wren if it had ever been completed, it was only the centre-piece and focus of a great scheme of radiating avenues, ornamental ponds, statuary, fountains, and formal gardens, standing in 3 square miles of parkland girdled by the wide river. Although the scheme was never finished in every detail, it is the most "royal" lay-out we have. The chestnut avenue a mile long, the 9 miles of plane-tree avenues, the "Long Water," the great gates, Tijou's marvellous ironwork screens by the river, the statues in stone and metal, are all impressive in their dignity and magnificence, while the more intimate charm of the gardens round the palace satisfies the domestically-minded.

Outside the immediate precincts of the palace there are the Royal Mews, a composite brick building retaining some relics of the Tudor period; "The Old Court House" near the bridge, where Wren lived in retirement and died in 1723 at the age of ninety-one; Hampton Court House and the old house east of it on the Green; Queen's Lodge or Bushy House, now the head-quarters of the National Physical Laboratory, on the north side of Bushy Park; and several others of note. The Hampton Urban District Council Offices occupy an old house, Rose Hill, near the station, and there are other buildings of historical interest near the church.

On the river-bank approaching Hampton is a charming group including "Garrick's Temple" and garden, acquired for the public in 1932. Behind it, across the main road, lies the large house which Adam altered and embellished, and beyond stands the dull brick church of Hampton, so surprisingly picturesque from this point of view.

Sunbury Church was rebuilt in 1752, and has a disappointing interior, but its picturesque tower and cupola, strangely Dutch in appearance, appears to advantage in distant views. Shepperton Church, though old in parts, has a somewhat crude brick tower of 1710, and owes its main attraction to its surroundings. Littleton Church, by far the most interesting of the three, has a thirteenth-

SHEPPERTON

century nave and chancel, with an interesting brick clerestory and tower of *c.* 1500. The ugly top stage of the tower is an eighteenth-century addition. In the churchyard may be seen the most ornate mausoleum in the county.

The Sunbury district is unaccountably short of historical houses of any size, but Sunbury Court, formerly Sunbury Place (now a boarding-house for "decayed gentlemen") is a typical mansion of the late eighteenth century, and there are many pleasant old buildings of no special importance near the riverside.

BOOKS ON LOCAL HISTORY AND TOPOGRAPHY

CARTWRIGHT, JULIA	Hampton Court	London	1910
GARSIDE, B.	History of Hampton Grammar School (1556–1700)	Cambridge	1932
GODDARD, C. E.	Historical account of the parish [Sunbury]	Sunbury	1890
HUTTON, W. H.	Hampton Court	London	1897
JERROLD, W.	Hampton Court	London	1912
KEATE, E. M.	Hampton Court Palace: a short popular guide	London	1932
LAW, ERNEST	History of Hampton Court Palace (3 vols.)	London	1890
	Hampton Court Illustrated: a popular guide	London	1910
	The Chestnut Avenue, Bushy Park	London	1919
	A Short History of Hampton Court	London	1924
	"My Lorde Cardinall's Lodgynges," Hampton Court	London	N.D.
	Hampton Court Gardens: Old and New	London	1926
RIPLEY, H.	History . . . of Hampton-on-Thames	London	1884
[SUNBURY U.D.C.]	Sunbury and Shepperton: Official Guide	London	N.D.
WOOD, W. M.	Littleton, Middlesex [a guidebook]	——	N.D.
Also:			
TIPPING, H. A.	Article on Garrick's Villa, Hampton, in *Country Life*, Vol. XL	London	—
	Article on Hampton Court Palace in *Country Life*, Vol. XIII	London	—

CHAPTER XXVIII

STAINES

INCLUDING ASHFORD, LALEHAM, POYLE, STANWELL, AND WEST
BEDFONT

THERE seem to be two different views about the town of Staines.
The lively author of *Highways and Byways in Middlesex**
supports the opinion of an older writer that it is "quiet, clean,
and commonplace," but he was speaking of its condition in 1909,
before the Petrol Age had begun, and he would certainly withdraw
his first adjective nowadays, when its streets are filled with an
endless roar of motor traffic. Then there is Mr. Donald Maxwell,
who boldly describes it as "The Bruges of Middlesex,"† and
supports his claim with a delightful sketch of one of its little streams
and bridges, taken from the top of the porch of the Great Western
Station. But things have changed for the worse since his day, an
ugly concrete building now occupying the centre of his Bruges
fantasy.

Admittedly the town is ancient, yet in itself it has little intrinsic
charm, the view of Church Street being perhaps its most attractive
aspect. But the modern urban district of Staines comprises, as is
usual in modern Middlesex, much more than the limited area of
the town, and extends over more than 8,000 acres, including the
charming villages of Poyle and Stanwell, the sprawling suburban
settlement of Ashford, a considerable length of the Thames, and
of the streams which together form the River Colne. Staines, in
this sense, really means the south-west corner of Middlesex, and
it contains some beautiful scenery. But its little capital has not yet
had time to tackle all the responsibilities that it will assuredly have
to shoulder in the future. There is no public library, no museum
where records of local history may be preserved for the future

---

* W. Jerrold, *Highways and Byways in Middlesex* (1909), p. 173.
† D. Maxwell, *A Pilgrimage of the Thames* (1932), p. 117.

T

information of its cosmopolitan and immigrant populace, and—as yet—no enthusiast who has taken the trouble to write its story. A town-planning scheme has been adopted, but frequent changes in the administrative boundaries of the district have complicated this work.

The name of Staines, like its character, is disputed by various authorities. Mr. Gover, from whose book* I have drawn most of the derivations of old place-names given here, gives its early forms as "Stana" in 960, etc., and "Stanes" in Domesday, interpreting these as "at the stone," and adding the suggestion: "referring to some boundary mark, perhaps the point where the Colne flows into the Thames." Mr. Gover may or may not have been aware, when he wrote thus, that there is in fact such a boundary-stone existing. It stands at the exact point of junction of Middlesex, Buckinghamshire, and Surrey, close to the bank of the river where a small branch of the Colne joins the Thames. It bears the surprising inscription, "God preserve ye City of London" and the date 1280, while the modern base is inscribed "Conservators of the River Thames, 1857." One wonders what the City of London has to do with this remote corner of the county of Middlesex; the fact is that the stone marks the limit of the authority of London over the river, and also the division between the Upper and Lower Thames.

But Sir Montagu Sharpe† offers a very different explanation of the name "Stanes," which, he says, refers to "the stone-paved way carrying the road through the marshland where the mouths of the Colne and Exe joined the Thames." This derivation reminds one of the Roman "Stane Street" and of "Stangate" in Lambeth where Watling Street crossed the marshes between London Bridge and Westminster. There is, of course, no doubt that there was such a paved Roman road, 24 feet wide where it has been uncovered, from London through Staines to Silchester, and Sir Montagu Sharpe adds that there must have been an inn and a posting-house

---

* J. E. B. Gover, *The Place-names of Middlesex*.

† Sir Montagu Sharpe, *Middlesex in British, Roman, and Saxon Times*, p. 74.

at the same point. The Roman name for Staines was *Pontes*, indicating that there was more than one bridge here.

"Stanwell" sounds much like "Staines," and occurs as "Stanwelle" in Domesday, but means simply "stony well." Ashford, spelt as "Exforde" in Domesday, may signify a crossing over the little River Exe or Axe, still to be seen; but curiously enough, there is an earlier spelling, "Ecclesforde" (969) which survives even in 1535 as "Echelford," and thus confounds us. Laleham,

CHURCH STREET, STAINES

another very old name, may be derived either from Anglo-Saxon *lœl* (= twig) or from some personal name as prefix. Poyle commemorates the Norman family of Poille or Puille.

The area of the Staines district amounts, as already stated, to 8,268 acres, or nearly 13 square miles, and will be increased by some 300 acres near Ashford if the recent recommendations of the County Council are accepted. A substantial part of this area is occupied by the huge reservoirs of the Water Board. The boundaries of the district consist very largely of watercourses: the Thames, the Colne and its branches, the Duke of Northumberland's River. In one respect at least the Thames boundary seems irrational, for at two points Middlesex crosses the river and takes a bite out of the Surrey side, while, near Chertsey Bridge, Surrey returns the compliment. This apparent inconsistency is explained by the changes since Saxon times of the course of the Thames which, quite properly, formed the original boundary. The landlord of the hotel at Chertsey Bridge told me of a curious result of the river frontier. It seems that Middlesex and Surrey have a different

POYLE

scale of bonus to be paid to persons who recover corpses from the river, the Middlesex tariff being distinctly more favourable. For some time it was regarded as singular that corpses were invariably washed up on the Middlesex side, until a catastrophe happened one night when a hopeful angler was found punting a somewhat decadent body across the channel and it came to pieces in midstream. Thus the secret was revealed.

There are well-kept locks on the river at Chertsey and at Penton Hook, the latter being the most striking loop on all the Thames. The lock-keeper at Chertsey has told me that the barge folk, especially the women, are among the hardiest and most

powerful people in England, due to constant practice in opening
and closing the lock-gates, an operation requiring strength as well
as skill. Swans are numerous on this part of the river, and seem
to sleep quite unconcernedly with their heads tucked under their
wings while drifting downstream. Although far inferior scenically
to the Thames, there are attractive reaches of the Colne in the
district, well worth preserving.

Staines Bridge, which carries the Roman Road across the Thames,

STANWELL

was designed by Rennie and opened in 1832. It is a dignified
structure, but less graceful than the rather steep and narrow bridge
at Chertsey which was designed by the architect James Paine, and
opened in 1785. Fortunately, the construction of a new bridge to
carry the New Chertsey Road over the river will avoid the necessity
of widening the old one. The enormous reservoir between Staines
and Stanwell, more than a mile long, is traversed by a right-of-way
which provides good views of the flocks of water-birds which
breed here in quantities, as on the reservoirs at Ruislip and in the
Lea Valley. Sportsmen, so-called, will be glad to hear that a silly
stag, which had swum a mile in this water to escape his pursuers,

was eventually captured, his antlers sawn off, and himself returned to the Berks and Bucks Staghunt in a van for future "sport." This was in 1933.*

The population of this interesting district, composed of the parishes of Ashford, Staines, Stanwell, and Laleham, was only 3,279 in 1801 and 5,434 in 1851, Staines itself accounting for about half the total. It grew steadily till 1891, then increased rapidly to 14,214 in 1901. The next twenty years showed a gradual rise, but there was a sharp increase from 16,979 in 1921 to 21,209 in 1931. Building is proceeding briskly in the dormitory town of Ashford, and to some extent round Laleham and Staines, while Stanwell remains a small village and Poyle a mere hamlet. There is not much industry in the neighbourhood, the linoleum factory at Staines being the principal centre.

The number of historical buildings in Staines is small for so old a market-town. St. Mary's Church is picturesquely placed, but was rebuilt in 1828 except the lower part of the seventeenth-century brick tower, and has few monuments of interest. There is a charming old brick house at the end of Church Street, known as "Corner Hall," which in summer is almost concealed by an enormous wistaria with a trunk 80 feet long, shielded with lead and hung from the parapet by steel ropes. The owner states that this wistaria was one of the first half-dozen plants brought from Japan to England three hundred years ago. "Duncroft," now a nursing home near the church, has legendary associations with King John's signing of Magna Charta at Runnymede near by. It comprises a building of 1621 which has been greatly altered and extended in recent years. Among modern buildings, Staines has a charming new post office, but the Town Hall is only surpassed in hideousness by the fearful structure across the river which, Mr. Walter Jerrold artlessly informs us, is "an ugly gasometer." The railway bridge is hardly less offensive.

Stanwell, even to-day, is a beautiful village. The church stands on the village green and is one of the finest in the county, its noble tower and spire being surpassed only by that of Harrow.

* Reported in *The Times*, October 30, 1933.

The building has been drastically restored, but retains many notable features, including a canopied altar-tomb used as an Easter sepulchre (1486), and a grandiose monument, carved by Nicholas Stone, to Lord Knyvett (who died in 1622) and his wife. Lord Knyvett also founded the little school, consisting of a schoolroom with a master's house (on the right). There are some quaint old houses in the village.

Laleham Church, famous through its associations with Thomas

STANWELL: THE OLD SCHOOL

Arnold and his son Matthew, who is buried there, is an old but not very attractive building with a curious brick Georgian tower at the west end. Ashford is becoming sadly suburban, but Poyle, a scattered hamlet near the Colne, contains a few charming old buildings.

The area of public open spaces owned by the Staines Urban District Council amounts to about 370 acres, of which Staines Moor (290 acres) is by far the largest item. This wild common has a name characteristic of the north and west of England rather than of Middlesex, though one finds "Moor Mead" at Twickenham, "Moorfields" and "Moorgate" in London, also "Stanwell

Moor" near Staines. It consists of level and sparsely wooded ground north of the town, and is traversed by several arms of the Colne, of which the Wyrardisbury River is the most important. The Staines Recreation Ground, formerly the Lammas Fields (see page 182), is a pleasant space by the riverside with the "London Stone" standing on the bank. One could wish that the enormous gasholder across the river did not overpower and spoil an otherwise attractive view. Recently the Council has acquired for its own purposes a small area at the north-east corner of the bridge, thus securing another short length of river frontage. The remaining public open spaces are of no special interest or importance.

Under the local town-planning scheme, the recommendations of the West Middlesex Regional Report have been accepted for the most part. A strip between the Great Western Railway and the Wyrardisbury River has been scheduled as a public open space, also a strip along the bank of the Duke of Northumberland's River, and various areas in Ashford and Stanwell. The only portion of these reservations which has any real scenic value is the beautiful bit near "Mad Bridge" at Poyle.

More important than any of these proposals is the question of preserving the banks of the Thames from the projected New Chertsey Road bridge to Staines Bridge. From Staines to Laleham, that is for nearly half the river frontage in question, most of the banks are already occupied by houses and gardens, and no reservation was recommended in the regional plan. From Laleham to Chertsey Bridge, a distance slightly over a mile, is a lovely stretch of open country, where there is a wide strip of grass between the road and the river. On summer Saturdays and Sundays, from noon until dusk, this becomes a motor park from end to end, the cars being lined up in a continuous row. While they are there they belch forth a non-stop programme of canned music, and when they go they leave an incredible display of litter behind them. This used to be the most peaceful and beautiful reach of all the lower Thames, especially on the Middlesex side, but now it is more like Blackpool. However, this horde of up-to-the-minute hooligans does not stay long; after dark, peace descends again, and

the swans have the river to themselves once more. The noisy
invasion is limited to summer week-ends.

It is proposed to reserve a strip of land 150 feet wide, east of
the existing road, from Laleham to Chertsey Bridge, as a public
open space. This follows the Thames Valley Regional Report in
the main, but falls short of it by limiting the reservation to a mere
strip, whereas the Thames Valley Report recommended the
additional acquisition of the fine grounds of Laleham House, now

CHERTSEY BRIDGE

a convent. Doubtless the Staines Urban District Council has
adopted a less ambitious plan as being more suited to the resources
of a comparatively small community administering a large semi-
rural area. The local boundaries have been so often modified, and
their ultimate destiny is still so uncertain, that one cannot blame
the various authorities for adopting a somewhat conservative attitude
towards their town-planning commitments. One way and another,
the Staines Urban Council has acquired or reserved between 600
and 700 acres of open spaces and allotments, a figure not far short
of the 750-odd acres required to fulfil the ideal ratio of 10 per cent

of the total area of the district (after deducting the large acreage of water that it contains). It is only in connection with riverside reservation that there is any need for anxiety, and even in that respect it seems only necessary to beg the burgesses of Staines to save every possible inch remaining of the banks of the Thames, to consider whether a larger area of the meadows at Laleham which Matthew Arnold loved can be acquired, and to preserve the meadow south-east of Chertsey Bridge.

Across the river, on the Surrey side, "bungaloid growth" is more advanced, though there is a long and welcome hiatus north of Chertsey Bridge. Mention of the word "bungalow," which somehow seems to rouse the worst passions on either side in the bitter conflict between idealists and "practical" people about rural preservation, suggests a few reflections with which this study of modern growth may fitly conclude. Why, exactly, is there all this fuss about bungalows, whether on the banks of the Thames or elsewhere, and what has town-planning got to do with bungalows?

Obviously, there can be nothing intrinsically wrong in the form of a bungalow, a one-storey house. In fact, such a building plays a less aggressive part in a landscape, especially a low river landscape, than a house of two or three storeys. Yet most intelligent people seem to agree that the rows of gay little bungalows along the riverside, in spite of their geraniums by day and their cheerful Chinese lanterns at night, are a blot upon the restful charm of the Thames. If the secret does not lie in strictly architectural attributes, perhaps that word "restful" contains it. Doubtless every type of mentality is represented among the crowds of those who come sculling and punting and sailing up the river in the summer months, but, if one excepts the steamer folk and the motorists and the owners of speed-boats, they nearly all come to be quiet. Even those boating people who must carry gramophones and loud-speakers object to undue competition from owners of more highly powered noise-machines on the banks. And restfulness on the river implies an absence of people, of noises, and therefore of frequent houses along the bank. The preservation of a riverside strip is only necessary to prevent rows and rows of little buildings.

It is unnecessary where great velvety lawns slope down to the water's edge, as at so many points along the Thames. It is unnecessary, for example, at Cliveden Woods, and nobody finds fault with Lord Astor as a riparian owner. But even in those places some guarantee is needed that the peaceful beauty of the Thames will not be thoughtlessly spoiled by indiscriminate development, accompanied by all the blatancy of hoardings and house agents' and builders' vulgarities. Some buildings are inevitable, but they should be limited in number and restrained in their manners. Near Sunbury, for example, is a startling imitation in miniature of a Moorish mosque, complete with dome and minaret. Nobody could possibly claim that this adds to the restfulness of the Thames. Rows of wretched little suburban shacks, each determined to outshine and outshout its neighbour, must lower the tone of the riverside.

"It should be our object," says the Thames Valley Regional Report, "so to order the incidence of open space and built-up areas along the banks . . . that houses and bungalows shall not so monopolize the river frontage as to turn the gentle river-banks into the likeness of suburban streets." . . . "To the thousands who spend their leisure time on or about the river it is a matter of first-rate importance that the character of the river should not deteriorate into the squalidity of a bungalow town."

In each chapter of this book we have seen a village, or a group of villages, grow into a sprawling suburban town within a period varying from ten to fifty years. The population of Middlesex has doubled itself twice in half a century, and shows no sign of abating its feverish growth. There has been nothing like it in our history and, as was suggested in the first chapter, it is to be hoped that nothing like it will ever occur elsewhere. But if Middlesex has grown too fast, if it has lost much of its former rural charm in the process, it provides an object lesson for other counties whose more leisurely growth gives the authorities time to meet their troubles half-way. Given reasonable foresight and an intelligent application of the principles of town-planning as we now understand that often misunderstood science or art, there is no reason why all the charm of the past should be sacrificed to the needs of the present, or why the full development of modern civilization and transport should be hampered by the trammels of the past. What is needed in this, as in so many aspects of modern life and industry, is a mutual understanding between scientific progress and artistic judgment.

If in these pages the speculative builder and the house agent have sometimes come in for criticism, the necessity of their functions has never been questioned. We must realize that Middlesex is destined to have a population of several millions before it stops growing, we must realize that most of its people have to live in small houses built close together, and that practically all its rural lanes will go. But it remains a fact, in spite of the attractiveness and internal comfort of many of these small houses, that they might have been so disposed as to preserve green girdles of open spaces and valuable market-gardens close to the London markets had there been more vision on the part of those concerned and less greed all round. Town-planning keeps up values, and avoids ruinously expensive widenings and purchase of land for public purposes at an enhanced value. It is not merely a wild dream of fanatical visionaries.

Finally, it has been my object throughout this book to interest the vast body of people in Middlesex who, like myself, have been born elsewhere, in the history and growth of the new townships where they now live and work, townships whose landmarks and traditions are daily being obliterated by the thoughtless Juggernaut of modern progress.

BOOKS ON LOCAL HISTORY AND TOPOGRAPHY

[STAINES CHAMBER OF COMMERCE]   Staines: Official Guide   London   N.D.

INDEX

[* *An asterisk denotes an illustration*]

Aberdeen, Lord, 167
ACTON, Chapter XV, 168–76
— almshouses, 175
— Berrymead Priory, 170, 172, 175
— Derwentwater House, 171
— East, 170, 173*
— "Elms, The," 171, 175
— Friars' Place Farm, 171
— Green, 171
— Horn Lane, 171, 173
— House, 171
— Housing Schemes, 173
— Manor House, 170, 174–5
— Parish Church, 175
— Park, 174
— Steyne, 170, 173
— Wells, 171
— Windmills, 171
Adam, R., architect, 38, 77, 262, 286
Alexandra Palace, 41, 104–6, 114
Alfred, King, 57, 95
Alperton, 31, 154
Amelia, Princess, 252
Angel Brook, see "Pymme's Brook"
Arkley, 47
Arlington, peerage of, 222
Arnold, Matthew, 295, 298
— Thomas, 295
Ashford, 289, 291, 294–5, 296
Axe, River, see "Exe"
Ayrton, O. M., architect, 268

Bacon, Francis, 264
Baird, T., *quoted*, 238, 245, 258
Baliol, John, 97
Ballard's Lane, 124
Barnet, 24, 46–7, 110
— Battle of, 52
— Bypass Road, 35, 51, 112, 133, 135
— Gate, 39, 47, 132, 134
Barnett, Dame H., 140–1
Barn Hill, 155

Bath Road, 169, 215, 246, 257
Bedford Park, 172, 243
Beech Hill Park, 58, 61, 69
Bentley Heath, 48
— Priory, see "Stanmore"
Bigley Ditch, 214
Bishop's Wood, 28, 113
Bolingbroke, Lord, 222, 226
Bollo Brook, 170, 246
Boston, Lord, 250
Boston Manor, see "Brentford"
Botany Bay (near Enfield), 55, 61
Botwell, 222
— Common, 225
Bounds Green Brook, 81, 120
Bowes Park, 79
Brent, River, 24, 30, 47, 132–3, 145,
        162, 182–4, 246, 249
— Bridge, 132, 137
— Reservoir, see "Welsh Harp"
BRENTFORD, Chapter XXIII,
        240–53
— Battles of, 241
— Boston House, 247*, 248, 249, 250
— Bridge, 247–8
— Chapel, 247–8
— Clifden House, 253
— Custom House, 241
— Docks, 241*, 246
— Gasworks, 242
— High Street, 247
— Houses demolished, 249
— Memorial at Ferry, 241
— "Old England," 32, 246
— Parish Churches, 249
— "The Butts," 253
— Three Pigeons Inn, 247
— Zionist Colony, 242
Bridgman, Sir O., 277
Brimsdown, 35, 56, 60
Brittain, F., *quoted*, 45, 48–9, 52–3
Broad Mead (Tottenham), 94

Brockley Hill, 33, 132, 148
Brondesbury, 161, 164
— Manor House, 166–7
Brooks, J., architect, 115
Burlington, Lord, 242, 248, 249, 251
Burnt Oak, 129, 141
Bushy House, 275, 286
— Park, 265, 269, 274–5, 283
Byng, Admiral, 52

Caesar, Julius, 241
Cambridge Road, New, 35, 58, 64, 76, 91, 95–6
Camlet Moat, 66
Campe, Laurence, 121
Canals, Middlesex, 31
Canon's Park, 35, 139, 145, 146, 152
"Cardinal's River," see "Longford River"
Caroline, Queen, 272
Carr, Jonathan, 243
Cary's atlas quoted, 51, 64, 72, 91, 125, 126, 146, 169
Cassivelaunus, 62, 241
Catuvellauni, 61
Chambers, Sir W., architect, 264
Chandos, Duke of, 149–50, 153
Charles I, 31, 241
Charles II, 52, 251
Chelsea, Beaufort House, 252
Chequers Green, 81
Cherry Tree Wood, 109, 113
Chertsey Bridge, 25, 282, 292, 293, 296, 297*
— Lock, 292
— Road, New, 247, 248, 250, 268, 284, 293, 296
"Chevy Chace," 230
Child family, 262
Child's Hill, 129
CHISWICK, Chapter XXIII, 240–53
— Ait, 170, 246
— Boston House, 250
— Brampton House, 251
— Bridge, 249
— "Burlington Arms," 251
— Burlington Lane, 248, 250

CHISWICK—continued
— "Duke's Meadows," 248
— Hogarth House, 245*, 250
— House, 170, 242, 249, 251*
— Mall, houses on the, 242, 243*, 251
— Parish Church, 249
— Walpole House, 242, 251
Cibber, Colley, 264
Clarendon, Lord, 272
Clarke family, 210
Clay Hill (Enfield), 56, 58, 69
Clendish Marsh (Tottenham), 94
Clifden, Lord, 253
Clitherow family, 250
Clive, Kitty, 271
Cnut, King, 241, 252
Cockfosters, 35, 57, 58, 61, 64, 79, 80, 85, 87
Coldfall Wood, 113, 114
Colham Green, 199
Colindale, 129
Colnbrook, 31
— Bypass, 35, 216
Colne Brook, The, 31, 214
— River, 24, 25, 30, 31, 47, 49, 145, 199, 202–3, 214, 216, 262, 289
Colney Hatch, 34, 110, 119
— Asylum, 119, 120, 180
Compton, Sir W., 97
Cook's Ferry, 75
Copse Hill, 192, 194
Coston family, 184
Coway Stakes, 282
Cowley, 199, 200, 201, 211
— Packet Boat Inn, 203
— Parish Church, 207
Crane, River, 30, 31, 145, 221, 259, 260, 262, 268–9
Cranford, 221, 222, 224
— Bridge, 23, 221*, 224
— Parish Church, 226
— Park, 224–5, 226
Cranley Gardens, 112
Cranmer, Archbishop, 227
Cresswell, Dr., 83
Crews Hill, 58, 61, 69

Cricklewood, 129
— aerodrome, 136
Crouch End, 34, 92, 107, 109*, 110, 117
— playing-fields, 110, 114
Cruchley's map *quoted*, 92, 103, 230
Cuffley Brook, 32, 58

Dance, G., architect, 185-6
Dancer's Hill, 48, 50
David I, King, 96
Dawley, 215, 222
— Court, 226
Dean's Brook, 133, 134
Denham Lock, 203
Derby, Countess of, 208
Devonshire, Dukes of, 171, 248
Dickens, Charles, 265
Dollis Brook, 124, 125*, 126, 132
Dollis Hill, 161, 162, 164-5
— Farm, 163*
— Lane, 166*
Domesday Book *quoted*, 45, 143-4, 178, 180, 194, 222, 234-5, 255, 290
Draper, W., *quoted*, 244
Dudden Hill, 161
"Duke of Northumberland's River," 31, 214, 268, 291
Duval, Claude, 258
Dyrham Park, *see* "South Mimms"

EALING, Chapter XVI, 177-88
— Christ Church, 180, 185
— Common, 183
— "Fordhook," 179, 182
— Green, 179, 180, 185-6
— Hanger Hill, 181, 182
— Lammas Park, 182-3
— Little, 179, 186
— Old Inns, 179
— Parish Church, 179, 184
— Park, 179, 186
— Pitzhanger Manor, 185*
— Rochester House, 179, 186-7
— Walpole Park, 183
— Westfield House, 186

East Bedfont, 234
— Parish Church, 239
Eastcote, 35, 190, 194, 197
— "The Barns," 195*
East Finchley, 110, 126
Edgware, 130, 131, 139, 143, 152-3
— almshouses, 140
— Brook, 133, 145
— "Chandos Arms," 152
— High Street, 33*, 152-3
— Parish Church, 138
— Road, 33, 40
Edmonton, The Merry Devil of, 70
EDMONTON, Chapter IV, 70-8
— "Angel," the, 74
— Bury Hall, 76
— Bury House, 76, 78
— Fair, 74
— Green, 75
— hundred, 72, 264
— Lamb's Cottage (*Frontispiece*), 70-1, 78
— Parish Church, 71*, 78
— Pymme's Park, 74, 77-8
— Refuse dump, 75
— Salisbury House, 76, 77*, 78
— Wash, 75
— Wyre Hall, 76-7
Edmund Ironside, 241
Edward III, 252
Edward VI, 66
Edward VII, 248
Edward the Confessor, 230
Eel Pie Island, *see* "Twickenham Ait"
Elizabeth, Queen, 50, 66, 121, 239
Elstree, 47, 130, 131-2
Elthorne hundred, 180, 200, 264
ENFIELD, Chapter III, 55-69
— Bush Hill Park, 64
— Chase, 28, 46, 58, 60-3, 79, 119
— Gentleman's Row, 57*, 66, 69
— Grammar School, 66
— Lodges, 62
— "Oldbury," 62
— Old Inns, 62-3*, 66
— Old Palace, 66

ENFIELD—*continued*
— Old Park, 68–9
— Parish Church, 56*, 65
— White Webbs Park, 58–9, 64, 69
— Windmill, 66
Ermine Street, 33, 50, 62, 64
Evelyn, John, *quoted*, 63
Exe, River, 290, 291

Fabell, Peter, 70
FELTHAM, Chapter XXII, 234–9
— Borstal School, 234
— Council Offices, 234
— Lower, 237*
— Modern buildings, 239
— Parish Church, 238
— R.A.S.C. Depot, 234, 237
— St. Catherine's Church, 239
Fenton, J., 98
Fielding, J., 182, 264
— *quoted*, 126, 182
FINCHLEY, Chapter X, 123–8
— Bridge, 132
— "Brookside Walk," 126
— Common, 34, 113, 126–6
— Manor House, 127–8
— Nether Court, 123, 132
— Parish Church, 127
— Park House, 128
— Spaniard's Tavern, 127*, 128
— Squire's Lane, 128
Finchley Road, 34, 124, 135
Finsbury Park, 108, 112, 114, 115*
Firth, J. B., *quoted*, 227
Flaxman, J., sculptor, 249
Flitcroft, J., architect, 277
Foot, P., *quoted*, 182–3, 238, 244
Fortee, Sir H., 56, 67, 108
Fortis Green, 108, 113, 115, 125
Fortunes of Nigel, 66
Forty Hall, 42, 58, 67*, 69
Forty Hill, 32, 56
Frays Water, *see* "Uxbridge"
Freezy Water, 56
FRIERN BARNET, Chapter IX, 119–22

FRIERN BARNET—*continued*
— almshouses, 121*
— Bethune Park, 120
— Friary, 121
— Friary Park, 120
— Parish Church, 121
— "Priory," 121
Fuller, T., 226
Fulwell, 266
— Park, 265

Ganwick Corner, 52
Gardner, S., *quoted*, 148
Garrick, David, 139
Gaskell, Mrs., 221
Gay, John, 264
George V, 59
— Reservoir, 59
Gibbons, Grinling, 150, 208
Gilbert, M., *quoted*, 243, 250
Gilpin, John, 70
Gladstone, W. E., 167
Golder's Green, 129, 131*, 137
— St. Alban's Church, 138
— Station, 124, 136
Gordon Riots, 114
Gore hundred, 264
Gotch, J. A., *quoted*, 67
Gover, J. E. B., *quoted*, 45–6, 55–6, 79, 107–9, 119, 130, 143–4, 154, 161, 178, 189, 199, 213, 222, 230, 235, 242–3, 255, 266, 275, 280, 290
Grand Union Canal, 31, 182, 193, 202, 215–16, 224, 229, 246
Gray, John, 158
Great North Road, 45, 46–7, 49–51, 113, 120, 124, 128
Great West Road, 30, 216, 244, 247, 256, 257
"Green Girdle," The, 22, 59, 136, 144, 148
Green Lanes, 81, 82, 102
Greenford (Magna), 26, 177, 178–9, 180–1
— Parish Church, 184
Greenford Parva, *see* "Perivale"

Gresham, Sir T., 262
Grim's Dyke, 24, 144, 148
Grove Park (Chiswick), 244
Gunhild, 243, 252
Gunnersbury, 243
— Lane, 244, 247
— Park, 173, 174, 183, 248, 252
Gurnell, T., 185
Gwyn, Nell, 249

Hadley, 46, 50, 60
— Woods, 61, 86
Hale, The (Hendon), 129
Halliford, 280
Ham House, 270
Hamilton, Duchess of, 175
Hampstead Garden Suburb, 40, 123,
       124, 132, 140–1
— Golf Club, 127
— Lane, 114, 116
HAMPTON, Chapter XXVII, 279–88
— Court, 31, 247, 274, 280*, 281–2,
       284–6
— Court House, 286
— Garrick's "Temple," 281*, 286
— Mitre Hotel, 282
— Old Court House, 286
— Parish Church, 286
— Rose Hill, 286
— Royal Mews, 283*
Hampton Wick, 274–6
Handel, G. F., 150, 153
Hanger Hill, see "Ealing"
Hanwell, 26, 177–9, 180–1
— Asylum, 180
— Brent Lodge, 183, 187
— Parish Church, 182, 185
Hanworth, 31, 234–5
— Air Park, 234, 236–7
— Palace, 239
— Parish Church, 238–9
— "Tudor Court," 239
Harefield, 28, 199, 200, 202, 205,
       206, 211
— almshouses, 203*, 210
— Parish Church, 201*, 208
Harlesden, 31, 161, 164

HARLINGTON, Chapter XX, 220–7
— Parish Church, 223*, 226
Harmondsworth, 213, 214, 216,
       257
— Barn, 213, 218
— Old House, 217*, 218
— Parish Church, 217–18
Harper, C. G., quoted, 205, 220, 228
Harringay, 92, 107, 110
HARROW, Chapter XII, 142–53
— Byron's tomb, 148
— Hill, 142, 144
— King's Head Inn, 150
— Parish Church, 143*, 145*, 148
— School, 142, 144, 145, 148, 149*,
       150, 155, 158
— Weald, 143
Haste Hill, 192–3
Hatch End, 143, 151
Hatton, 235
HAYES, Chapter XX, 220–7
— Barra Hall, 224–5
— Housing schemes, 220
— Manor House, 227
— Parish Church, 225*, 226
— Railway bridge, 220
— Wood End Green, 225
Hayles, J., quoted, 178
Headstone Manor, 143, 150, 151*
Heathrow, 213, 218, 258
— aerodrome, 213
Helder, E., 68
HENDON, Chapter XI, 129–42
— aerodrome, 136
— almshouses, 139
— Burroughs Pond, 132, 138–9
— Church House, 139
— Clitterhouse Farm, 138
— Greyhound Hill, 138*, 139
— Hodford Farm, 138
— Hall, 139
— Parish Church, 137–8
— Tenterden Hall, 139
Henry IV, 60
Henry VIII, 24, 97, 239, 284
Hertfordshire–Middlesex boundary,
       24, 47, 57

HESTON AND ISLEWORTH, Chapter XXIV, 254–63
Heston Airport, 254, 257, 259
— Parish Church, 260, 261*
Highgate, 108
— almshouses, 116
— Archway, 34, 111, 112, 113*
— Cromwell House, 116
— Fairs, 111
— "Gatehouse," the, 111
— Golf course, 109, 114
— Hill, 108*, 110, 116
— North Hill, 116
— Old Manor House, 116–17
— School, 116
— Wood, 113, 114
Highwood Hill, 132
High Wycombe, 204
Hill, Sir R., 98
Hillingdon, 199, 200, 205, 206
— Cedar House, 211
— Heath, 204
— Parish Church, 208
Historical Monuments Commission, 36
Hogarth, W., painter, 242, 249, 250
Honeypot Lane, 146
Hood, T., quoted, 84
HORNSEY, Chapter VIII, 107–18
— Eagle House, 117
— Parish Church, 114, 115, 117*
— Wood, 113
Horsendon Hill, 32, 182, 183
— Wood, 183
Hounslow, 31, 254
— Baber Bridge, 260
— Barracks, 254
— Carville Hall, 260
— Heath, 34, 213, 215, 238, 254, 257–9
— Priory and Church, 261
Hunt, Leigh, 87
— quoted, 84
Hunter, Dr., quoted, 125
Hyde, The (Hendon), 130

Ickenham, 39, 199, 200, 205–6

Ickenham Marsh, 206
— Parish Church, 207*, 208
Isaacs, Rev. F. W., quoted, 243
ISLEWORTH, Chapter XXIV, 254–63, 255*
— hundred, 264
— London Apprentice Inn, 263
— Mills, 32, 254
— Parish Church, 260
Islip, John, 190
Islip Manor, see "Northolt"

James I, 63, 262
James II, 272
James, John, architect, 271
Jerrold, W., quoted, 205, 228, 288, 294
Jersey, Earl of, 262
John, King, 294
Johnson and Forsyth, architects, 208
Joinville, Prince de, 265
Jones, Inigo, architect, 67–8, 252, 262
Jonson, Ben, 247

Kempton Park, 279, 280, 283–4
Kensal Green, 161
Kent, W., architect, 249, 252
Kenton, 154
Ken Wood, 114
Kew Bridge, 245, 248
— Gardens, 242
Kilburn, 25, 161, 162–3
— Bridge, 163
— Priory, 165–6
— Wells, 163
Kingsbury, 26, 134, 154, 156–7
— Green, 158
— Hill, 155
— Parish Church, 155*, 157–8
— Plough Inn, 158
Kingston Bridge, 274, 276
Kneller, Sir G., painter, 264, 271
Knyvett, Lord, 295

Laleham, 291, 294, 298
— House, 297
— Parish Church, 295

Lamb, Charles, 70-1, 78
— quoted, 71, 84
Lampton, 255, 259
Lancaster, Duke of, 60
Law, Ernest, 284
Lea, River, 24, 25, 57, 72, 73*, 94-5
— Marshes, 59-60, 61, 72, 75-6, 78, 94-5
— Navigation Canal, 31, 75, 94
Little Stanmore, see "Edgware"
Littleton, 280, 281
— Parish Church, 287
— Park, 238, 279
— Reservoir, 31
Lloyd, T. A., architect, 173, 220
Lodge Hill, 114
Londinium, 24, 129, 169
London, Bishop of, 110, 111, 113, 114
— City of, 19-21
— County of, 19-21, 25
Longford, 31, 213, 215, 218
— River, 31, 285
Lyon, John, 158
Lysons, Rev. D., quoted, 74, 107, 126, 245
Lytton, Lord, 175
— quoted, 126

Maiden's Bridge (Enfield), 32, 58, 65,* 68-9
Mair, G., architect, 271
Manoel, King, 265
Manor House Station, 112
Mansfield, Lord, 114
Mapesbury Manor House, 166
— Windmill, 165*, 166
Marble Hill, see "Twickenham"
Maxwell, D., quoted, 289
Mercia, 24
"Metroland," 28, 146, 189
Middlesex, boundaries of, 19-21, 23-6
— Forest of, 28, 61, 102, 194
— Geology of, 48, 132
— Guildhall, 20
— hundreds of, 72, 180, 264
Middleton quoted, 203-4

Mill Hill (Hendon), 130-1, 132, 137, 140
— almshouses, 140
— Angel Pond, 132
— Belmont, 130
— Broadway, 133*
— Copt Hall, 140
— Goldbeaters' Farm, 140
— "Green Man," 135*, 140
— Goodhew's Farm, 40, 130*, 140
— Hale End Farm, 29*, 140
— Hendon Park, 137, 140
— Holcombe Hill, 41*, 140
— King's Head Inn, 140
— Laurence Street Farm, 37*, 140
— "Littleberries," 140
— Old Mill Field, 130
— Ridgeway, 33, 130, 140
— St. Paul's Church, 138
— School, 136, 140, 142
— Sheepwash, 132
Mill Hill Park (Acton), 171
Mimms, South, see "South Mimms"
— Wash, 32, 49, 50
— Wood, 48
Moat Mount, 136
Mohun, Lord, 175
Monasteries, Dissolution of, 25, 32, 119, 261
Monk, General, 52
Morden's map, quoted, 145-6
Morris, R., architect, 272
Moselle Brook, The, 30, 93-4, 103, 110
Muswell Hill, 34, 110, 114, 117
— Golf course, 104
Mutton Bridge, 32, 132
— Brook, 126, 132
Myddelton, Sir H., 60
Mymmshall Brook, 49, 53

Nash, J., architect, 86
Neasden, 161, 167
— Golf Club, 165
— Manor House, 167
— Spotted Dog Inn, 167
Nemours, Duc de, 265

New Bedfont, 216

"New River," The, 32, 60, 80, 102–3, 114, 115*

New Southgate, 119

Norden, *quoted*, 27, 34, 111

Norman, P., *quoted*, 116

North Circular Road, 35, 74, 75, 76, 81, 109, 112, 120, 124, 127, 135, 164, 181, 247

North Middlesex Golf Club, 120

Northolt, 31, 177–9, 180–1, 184, 200

— Islip Manor, 183, 189–90

— Junction, 192, 195

— Parish Church, 183*, 184

Northumberland, Dukes of, 262

Northwood, *see* "Ruislip and North-wood"

Norwood Green, 228, 229*, 231–2

— Bridge House, 232

— Parish Church, 232

— School, 232

Nut Wood, 133

Oakington, *see* "Wembley"

Oakleigh Park, 119

Oakwood Park, *see* "Southgate"

Offa, King, 231

Olaf, King, 283

Old Brentford, *see* "Brentford"

"Old England," *see* "Brentford"

Old Fold Golf Club, 51

Old Oak Common, 168, 169, 170, 172

Orleans, Duc d', 265

Ossulston hundred, 264

Osterley Park, 42, 228, 255, 256, 257*, 259*, 260, 262–3

Oxgate Farm (Willesden), 167

Paddington Canal, 31

Paget family, 218

Paine, J., architect, 293

Palladio, A., architect, 252

Palmer's Green, 79, 82

— "Thatched Cottage," 83*, 88

Paris, Comte de, 265

Park Royal, 162, 173

Pearce, T., 187

Penton Hook Lock, 292

Pepys, S., *quoted*, 209–10, 222

Perivale, 26, 31, 178–9, 181

— Bridge at, 179*

— Parish Church, 181*, 184

— Wood, 31

Perry Oaks, 217

Perryn, John, 175

Pilgrim Fathers, The, 36

Pin, River, 145, 189, 194, 203

Pinner, 129, 143–4, 148, 151

— Dear's Farm, 147*, 151

— Fair, 151, 153

— High Street, 27*, 151

— Hill, 144

— Parish Church, 148

Pinnock, *quoted*, 96, 142, 146, 168, 178, 228

Ponder's End, 56

— Mill, 59*, 66

Poor Robin's Almanack, 111

Pope, Alexander, 187, 222, 226, 242, 264, 271

POTTERS BAR, Chapter II, 45–54

— War cemetery, 53

— Wyllyott's Manor, 45, 51–2

Poyle, 214, 289, 291, 292*, 294, 295

— "Mad Bridge," 296

Preston, 154

— Lyon's Farm, 157*, 158

Pymme's Brook, 30, 58, 74, 76, 78, 80

Queen's Wood (Highgate), 110, 113, 114

Quiller-Couch, Sir A., *quoted*, 48

Rammey Marsh (Enfield), 59

Raynton, Sir N., 65, 67

Reade, Charles, 277

Reade, Lady, 250

Rennie, Sir J., engineer, 293

Reynardson, Sir A., 99

Richmond Bridge, 268

"Robert the Bruce," 97

Robinson, H. C., *quoted*, 83–4

Rocque's map, *quoted*, 125, 169, 230

Roe Green, 158

Roman roads in Middlesex, 28, 33, 50, 64, 163-4, 169, 246, 257, 290

Rothschild family, 252

RUISLIP AND NORTHWOOD, Chapter XVII, 189-98

Ruislip Association, 189

— Hunting Park, 194

— Manor Farm, 193*, 196

— Parish Church, 191*, 195-6

— Park Wood, 194

— Poor's Field, 194

— Reservoir, 30-1, 194

— Woodman's Farm, 197*

Russell, Francis, 61

Ryslippe, John, 189

St. Albans, Abbot of, 24, 47

St. Margaret's, New Bridge, 255, 257, 268

Salmon Brook, 74, 80

Scott, Sir Gilbert, architect, 85, 105, 185, 195-6, 208, 226

Scott, Sir Giles, architect, 138

Scratch Wood, 136

Scrattage, 255

Seabrook, H., *quoted*, 52

Selborne Society, 31

Sharp, Becky, 242, 250

Sharpe, Sir M., *quoted*, 24, 32, 34, 57, 190, 241, 264, 282, 290

Shaw, Norman, architect, 173

Sheppard, Jack, 126

Shepperton, 279, 280, 281, 282

— Parish Church, 287*

— "War Close," 283

Short, S. G., *quoted*, 230

Silk Stream, 133, 145

Sipson, 213, 216, 218

Slade Brook, 162

Sloane, Sir H., 252

Soane, Sir J., architect, 185-6

SOUTHALL-NORWOOD, Chapter XXI, 228-33

Southall Bridge, 232

— Dormer's Wells Farm, 232

— Gasworks, 229

— Grove House, 232

Southall—*continued*

— Manor House, 231*

— Mill, 232

— Mount Pleasant, 230

— Old Inns, 232

— Railway Bridge, 232

SOUTHGATE, Chapter V, 79-89

— Arnos Grove, 81, 86

— Broomfield Park, 81, 82, 85*, 86

— Eagle Hall, 87

— Essex House, 87*

— Grovelands, 86

— Minchenden School, 88

— Oakwood Park, 86

— Old Smithy, 80*, 85

— Parish Church, 85

South Marsh (Enfield), 59

SOUTH MIMMS, Chapter II, 45-54

— Castle, 51

— Duke of York Inn, 47*, 52

— Dyrham Park, 49, 52, 53*

— Knightsland, 51

— Mimms Hall, 52

— Parish Church, 46*, 51

— Wrotham Park, 49, 52, 53

Spaniard's Tavern, *see* "Finchley"

Spelthorne hundred, 264

Sprignell, Sir R., 116

Spring Grove (Isleworth), 255

Stag Lane aerodrome, 136, 157

STAINES, Chapter, XXVIII, 289-300

— Bridge, 290, 293

— City Boundary Stone, 23*, 290

— Church Street, 288, 291*

— Corner Hall, 294

— "Duncroft," 294

— Moor, 295-6

— Parish Church, 294

— Recreation ground, 296

— Reservoir, 293

Stanmore, Great, 143,144, 146, 147,153

— Bentley Priory, 152

— Heath, 144

— Manor House, 151

— Parish Church, 148-9

— Park, 152

Stanmore, Little, *see* "Edgware"

Stanwell, 257, 289, 291, 293*, 294

— Old School, 295*

— Parish Church, 294–5

Stone, N., sculptor, 65, 149, 295

Stonebridge, 161, 164

Stone Grove, almshouses, 140

Strafford, Earl of, 52

Strand-on-the-Green, 32, 243, 249, 252

Strawberry Hill, 264, 266, 273

Street, G. E., architect, 51

Stroud Green, 109, 113

Sudbury, 154

— Hill, 32

Suffolk, Countess of, 272

Sulloniacae, 148

SUNBURY, Chapter XXVII, 279–88

— Common, 284

— Court, 287

— Parish Church, 285*, 287

Surrey, boundary of, 25, 292

Sutton (near Heston), 255

Swakeleys, *see* "Uxbridge"

Swift, Dean, 222, 226, 264

Syon House and Park, 42, 254, 259, 260–2

Syon Monastery, 31, 261

TEDDINGTON, Chapter XXVI, 274–8

— Elmfield House, 277

— Lock, 275, 276, 277*

— National Physical Laboratory, 275, 286

— Parish Church, 276–7

— St. Alban's Church, 277

— Trowlock Island, 276

Thames, River, pp. 240–300 *passim*

Telford, T., engineer, 34, 50

Tennyson, Lord, 265, 272

Thackeray, W. M., 175, 251

Thorney Weir, 213

Thornhill, Sir J., painter, 86

Tijou, J., 286

Tite, Sir W., architect, 140

Tooke, Horne, 249

TOTTENHAM, Chapter VI, 90–101

— almshouses, 99, 100

— Bruce Castle, 90, 97*, 98

— Bruce Grove, 91, 92, 97, 100

— Cemetery, 93

— Grove House, 100

— Hale, 95

— High Cross, 98–9

— Housing schemes, 92

— Mills, 93*, 100

— Northumberland Row, 101

— Parish Church, 91*, 96–7

— Priory, 98, 99*

— Seven Sisters Road, 91, 92, 95, 109, 112

— Tournament, 96

— Wood, 102, 104

Totteridge, 24, 47, 125

Tree, Sir H. Beerbohm, 242, 251

Trent Park, 42, 61, 86

Trinobantes, 61

Trotter's Brook, 49

Turner, J. M. W., painter, 265

Turnham Green, 243

Turpin, Dick, 126, 140

"Turpin's Oak," 126

TWICKENHAM, Chapter XXV, 264–73

— Ait, 270

— Arragon House, 273

— Bridge, 257

— Cambridge House, 273

— Crossdeep Lodge, 270, 273

— Embankment, 267*

— Ferry House, 271*, 273

— Fortescue House, 273

— Green, 268, 269

— Heatham House, 273

— King Street, 265

— Kneller Gardens, 269

— Marble Hill, 267, 268–9, 272

— Montpellier Row, 272

— Moor Mead, 269

— Orleans House, 265, 272

— Parish Church, 270–1

— Park, 271

TWICKENHAM—*continued*
— "Pope's Villa," 270
— Poulett Lodge, 270
— Radnor House, 270, 273
— Sion Row, 272
— York House, 265, 269, 272
Twyford, 154, 178
— Abbey, 158, 159*
Tyburn, 170

Unwin, Sir R., architect, 141
Uvedale, Dr. R., 66
UXBRIDGE: Chapter XVIII, 199–212
— Bridge, 199, 202, 205
— Clark's Meadow, 217
— Common, 206
— Frays House, 211
— Frays Water, 202, 214
— High Street, 200*, 204–5
— Market House, 211
— Parish Church, 208
— Swakeleys, 206, 208, 209*, 210
— "Treaty House," 210–11

Verulamium, 24, 33, 129, 141
Victoria, Queen, 186
Villa Capra (Italy), 252
Villiers, Barbara, 251
Voltaire, 222, 226
Vyner, Sir R., 209

Walpole, Horace, 263, 264, 272, 273
Walter, John, 277
Waltham Cross, 64
Waltheof, Earl, 96–97
Walton-on-Thames, 25
Ware, Isaac, architect, 52
Waterlow Park, 114
Watford Bypass Road, 35, 133, 135
Watling Estate, 29, 40, 94, 133, 141
Watling Street, 33, 50, 129, 131, 134, 139, 145, 156, 162–4
Way, T. R., 272
Wealdstone, 143, 144, 148
— Brook, 145, 155
Webb, J., architect, 252

Wedmore, Treaty of, 129
Wegg, Samuel, 175
"Welsh Harp" Reservoir, 30–31, 132, 133–4, 155–6, 162*, 163
WEMBLEY, Chapter XIII, 154–60
— Exhibition, 154, 156, 159, 160
— Green Man Inn, 158
— Hill, 155
— Oakington Manor Farm, 158
— Park, 158–9
Wesley, John, 226
WEST DRAYTON, Chapter XIX, 213–19
— Gatehouse, 218
— Green, 216
— Mills, 214
— Parish Church, 218
West End (Northolt), 184
West Middlesex Golf Club, 231
Western Avenue, 174, 181, 204
Westmacott, Sir R., sculptor, 249
Whetstone, 34, 110, 120, 122, 124, 127, 128
Whitaker, *quoted*, 61
Whitchurch, 144
— almshouses, 150
— Parish Church, 149–50
White Webbs Park, *see* "Enfield"
Whitton, 265, 266, 268, 271
— Kneller Hall, 269, 271–2
— Murray Park, 269
Wilberforce, Wm., 137, 138
WILLESDEN, Chapter XIV, 161–67
— Gladstone Park, 165
— Grange, 167
— Green, 164
— Manor House, 166
— Mount Pleasant, 162, 164
— Parish Church, 166
— Roundwood Park, 165
William III, 285
Winchmore Hill, 79, 82–3, 87–8
— Friends' Meeting House, 88
— Rose Cottage, 84, 87
Woffington, Peg, 277
Wollaston, Sir J., 116
Wolsey, Cardinal, 31, 284

Wolstenholme, Sir J., 149

WOOD GREEN, Chapter VII, 102–6

— almshouses, 103–4, 105

— Common, 103

— Devonshire Hill Farm, 104, 105*

— St. Michael's Church, 103, 105

— Town Hall, 105

"World's End" (Southgate), 80

Wortley-Montagu, Lady M., 264

Worton (Hounslow), 255

Wren, Sir C., architect, 68, 260, 284–6

Wright, E., 209

Wrotham Park, *see* "South Mimms"

Wyatt, J., architect, 252, 262

Wykeham, William of, 271

Wyrardisbury River, 214, 296

Yeading, 220–1, 222

— Brook, 145, 192, 203, 206, 224–5, 237

— Refuse dump, 31, 221, 225

YIEWSLEY, Chapter XIX, 213–19

— Otter Dock, 216

— Recreation grounds, 216

— Refuse dump, 215

Zoffany, J., painter, 242